MW01533870

BREWED

A GUIDE TO THE
CRAFT
BEER
OF NEW ZEALAND

JULES VAN CRUYSEN

pb potton & burton

SUM
James

three boys
Ale
Golden:

Golden Ale is a modern style invented by
ms to counter global brands. Pale golden
aroma, this style combines the intricacy
the refreshing qualities of lager. Three Boy
Canterbury malt and 100% Nelson hops
a genuine Kiwi brew. A perfect match for
r - or anytime!
ml.

SPEIG
MASTER
BREWER
SINCE 18
James
SUMM
ALE
FTED BATCH BR

BREWING
ALL DAY ALE
Extra Session Ale

MAC
SINCE 1981

GRE
[CL

330ml

BEER
CIDER
AWARDS
GOLD
2014

SOUR ALE
948ml/32 oz 3.7% ABV

BREWING

CRISP
Emersor
PILSNER
Naturally brewed from
finest NZ grown hops
and malt
NEW ZEALAND PILSNER

Golden
Golden Ale

BI
PO

MOA

NEW ZEALAND

DONELA... X2

...BREWERS COLLABORATION... DOWNSHE...

Hadox

PILSNER
...refreshing sur...
...with zesty...

...ASTIE OYS
...TAL IPA

SINCE 1981
MAC'S

HOP ROCKER
(PILSENER)

Hop Rocker is Mac's own Pilsener, with a full
...plement of Cascade & Nelson Sauvin hops for
...rounded complexity. Bitter, but in a good way.

BEST beFORE
08:12 0212

...OLD...

...TY
RS
...ting

SINCE 1...
MAC'S

Contents

Acknowledgements

I want to thank all of the people and businesses that backed the publishing of this book via Kickstarter (a full list of names can be found at the back of the book). I also want to thank all of my esteemed colleagues who write about and comment on beer in New Zealand. You have given me so much inspiration, support and help in many different ways.

My biggest thanks go to the book's designer, typesetter, sub-editor and my partner, Lauren Costello, for all her encouragement, support, cajoling and sacrifice (among other things, she moved us into our house while I drank beer and visited breweries in Auckland), and for making this book look amazing. I wouldn't and couldn't have done it without you.

A huge thanks also to Robbie and the team at Potton & Burton for publishing the book, and especially for allowing Lauren and me the independence to create a book designed to educate and inspire beer drinkers rather than one that would be watered down by the needs of marketing boffins.

To Geoff Griggs, of all the financial contributors to the book, your endorsement meant the most to me. Without you, the industry would not be as developed and exciting as it is.

To Neil Miller, thank you for challenging me. I have looked up to you for a long time and I hope you enjoy this book.

To Michael Donaldson, thank you so much for your contribution to writing about beer in New Zealand, especially your excellent book *Beer Nation*, without which I would have not been able to write the section on the history of New Zealand beer.

Huge thanks also go to David Wood (president of SOBA), Dale Cooper, Stu McKinlay, Jono Galuszka, Dominic Kelly, Sean Golding and many others in the craft beer industry for your knowledge and encouragement throughout this project.

Thanks also to SOBA, who made the largest single contribution I received. Without that support I would not have been able to travel and visit as many breweries as I did or have dedicated to the project as much time as I have. Your endorsement of this project means a lot to me.

A special thanks to my son Remy (who at the time of publication will have just turned eight). Thanks for putting up with a distracted father for six months, for being patient with me when I needed you to be, and for being so proud of me all of the time – I hope by the time you start to drink beer (responsibly) you will enjoy the book.

Cellphone collection at the Mussel Inn, Golden Bay.

Introduction

This book attempts to document every brewery and brewing company producing beer in New Zealand as of 1 January 2015. Undoubtedly, there will be new companies bursting onto the scene between this date and when the book is published. Likewise, some may close, change ownership and/or release new beers. To keep you up to date, an app has been launched to complement the book. It will have a taste of the same content: abridged brewery profiles and beer notes, as well as the beer destinations, but also enhanced content, such as profiles of new breweries and tasting notes for new beers.

While the majority of breweries featured are craft breweries, this book is by no means restricted to them alone.

You'll see notes on Kiwi beers that are regularly available on the market. Capturing all beers, especially historical ones, would be an impossible task, and it would also make the book unwieldy, hard to read and too expensive.

As such, the book includes detailed profiles of 140 breweries and brewing companies, as well as tasting notes for over 400 beers and informa-tion on 15 cider producers. I have chosen not to include international beers brewed under contract in New Zealand (like Heineken or Guinness, for example), nor have I included notes for house beers at bars, restaurants and chains, as the vast majority of these are brewed by one or other of the larger breweries (or, if you are lucky, a larger craft brewery), then relabelled for the particular outlet.

Terminology

Where I use the term 'brewery', I am referring to either a physical brewery or a company that owns one. Beer producers without a physical brewing space will be deemed a 'brewing company' or 'contract brewer' interchangeably. Sometimes these brewers prefer the term 'gypsy brewer'. Where a commercial entity has more than one range of beers, as is the case with the three large industrial breweries, I will refer to each imprint as a 'brand'.

Beer in New Zealand

The history of brewing in New Zealand has mirrored that of the USA, albeit on a smaller scale. At the end of the nineteenth century, there were approximately 100 brewers operating in New Zealand. Beer did not travel well and every town of note had a local brewery, if not several. By 1971, there were only two: Lion and Dominion Breweries (DB), both making very similar industrial beer.

This finally changed in 1981 when ex-All Black Terry McCashin established the Mac's Brewery in Nelson, brewing all-malt beers (before being bought out by Lion – but that's another story). Since then, the number of brewing entities has grown exponentially, and in the four years between 2011 and 2015 it has more than doubled, growing from around 60 to over 140, but this also includes brewing companies releasing beer brewed under contract at other facilities.

This explosion in the number of breweries, brewing companies and brands on the New Zealand market has caused a similar-sized boom in the number of beers available on the market. This said, while the market for craft beer continues to grow, it can grow only so much in any given market, especially one as small as New Zealand's.

Dominic Kelly (beer importer, distributor and publican) believes that even if the industry is not consolidating, consumers are.[1] He points out that as 2014 progressed, consumers tended to purchase increasing amounts of a handful of beers, notably from his portfolio Liberty and Panhead, and especially their more approachable beers. 'There seems to be a lot more people taking home six-packs of Oh Brother Pale Ale or Quickchange XPA where they might have taken a mixed bag of different beers a year ago.' He goes on to say that many of craft beer's 'early adopters' are 'settling down with a few staples and experimenting less'.

What is the cause of this? Kelly acknowledges that the success of the brands he mentions (and undoubtedly other similar brands) is that 'their quality has been consistently very good'. While this is true, this is only part of the story. Today there is just so much choice that consumers are more discerning, not only about the quality, consistency and style of the beers they drink, but who they buy them from as well. The breweries that succeed are those that engage and communicate with their market, both face to face and via the traditional and digital media platforms available to them.

As the market grows, breweries can afford to pursue particular chunks of this already niche market, sometimes even compromising their ability to sell to other segments. Andrew Child's Behemoth is an example of this: an ex-lawyer, Child has the sense of humour of a 14-year-old boy but, unlike most 14-year-old boys, he has an outlet for it. He regularly uses promo girls at beer events, has T-shirts that proclaim things like 'IF YOU DON'T LOVE HOPS THE TERRORISTS WIN', and releases beers with names such as The Nuts, The Tits and Sacrilegious Saison (featuring an image of The Buddy Christ). Needless to say, this behaviour does not endear him to some parts of the market, but with other segments it works perfectly.

Likewise, regionalism is also becoming more important. The success of both Panhead and Garage Project is in no small part due to their focus on, and participation in, their local market, as well as to both breweries' ability to stand out in the crowded national market. With active brewing and primary industries supporting brewing, this is especially the case in Christchurch and Nelson, but is also becoming of a factor in regions not typically associated with craft beer, like Hawke's Bay and the Waikato.

What is craft beer?

Craft beer (referred to as micro-brewing in the US and other markets) is an elusive term and one that is beginning to lose its meaning as industrial brewers create craft-like brands and buy already-established craft breweries – a phenomenon known as 'craft-washing'. Craft brewing originally defined itself in relation to the industrial breweries that had taken over the marketplace, its essence being the pursuit of high-quality beers, made traditionally, with (largely) traditional ingredients and usually by smaller breweries. For example, where industrial breweries will regularly brew beers with adjuncts to reduce the cost and to create light beers with very little character demanded by some sectors of the market, a typical craft beer is made from all malt and any adjuncts are used only to enhance the character and flavour of the beer.

The New Zealand market has historically been dominated by two foreign-owned indus-

trial brewing companies: Lion Nathan (owned by the Japanese beer giant Kirin) and DB (Dominion Breweries – owned by the Heineken conglomerate).

More recently, Independent Liquor has emerged as a third major player. These breweries represent up to 98% of the market as of August 2014.[2] Similarly, while the amount of beer consumed dropped by 10% between 2008 and 2013, the market for craft beer has grown 25% year on year.[3] This is similar to market trends all around the world, particularly in North America, the UK, Australia and Japan. Craft beer, conversely, represents up to 10% of the market, if you include the craft and craft-like market. It is estimated that there are approximately 130,000 craft beer drinkers in New Zealand; or 250,000 if you include those who drink craft-like offerings from one of the three major breweries.[4]

To refer to these large breweries, I have used the term 'industrial' because, unlike craft brewers, they are more likely to use industrially produced ingredients, such as malt and hop extracts. Typically, these industrial breweries will have more than one production facility.

'Industrial' should not be read as a pejorative term, though. There are a lot of positives to be said of good industrial breweries (of which I include both DB and Lion). Their beers are consistent, even excellent (Speight's Triple Hop Pilsner and Monteith's Black being two personal favourites), which keeps consumers buying them.

It has also been with the help of the industrial breweries that beer events such as Beervana and the Brewers' Guild Awards can happen and grow, which, in turn, help other aspects of the industry to grow. Likewise, they have been a welcome resource for many craft breweries, sending out trained, skilled brewers into the world. There can also be a lot of negatives about these breweries, notably that they tie up taps by providing incentives (some would call them bribes) to pubs and bars to stock only their beers. Needless to say, it is a double-edged sword.

Corporatisation

While larger breweries have bought up smaller ones since time immemorial, there is a growing trend for industrial brewers to buy craft breweries but, rather than turn them into brand imprints, to leave them as craft beer offerings true to the original principles and style of the former owner, as is the case with Lion's purchase and subsequent treatment of Emerson's. DB has also re-established their West Coast-based Monteith's brand after much consumer pushback and has launched a range of craft-like beers.

A number of larger craft breweries have also used various means to raise capital. In late 2010, the Scott family of Alan Scott wine fame sold 47% and 23.5% of Moa Brewery (established by their winemaker son, Josh) to 42 Below Vodka founder Geoff Ross's Business Bakery and Pioneer Capital, respectively.[5] Two years later, Moa launched an initial public offering (IPO) and managed to raise $16 million for expansion into international markets. Similarly, in 2013 Wellington's Tuatara saw an influx of capital from the sale of 35% of the business to investment firm Rangatira for 'about $5 million'.[6] Marlborough's Renaissance and Yeastie Boys (in late 2014 and early 2015, respectively) both used the newly allowed crowd-equity funding model to raise just over $500,000 apiece, largely from lovers of these breweries.

Many have questioned whether those breweries who have sold outright, such as Emerson's and Founders, or who have received large corporate cash injections, like Moa or Tuatara, will retain the right to call themselves craft breweries. Emerson's and Tuatara have more or less maintained their quality levels and kept up business as usual (and, in fact, have increased their production of more experimental beers). On the other hand, Founders has become little more than a premium range of craft-like beers for Independent Liquor. With Moa's PR gaffes, alienating both traditional craft beer consumers and women in general, distribution issues and substantial losses ($5.4 million in the year to March 2015), to say the brewery has struggled would be an understatement.[7] Whether it continues to be run as a 'craft brewery' remains to be seen.

Contract brewing

Contract brewing is a growing section of the industry. It refers to 'brewing companies' that do not own physical breweries but choose to rent space and sometimes manpower in other breweries to brew beers they have designed or created.

Due to the rise of this trend, the barriers to entry into the beer market have dropped considerably and the number of contract brewers popping up (and then subsequently disappearing, sometimes after only one commercial release) has been difficult to monitor. There are several very important brewing companies in the New Zealand market for whom contract brewing is their modus operandi, most notably Yeastie Boys and Epic Brewing Company.

There are also a number of now-established brewers who have used contract brewing to test the market for their beers and continue to use it as a platform to establish their own breweries, such as ParrotDog and North End, both Wellington-based. In a similar vein, Søren Eriksen started 8 Wired by working as assistant brewer at Renaissance and established his brand by brewing his own beers in the brewery's downtime. He has since moved to his own facility north of Auckland. It is also common for a smaller brewery to brew a larger batch of beer off site if their own premises won't allow such high-scale production – this has recently been the case for Wellington's Fork & Brewer.

For larger breweries, the ability to contract out some of their excess capacity can be a boon, as it allows them to get more value out of their assets, expand their business and employ more full-time staff. Some breweries, such as Steam (where Epic brews) in Auckland, Stainless Brewing in Christchurch and, to a certain extent, Invercargill Brewery (where Yeastie Boys brews) have made this a part of their business model; while they brew their own beers, a large proportion of their income comes from brewing beers for other brands.

As more and more contract brewers go into production, there is a growing conflict between them and the smaller breweries over the same small slice of the market. In the process of interviewing brewers for this project, I had a number of negative comments about contract brewing; one smaller brewer summed up the general feeling about these beers: 'The current cyber/contract brewing craze, where everyone from accountants to waiters are getting beer brewed at a "brewing facility" and putting a label on it, is misleading and just plain wrong!'

Likewise, in order to establish new businesses and/or expand existing ones, brewers are teaming up to build shared facilities, thus creating the economies of scale of having a larger brewery. When brewer Steve Plowman of Hallertau wanted to expand his business, he teamed up with Liberty's Joe Wood, who also needed a production facility. The result was The Beer Fountain. The benefit of having a large brewery (to meet demand for their popular beers), but with two producers sharing the space and staff, and being able to contract out excess capacity to other Auckland breweries, is much more viable than having one (or two) smaller breweries. Tiamana and Wild and Woolly in Wellington have a similar story: neither had enough capital to build their own brewery but together they have been able to establish a physical one. I imagine that these alliances are also creatively beneficial.

The New Zealand beer industry is a dynamic one – full of larger-than-life, passionate characters; from loveable rogues through to mad scientists. Our beers are just as diverse. One can now find examples of any international style you would care to imagine, as well as others we have thought up ourselves. Our beers range from fiercely traditional through to post-modern.

Our industry now celebrates many facets of New Zealand culture and brewing traditions: from beers inspired by the country's first settlers, incorporating indigenous ingredients, to those that borrow from the brewing traditions of the various migrants to New Zealand, particularly the English, Dutch, Germanic, Slavic and North American.

CLOCKWISE FROM TOP LEFT Andrew Dixon at the Mussel Inn, Golden Bay; Simon Nicholas from Hop Federation, Riwaka; brewers enjoying beer at Deep Creek Brewing.

How beer is made and what goes in it

The brewing process

Grain is milled.

Grain is steeped in hot water to allow the enzymes in the grain to convert the starch to sugar. This is referred to as the **mash**.

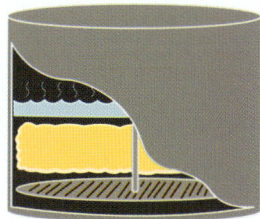

The liquid is then separated from the grain, usually by draining through a false bottom. This is called **lautering**. At the same time, hot water (or **wort**) is poured over the grain to extract all of the sugar from it – this is called **sparging**.

Then the liquid is boiled in a **kettle** or copper. Hops are added throughout this process depending on style. Boiling sterilises the wort and turns the acids in hop flowers into aroma and bittering compounds.

The liquid is then separated from the solids in a **whirlpool**, before (for hop-focused beers) being pumped through a vessel full of hop flowers or pellets. This is called a **hopback**.

This liquid is then chilled very quickly in a **heat exchange** because if it remains tepid (as is the case for some styles like Berliner Weiss) it can be infected by bacteria.

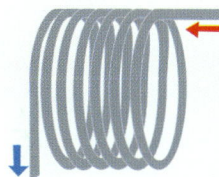

The wort is then pumped into a **fermenter** and yeast is added, converting the sugar into the alcohol.

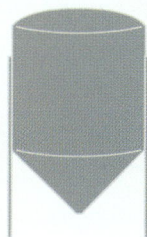

The wort has now transformed into **beer**. This is typically run through a **filter**.

Filtered beer is now pumped into **bright beer tanks** for **conditioning**, before being bottled, kegged or served (in brewpubs, beer is often served straight from the tank). Bottle- and cask-conditioned beers are carbonated by letting the yeast still present in the beer ferment just enough to carbonate the beer naturally in the vessel from which it is served.

Malt

Malt refers to any grain (but when it comes to brewing, it usually means barley and sometimes wheat or rye) that has undergone the process of malting.

In short, malting involves tricking a grain to germinate by creating a warm, moist environment that creates enzymes which can then convert the starches in the grains into sugar (which occurs during mashing), before stopping this process by the application of heat (brewers want sugar, not sprouting barley plants).

How this is done (and whether other steps occur, such as roasting and stewing, as is the case for speciality malts) creates a wide variety of types of malt, which, when carefully selected by a brewer, account for the colour and strength of a beer, as well as a great deal of the flavour, mouthfeel, body and aroma.

After water, malt is the second most abundant ingredient in beer. For every litre of beer brewed, a brewer will use approximately 150–200g of malt.

Types of malt

There are many types of malt and typically they fall into two categories: base malt, which gives the majority of the starch for fermentation and the enzymes that turn these into sugar; and speciality malts, which give colour, flavour and other unique aspects to beer.

Both the European/British two-row and North American six-row barleys can be malted and sometimes this will be specified. Likewise, there are also various different maltsters around the world, all of whom produce malt with a slightly different character.

Base malts

Pilser malt	Originally malted in the town of Pilsen, this is used as a base malt for the majority of lager styles. It is very lightly coloured, subtly malty and sweet.
Pale ale malt	Distinct malty flavour and warm colour, ideal for ale styles.
Maris otter	English variety that gives a distinctive malty character as a base malt, darker than traditional pale ale malts. It is in demand from specialist brewers for the unique character it gives British ale styles.

Speciality malts

Vienna malt	Pronounced malty character, biscuity flavour and ruby hue.
Munich malts	Darker than Vienna malt, it contributes a rich, nutty aroma and flavour to beer.
Carapils	Used in small quantities, it helps increase foam, improves head retention and enhances mouthfeel without adding colour.
Crystal malts	These malts come in a variety of colours and are produced by stewing so that the sugars in the grain begin to caramelise and then crystallise into long-chain sugars that cannot be fermented. Used judiciously, they add sweetness and caramel flavour, and make for a fuller-tasting beer. The darker of these malts add toffee, woody and dried fruit characters to beer.
Biscuit malt	Named for its predominant biscuit/toasted bread character. Gives a brown-red hue to beers.
Chocolate malts	Named for their colour and flavour, there are various chocolate malts, from light to dark. They typically add a chocolate/coffee character to beer as well as a deep brown colour. Aside from barley-based chocolate malts, wheat and rye malts can also be used.
Black patent	Roasted further than chocolate malt, this imparts astringent charcoal notes to black beers.
Black malt	This is a fairly neutral-flavoured malt that imparts a dark colour to beers.
Roasted barley	These are unmalted barley kernels that are roasted until black. They drive the distinctive astringency, bitterness and colour to stout beers.

Doug and Gabi Michael established Gladfield Malt on Doug's family farm, just west of Dunsandel, about half an hour south of Christchurch.

Producing high-end malt, Doug and Gabi equate themselves with the craft brewers they service, saying their philosophy is one of 'quality and service', repeating this mantra on multiple occasions.

They supply 120 New Zealand breweries and brewing supply stores, as well as exporting about 25% of their produce. Australia is a large market but other markets are growing, including the burgeoning Asian craft beer market.

As well as growing barley, Gladfield buy wheat and barley from 15 other growers in the area, giving them a much higher rate for their crop than they would be earning selling it for feed. Among the most rewarding aspects of the job, says Gabi, is to show a farmer how what they have grown translates directly into a physical product.

Among their most famous malts is the Organic Pilsner, which for a long time has formed the backbone of Emerson's Organic Pilsner (until demand for the beer outstripped Gladfield Malt's ability to supply organic malt – the beer is no longer organic). This beer for some time was rated as the best Pilsner in the world on ratebeer.com.

One of the things that makes Gladfield unique is their range of malts, especially the speciality malts they produce. Originally they were producing base malts only but with the growth in the craft beer industry in New Zealand there has been a similar growth in the demand for New Zealand-grown speciality malts. While unimaginable even five years ago, there is a growing number of New Zealand breweries that exclusively use malts from Gladfield.

Gladfield produce approximately 25 different malts – while most of these are analogous to malts from other maltsters, others such as their manuka-smoked malt have a uniquely Kiwi quality. They are constantly experimenting and have recently set up a nano-brewery in one of the sheds adjoining the maltings so that rather than send new malts out to brewers (who often don't have time to brew with them in their own breweries), they can come to Gladfield and experiment there.

In addition to these malts, Gladfield also blend base malts especially for particular customers and have recently introduced an American ale malt with a lighter body than their standard ale malt, making it ideal for hoppy American-style beers.

Gladfield INSIDE
WORLD'S BEST PURE MALT NEW ZEALAND

Hops

The hop, or *Humulus lupulus*, plant is the ingredient used in beer as a preservative, as a bittering agent and for the various flavours different varieties impart. The cultivation of hops dates back to the eighth century CE. However, they are not recorded as being used in beer until around 400 years later. Hops are dioecious, meaning that plants are either male or female, although only the female plants produce the cones that have the aroma and bittering components needed to produce beer.

Hops are used at various stages of the brewing process and come in two main classes. Bittering hops are added to boiling wort at the beginning of a boil, as this converts the insoluble alpha acids (humulones) into soluble, bitter compounds. These alpha acids are extremely antibacterial and act as a beer's preservative. Aroma hops are added toward the end of the boil, in the whirlpool (see page 17) and to fermented beer (dry hopping). Adding hops at these stages allows the essential oils (beta acids) within the hops to dissolve into the beer, resulting in high levels of hop aroma. These essential oils are extremely volatile and, as a result, highly aromatic beers are particularly sensitive to heat and lightstrike, which can convert the iso-alpha acids into off or 'skunky' flavours. As well as aroma and bittering hops, dual-purpose varieties also exist and are able to be used for both bittering and aroma. Some New Zealand varieties, such as Sauvin, Wakatu (Hallertau Aroma) and Waimea, are especially prized for these qualities.

Fresh hops are notoriously fragile and will often begin to deteriorate within hours of being picked. So hops are usually preserved by kiln drying and packing as hop pellets – pulverised dry-hop flowers that are then sealed in foil and further protected by inert gas and refrigeration. Beers brewed with freshly picked hops are generally referred to as 'wet hopped' or 'harvest' beers and are typically made only by breweries in or extremely close to hop-growing regions. These beers have a uniquely delicate hop profile with a distinct green, chlorophyll-like character.

Hop extracts are used by both industrial brewers and some extreme craft brewers for double (and bigger) India pale ales (IPAs). In order to create these extracts, hops are washed with carbon dioxide to extract all of the hop compounds used in brewing. Using these products has several advantages: beers are brewed to have more precise bittering than with whole hops and can be brewed to have a much more assertive hop character than beers brewed without them. Likewise, hops in this form can be manipulated to be light-stable and thus beers brewed with them can be packaged in clear bottles, as is the case with many Mexican lagers.

Hop varieties

As previously mentioned, hops are grown in many parts of the world. Often hops from particular regions or countries share certain characteristics. Here are the characteristics of some of the more important hop-growing regions.

German

Germany has four main hop-producing regions: Hallertau, Elbe-Saale, Tettnang and Spalt, and has the largest overall area under hop cultivation. Other than the Elbe-Saale, all of these have noble hop varieties named after them (the fourth is Saaz, named for the town in the Czech Republic from which it originates). Of these, the Hallertau represents the majority of hop production and is also a centre for hop research. Hallertau is arguably the most famous hop variety, both in Europe and around the world. It is floral with spicy and woodsy characters. Tettnang has citrus zest characteristics with spicy, earthy and grassy notes, and Spalt is softly aromatic, woodsy and peppery.

Czech

Saaz is the pre-eminent hop grown in the Czech Republic and is known for the uniquely spicy, bitter, aromatic character it gives to Pilsner beers.

English

England is one of the cooler hop-producing regions in the world and as such hop varieties from here have distinctive characteristics. English hops are regarded as more subtle than those from other regions (especially the US, Australia and New Zealand). They are typically lower in alpha acids and have flavours that range from earthy and woodsy, to subtle fruit flavours (stone fruit and lemon), to spicy and herbal (mint, pepper, tea). Goldings and Fuggles are among the most important varieties.

American

The unique character of American hops was created as a result of the hybridisation of English and native varieties. While production started in New England, by 1900 the industry had moved to the Pacific Northwest, where it remains firmly centred today; Washington, Oregon and Idaho are now responsible for 'almost all' hop production, with Washington's Yakima Valley being responsible for three-quarters of that.[8] The character of US hops ranges wildly depending on variety, and can include tropical fruit notes, stone fruit, woodsy and spicy characters, but the dominant flavours are often orange, grapefruit, pine and extremely aromatic florals. Among the wide variety of US hops available, some of the most important are Amarillo, Cascade, Citra, Willamette, Centennial, Chinook and Simcoe.

New Zealand

Almost exclusively grown in the hills around the Nelson–Tasman region, centering on Motueka, New Zealand hops represent less that 1% of the world's supply but are heavily in demand, especially from the craft beer industry. New Zealand hops have become internationally famous for a number of reasons but, in particular, because of how their relative isolation from other hops has resulted in low pest and disease pressure, making organic production viable. In addition, the active hop-breeding programme by the government-owned Plant & Food Research has led to the discovery of exciting new hop varieties, such Nelson Sauvin.

International bitterness units (IBUs) are the standard the brewing industry uses to calculate bitterness in beer. Beers typically range between 1 and 100 IBUs (although beers boasting much higher IBU levels do exist), with 1 IBU equalling approximately 1mg of iso-alpha acid per litre of liquid, or 1 part per million. IBU is an indication of actual bitterness rather than perceived bitterness, as the same level of bitterness would be perceived as less in a richer, sweeter beer. It is calculated by taking into account the original gravity of the wort (essentially how much fermentable sugar is in it), the quantity and alpha acid content of the hops, and how long they are boiled for. It does not take into account, for instance, bitterness from other sources, such as roasted malt.

New Zealand HOPS

New Zealand Hops is a grower co-op that represents the 17 commercial hop growers in New Zealand (all are located in the Nelson–Tasman region). While the individual farmers grow the hops, New Zealand Hops is responsible for processing them, and selling and marketing them both in New Zealand and around the world. As well as marketing local hops, it also imports and sells hops from other countries to service the growing New Zealand craft brewing industry.

Nelson–Tasman has a long history of hop growing, with the first plantings dating back to 1842. This turned the region into a centre of brewing. Until 2003, the marketing of hops was controlled by the then state-owned Hop Marketing Board; when this was disestablished, New Zealand Hops (previously NZ Hop Products, which sold pelletised and other processed hops) took over this role.

Due to the long history of hop growing in New Zealand, many of the hop growers who make up New Zealand Hops are fourth- and fifth-generation hop farmers; others include Kono, a Maori-owned food and drink business that covers all of New Zealand and whose activities include grapes and wine production, fisheries and orcharding.

As well as the processing, sale and marketing of hops, New Zealand Hops has taken an active role in the development of new and exciting hop varieties, as well as making sure the industry remains viable (much research is in pest and disease control). It works closely with Plant & Food Research, a Crown research institute, and has had a hop research laboratory in Riwaka since the 1940s.

The first new varieties were released in 1961, developed for their resistance to root rot. Since this time, many varieties have been commercially released, with 11 new commercial varieties between 1987 and 2012. Among the highest regarded of these is Nelson Sauvin, which was released in 2000 and was named for its aromatic similarity to Sauvignon Blanc. In 2014, Plant & Food Research's 'Hop Lab' commissioned a 50-litre brewery to experiment with new varieties, also enlisting the help of New Zealand breweries. In 2014, Wellington's Garage Project released three hop trial beers, each with previously unused (let alone commercial) hop varieties.

The demand for New Zealand hops is huge, both at home and internationally. In 2014, New Zealand Hops produced 765,000kg of hops across about 370 hectares, with 95% of the production sold prior to harvest and future harvest forecasted to be completely pre-sold.

New Zealand Hops has also become an important player in the market for organic hops, with approximately 3% of hops grown being organic varieties.

Water

Beer is about 90% water, so obviously the water a brewer uses will have a great effect on the outcome of the beer. In fact, many of the most famous historical styles of beer, notably Czech Pilsner, Irish stout and Burton IPA would probably have never existed without the particular water profiles of Pilsen, St James's Gate and Burton upon Trent, respectively. Today, the ability to brew particular styles of beer is no longer tied to geographical location – modern brewers can use a variety of chemical modifications to create a particular water profile suitable to the beer they intend to brew. These chemical additives are minerals that naturally occur in water.

At a basic level, most brewers in cities with chlorinated water will filter this through activated carbon to remove the chlorine, which would otherwise react negatively with enzymes in the malt. Among the various minerals used to change the profile of water are: calcium, magnesium, sodium chloride (salt), potassium, iron, zinc, bicarbonate, sulphate and chloride.[9] Sodium bicarbonate (baking soda), for instance, is used to raise the alkalinity of water, which means that yeast is less able to metabolise sugar, leaving the beer with a richer, sweeter feel. On the other hand, calcium (in the form of brewing salts such as gypsum) raises the acidity, which means the yeasts can metabolise more of the sugar, resulting in a beer that is much drier.

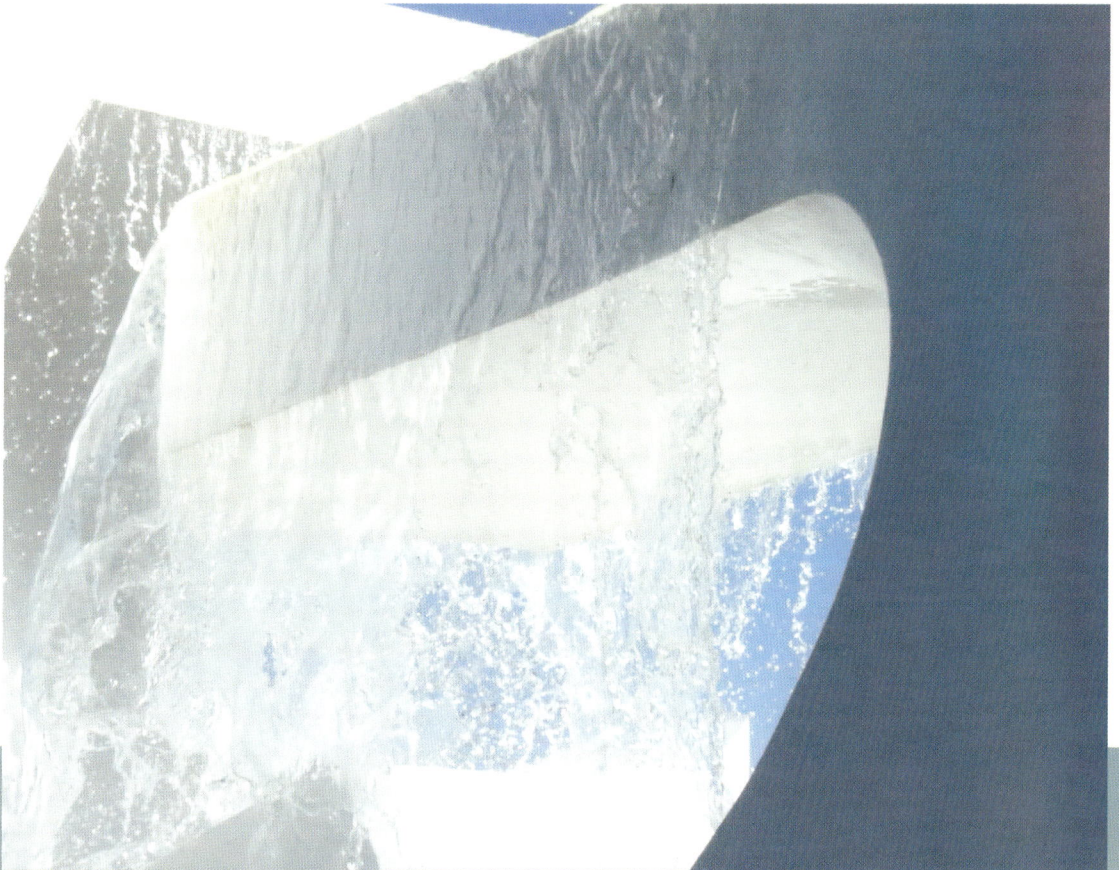

Yeast

Yeasts are single-celled fungi that convert sugar into alcohol and carbon dioxide. When it comes to beer, there are two families of yeasts. Those responsible for the production of ales (*Saccharomyces cerevisiae*) and those responsible for the production of lagers (*Saccharomyces pastorianus*), though other yeast strains are also able to convert malt sugar into alcohol and can thus be used in brewing.

Ale yeasts

While 'isolated' only in 1876, *Saccharomyces cerevisiae* is an extremely old family of yeasts used, probably throughout history, for both brewing and baking. Genetically diverse, *Saccharomyces cerevisiae* includes approximately 200 different varieties, which vary wildly in the character they give beers. *S. cerevisiae* is used throughout the brewing world but most commonly in the beers of Britain and Belgium, in the wheat beers of Germany, and in American-style craft beers. Ale yeasts ferment at warm temperatures and while they do so are responsible for the creation of esters, a group of flavour compounds present at various levels in beer. Most British and American styles of ale have relatively little ester flavour (most lager beers have even less), while wheat beers and Belgian ales derive much of their flavour from esters created during fermentation. These flavours range from fruity to floral, to earthy and spicy, depending on which esters are produced, which, in turn, is dependent on the yeast strain used and the nature of the wort that is fermenting.

Lager yeasts

Named *Saccharomyces pastorianus*, lager yeast is named after Louis Pasteur, who is credited for being the first scientist to understand the role yeast plays in fermentation. This yeast has sometimes been called *Saccharomyces carlsbergensis*, as it was most famously commercialised by Denmark's Carlsberg brewery in 1884. But *S. pastorianus* was the name first used in 1870 and is thus the most taxonomically correct.

Unlike ale yeasts, lager yeasts perform at relatively low temperatures; they also ferment from the bottom of the fermentation vessel (hence ales are often described as top-fermenting beers, and lagers bottom-fermented) and can metabolise sugars that ale cannot, resulting in a beer that is typically drier. Lager yeasts were commercialised much more recently than ale yeasts (although they have been described as early as the 1300s),

which means they are less genetically diverse than ale yeasts. Coupled with the fact that they ferment at lower temperatures, they also create much less flavour than ale yeasts, resulting in a pure, clean, fresh end result, which is shared by many lager styles.

Other yeasts

While other yeasts can convert the sugars in wort to alcohol, most of these also create various off-flavours and are thus often described as 'infections'. This aside, there is one other notable strain of yeast, *Brettanomyces* (or *'Brett'* for short), that is used in beer production. *Brett* lives naturally on the skins of fruit but is also notoriously hardy, and will grow in breweries (and wineries) and in brewing equipment, notably barrels (it is one of the few yeasts that can metabolise the sugars in wood). Unlike the winemaking world, where it is widely vilified, *Brett* is responsible for a number of traditional beer styles, such as the sour beers of Belgium, the unique character of British old ale (*Brettanomyces* means 'British fungi') and some abbey beers, notably Orval. It has been increasingly used by craft beer brewers for a variety of styles – it creates a wide range of flavours, from intensely fruity to very earthy (the most common descriptor is 'horse blanket').

While beer can be inoculated with commercial strains of *Brett*, many brewers will introduce it to a beer by fermenting or ageing that beer in a barrel previously containing a beer or wine infected by *Brett*. Although it is synonymous with sour beer production, *Brettanomyces* by itself (especially commercial strains) produces only small amounts of acidity (such as acetic acid in the presence of oxygen), to create truly sour beers it is usually combined with *Lactobacillus* and/or *Pediococcus* bacteria.

Other stuff you can put in beer

Other than the holy quartet of water, malt, hops and yeast, there are many different ingredients that brewers can add to beer. Typically ingredients are added to beers for one of two reasons. First, and most importantly, other ingredients such as fruits, spices and additional grains can be used to flavour beer. Second, more cost-focused or less scrupulous brewers often add sources of sugar that are cheaper than barley malt to boost the strength of a beer more cheaply.

Enzymes

Enzymes are proteins that can be used to catalyse the complex reactions throughout the brewing process. They occur naturally in brewing ingredients but can also be added at different stages of the brewing process to various effect.

Adjuncts

These are any non-malt 'fermentable' grains used in the brewing of beer, typically to raise the alcohol content of a beer without having to add more malt, but also often to give particular flavour or body characteristics.

In the case of many large, corporate, volume brewers, adjuncts are often used not only as they are a cheaper source of fermentable sugar than malt, but also used to create beers that are lighter in body and character than all-malt beers.

For more quality-focused breweries, adjuncts are used in traditional, historic and experimental styles to add particular characters to beer. For example, the 'extra dry' character of Japanese lager is due to a proportion of rice being added to the mash – malt has traditionally been taxed at high rates in Japan, making all-malt beers prohibitively expensive. Likewise, early American colonists often supplemented brewing mash with cooked pumpkin as it was an easy source of fermentable sugar, making way for the pumpkin beers that have grown in popularity, even here in New Zealand. Among the many adjuncts used in beer are: rice, corn, sorghum, honey, potato, taro, pumpkin and kumara. While all of these add fermentable sugars to a brew, they also impart unique flavour and textural elements.

Non-fermentables

In some cases, brewers will add sugar during the brewing process, not to add alcohol but to add body and/or sweetness. Both lactose (milk sugar) and maltodextrin are used for this purpose, with the former adding some sweetness and the latter adding little to no sweetness.

Fruit

Like adjuncts, fruits were an easy source of fermentable sugar for early brewers. They also had the added benefits of being able to flavour (or hide the flavour of) bad beer and, while we in New Zealand cannot claim alcohol as having health benefits, would have been a source of nutrition. Beers made with fruit would also have been preserved for seasons at a time. Today, fruit is used in beer brewing predominantly for flavouring. Almost every style can be flavoured with fruit. However, the most common are Belgian wheat beer, sour and black beer styles such as stouts and porters. Likewise, almost every variety of fruit can be used, although those traditionally used in beer, such as citrus fruit, cherries and berries, are still the most common today.

Herbs and spices

Before the use of hops to preserve beer, herbs and spices were traditionally used, and even today beers bittered by spice rather than by hops are called gruit (after the herb mixes used to flavour them). Today, brewers use as wide a palette of spices (and herbs) as chefs do, but usually in combination with hops rather than on their own.

Even after the introduction of hops, herbs and spices were still used for many purposes but usually for their purported medical benefits and in some beer traditions for their extra intoxicating potential.

Coffee, chocolate and tea

Coffee, chocolate and tea are used in a similar way to spices and herbs in brewing but need to undergo a transformation by fermentation and processing before they can be added as ingredients. Coffee and chocolate especially are often added to dark beer styles to intensify the characters already present in these beers, though lighter beers brewed with these ingredients also exist. Tea has only recently begun to be popular as a beer ingredient, almost as a reaction to coffee being used so widely. Beers brewed with teas will often take on their tannin structures but also their aromas. Green and herbal teas are often used in wheat beer styles, black and smoked teas in dark beers, and aromatic teas like Earl Grey in equally aromatic beers, such as IPA.

Bacteria and other microflora

While typically the enemy of brewers as they cause spoilage, bacteria are used in the production of several styles of beer, especially sour beer, where *Lactobacillus* and *Pediococcus* can be responsible for creating acidity, either before or after fermentation.

Other flavourings

Essentially anything you can eat (or is safe to eat) can be added to beer. If you can imagine something as a beer ingredient, it probably has been used as one. Bacon,[10] oysters,[11] whole chicken,[12] pizza,[13] gold,[14] bulls' testicles[15] and even civet poo (containing rather expensive coffee)[16] have all been used in beer production.

CLOCKWISE FROM TOP Jim Matranga at Golden Bear Brewing, Mapua; Peter Lines from Totara Brewing Company, Nelson; Chris Barber tasting brews at Zeelandt Brewery, Napier.

Beer styles

One of the reasons I decided to write *Brewed* is that beer can be confusing. And nothing confounds amateurs and professionals alike more than its many styles. Even brewers have trouble with this, and misnamed beer can cause a lot of frustration among consumers.

Is there a difference between a pale ale, an American pale ale (APA) and a session IPA? Yes, without a doubt. But there are also many beers that could be described as all three. Taking the pale ale example even further, here in New Zealand there is no clear definition between English and American styles, so classifying them as one or another seems pointless to me. While The Twisted Hop's Hopback IPA is quintessentially British and Epic's Armageddon a flag-waving Yankee drop, these are the two beers at the poles of the style scale – there are countless more that sit at different places on the spectrum. Regardless of this, I'm sure that buyers of a beer like Hopback IPA are much more likely looking for a 'hoppy ale' than a strictly British-style one and have thus categorised it as such.

I have created a style guide that will make sense to consumers but I have taken inspiration from various other guides and sources, including the 2014 Beer Judge Certification Program Draft Guidelines, The Brewers Guild of New Zealand Awards Style Guidelines, RateBeer, BeerAdvocate, *The Oxford Companion to Beer*, conversations with brewers and my own market experience. Please bear in mind the guide I have created is designed for the average engaged beer consumer in New Zealand. As such, there are some international styles that are largely ignored, while there are some New Zealand-specific styles (especially in regard to New Zealand hops) that feature in more detail.

There are some beers that probably should not be in the categories they are in. English-style pale ales and IPAs should probably be in the British-style ales category, Schwarzbier should probably be in the lager category, and 'Other weird and wonderful beer styles' is not really all that technical a definition of anything.

Because sour/wild beers are spread across all of the different style categories, they are included in the most relevant category (instead of having a separate, catch-all category).

Nomenclature

Beer is constantly evolving, and thus brewers are becoming more and more specific when describing their beers. There is a growing tendency to hybridise beer style names to describe a beer more accurately. In some cases, brewers use descriptors (say 'NZ' for New Zealand hops or 'Belgi' or 'Belgo' for Belgian yeasts) in addition to a style like IPA; in others they mash styles together, such as 'IPL' or India pale lager – a bitter, strong, hoppy lager.

Imperial and double

For bigger, stronger beers in already established styles, most brewers use one of two terms: imperial or double. These terms usually imply that whatever dominant characteristics the beer style originally has, this too will be amplified. Where use of these terms defines a beer style (as is the case with imperial stout or double IPA), there are specific style descriptors. Combining both descriptors: double imperial (or imperial double) implies the beer is stronger again, as does the use of triple and even quadruple.

Lager

The word 'lager' refers to cold storage and maturation, and has been a common brewing practice that dates as far back as medieval times. Brewers at that time used bottom-fermenting yeast, a practice that emerged in the early fifteenth century and became commonplace in Bavaria and Bohemia between 1860 and 1870.

Pale lager
This is one of the most commonly available styles of commercial beer and is generally what is meant when a beer is described as 'lager'. Pale lagers are typically light in body and straw to golden in colour, with little hop flavour and aroma. They are typically around 4% ABV (alcohol by volume).

American lager typically has a high proportion of maize, giving it a lighter, crisper body. Japanese lager often uses rice to similar effect.

Premium lager
Slightly stronger than pale lager, premium lagers are also commonly referred to as 'green bottle beers'. They have more obvious malt body and some hop flavour and aroma.

Pilsner (Pilsener)
This style was developed in the mid-nineteenth century when the British malting techniques that allowed for the creation of pale ales were combined with European brewing techniques. The first recorded example of this style is Pilsner Urquell, which was first brewed in the town of Pilsen (in modern-day Czech Republic) in 1842. Pilsner Urquell remains the pre-eminent example of this style. Pilsners are golden in colour with more pronounced malt flavour than pale and premium lager, and more pronounced hop bitterness.

Bohemian Pilsners are beers brewed with the traditional Czech Saaz hop, which gives the beer a spicy, slightly floral aroma.

German Pilsners are typically paler and lighter in body than Bohemian Pilsners and, as they are brewed with noble German hop varieties, are more bitter and less aromatic.

New world or international Pilsners are brewed using hop varieties cultivated in the US, New Zealand and Australia. Depending on the variety of hop used, they usually have a more vibrant hop profile, often with aromatic and/or fruity notes.

Munich helles
Named after the German word *hell*, meaning light, helles is a style of pale lager from Bavaria. Water in Bavaria had a much higher mineral content than that of Bohemia, and as a result Pilsner-styled beers tasted too aggressively bitter. This style was created with a much milder hop profile and despite the style being less than a century old it has become extremely popular. Helles are typically golden, with little bitterness but pronounced malt flavours.

Maibock (or helles bock) beers are a stronger example of this style brewed in May.

Vienna lager
Vienna lager takes its name from Vienna malt, which gives beer a distinctive copper colour and has a toasty/biscuit malt aroma. Vienna lager is a darker, richer style of lager but retains focused hop bitterness. As a result of nineteenth-century Austrian immigration, it is a style that has thrived in Mexico.

Märzen/Oktoberfest
Märzen is a Bavarian style of lager brewed in late March. The beer was originally cellared until late summer and, in order to age well, it would have either been high in alcohol, highly hopped, or both.

Since 1818, Märzen beers have been served at Oktoberfest and only the six breweries that have traditionally served their beer at the festival are entitled to call their beer Oktoberfestbier.[17] From 1872, a stronger version of the Vienna style was popularised and became the common style of the festival. Märzen/Oktoberfest beers are typically medium- to full-bodied and copper-coloured, with rich, malty flavours and a dry finish.

Munich dunkel
Dunkel is German for 'dark' and these beers, which range in colour from copper through to chocolate, are the traditional style of Munich. With an ABV between 4.5% and 6%, they are full-bodied beers

with enough bitterness to balance sweetness. They often have a noticeable malty flavour, which is achieved through decoction brewing.[18]

Bock and doppelbock

Bock was first brewed in the town of Einbeck in Germany and dates back to the fourteenth century. This dark malt ale was adopted by brewers in Munich around the seventeenth century and then adapted to the new method of lager brewing. Bock beers typically have malt-accented flavours, are relatively strong (6–7.5%) and range in colour from light copper to dark brown. Hops are used sparingly and only to give balance to this relatively sweet style of beer.

Doppelbock are 'double' or stronger (7–12%) bock beers. They were originally brewed for friars and monks to drink during Lent, acting as a liquid meal. Like bock beers, they range in colour but their aroma and flavours are derived from malt, with caramel and toasty notes in lighter coloured beers, ranging through to extremely fruity and chocolate/mocha flavours in darker examples.

Eisbock is made by partially freezing finished beer, then removing the ice to create a sweeter, richer and stronger end result.

Bock is traditionally associated with special occasions like Christmas, Easter and Lent.

New Zealand amber lager

Also often referred to as New Zealand draught and sometimes erroneously referred to as an ale, this is a collection of light-bodied amber/brown beers that are relatively sweet and are usually around 4% ABV. Typically, they have some bitterness but very little hop character. This is a style created and dominated by the two large brewing conglomerates in New Zealand – Lion and DB. However, there are also excellent craft examples of this style.

California common/steam beer

California common is a style of beer made by brewing with lager yeasts at warmer temperatures. It originated on the west coast of the US as brewers lacked refrigeration (and in some cases access to ice or even cold water). This style was pioneered by the San Franciscan brewery Anchor,

who now own the trademark to the term 'Steam Beer'. Anchor Steam is still regarded as the prototypical style of this beer: it combines the crispness of a lager with the weight of an ale, and uses hops that give the beer a bitter, woodsy flavour.

Wheat beer

Wheat beers are a family of beers that, needless to say, are defined by the presence of a high proportion of wheat malt or unmalted wheat. They usually fall into two categories: those originating in Germany; and those originating in Belgium. While they derive a significant amount of their flavour and structure from the wheat malts, they also derive their unique flavour profiles from the yeasts used, which create fruity, spicy aromas. In the case of the Belgian examples, they are also often flavoured with unmalted grains, fruits (especially citrus) and spices.

Witbier

Literally 'white beer', this is a beer style originally brewed in Flanders and France (where it is called bière blanche). It is typically made with unmalted wheat and sometimes other adjuncts, such as oats or spelt, and is commonly flavoured with spices like coriander and citrus peel. These beers are white in colour and have a low bitterness, with no hop profile, a light, effervescent body, and a citrusy/spicy aroma with mild acidity. Hoegaarden is the most famous international example of this style. These beers are usually between 4% and 5% ABV but stronger 'celebration beers' are sometimes made to commemorate holidays.

Berliner weisse

This is a style of sour wheat beer that originated in Berlin but shares several stylistic similarities with the sour beers of Belgium – it may have been brought to Germany by French immigrants via Flanders. It is an extremely dry, light beer (both in colour and strength), with a sharp, sour flavour created by the addition or cultivation of the same bacteria found in naturally fermented foods, such as sauerkraut. In Berlin, these beers are often served with a shot of fruit syrup and can be flavoured with fruit, such as citrus.

Gose

Like Berliner weisse, Gose (pronounced goes-uh) is another German beer style that is heavily influenced by the beers of Belgium. It has a distinct salinity, being fermented with salted water. It is normally flavoured with coriander seed (but outside of Germany it is often flavoured with other ingredients) and as such does not comply with the Reinheitsgebot.[19] Like Berliner weisse, these beers are often traditionally served with a shot of fruit syrup.

Lambic (non-fruit)

Native to the region surrounding Brussels, lambics are a family of wild sour beers, usually containing 30–40% unmalted wheat. Wort is traditionally left exposed to allow the microflora in the brewery to induce spontaneous fermentation. While hops are used as a preservative, these are traditionally aged hops that have lost much of their bitterness and flavour. Because of their natural fermentation, lambics have a distinctly sharp, sour character and as such are either aged and blended, as is the case with Geuze, or sweetened and pasteurised, as is the case with Faro. For fruit examples, see the 'Fruit beer' section on page 42.

Weissbier/hefeweizen

Weissbier also translates as 'white beer' and is the 'classical wheat beer of Bavaria'.[20] It is brewed traditionally with at least 50% wheat malt, and sometimes a much higher proportion, but outside of Germany can also be brewed with less. These beers are straw to amber in colour and typically cloudy (although kristalweizen is a filtered variation that is clear). They have a low bitterness and hop profile, and a vibrant fruity/spicy aroma and flavour profile typified by banana and cloves but also including smoke, nutmeg, vanilla and bubblegum.

Dunkelweizen

Brewed with darker malts than weissbier to create a chocolate-like colour, Dunkelweizen beers have a more complex, malt-driven flavour profile with chocolate notes subduing the otherwise vibrant fruit and spice esters. The high carbonation provides freshness.

Weizenbock

Weizenbocks are German wheat beers brewed to bock strength (7%+), depending on producer, and range in style from gold to very dark. They normally have a malty sweetness, vibrant clove and banana aromas, and some roasty elements. Like weissbier and dunkelweizen styles, the carbonation is high, which balances the full body.

Wheat ale

The term wheat ale refers to any beer brewed, typically in the new world, with a proportion of wheat malt that falls outside the German and Belgian styles. They are usually light in body and colour, have low to no ester aromas, and are often flavoured with any number of fruits and/or spices. Moderate to highly hopped examples are often described as American, hoppy or pale wheat ales (see 'Hoppy ale styles' on pages 36–37).

British ale styles

If there is one thing that defines the styles of brewing native to the United Kingdom and Ireland, it is balance. While balance is important to every beer style, the beers of this region balance malt and local hop varieties to create a wide selection of styles that form the basis for the majority of those championed by the craft brewing movement. Britain has a brewing tradition that dates back to the Anglo-Saxon colonisation in the fourth century CE. However, it has only been since the Industrial Revolution that the styles we typically associate with British beer were established.

Cask ale/real ale

This is a serving method rather than a style. Cask or real ale is an unpressurised, unpasteurised, unfiltered beer that has been naturally refermented in the cask it has been poured from via a beer engine (often referred to as a hand pull). Because these beers are refermented on their natural yeasts, they have a light carbonation and a unique depth of flavour, and are typically served at cellar temperature, which is cool but not cold. These beers are distinctly different to 'cold, fizzy' beers served out of bottles and pressurised keg systems, and are in fact sometimes derided as 'warm and flat'.

Here in New Zealand, Steve Nally of Invercargill Brewery has pioneered a system that simplifies the serving of these beers by packaging them in large bladders. While beers served this way are not true real or cask ales in the traditional sense, the system allows beers similar to the style to be served in bars and pubs that lack traditional hand-pull systems.

English golden and pale ales

English golden and pale ales (often confusingly referred to as IPAs, as is the case with Greene King IPA) are a golden light- to medium-bodied beer with subtle but balanced malt and English hop characteristics. Seasonal beers in this style are often made in the warmer months and described as summer ales.

Bitter

Among the most traditional of the English styles, this refers to a cask-conditioned beer typically tawny in colour. In New Zealand it can refer to a variety of beers made in a similar style, ranging in colour from deep gold to copper and served from cask, keg or bottle. These beers show moderate malt character balanced by clean bitterness and, occasionally, some hop aroma, usually from English hop varieties like Fuggles or Goldings. Brewed with English ale yeasts, some fruity ester characters can be present. For traditional producers, 'Ordinary' or 'Boys' usually denotes a beer between 3% and 4% ABV and 'Special' or 'Best' for a beer of around 4–5% ABV.

Extra Special Bitter (ESB)

Made famous by the Fuller's Brewery of London, this is a richly flavoured, malty copper-coloured bitter ale. Full-bodied, and it has an almost marmalade-like malt sweetness that is counterbalanced by focused bitterness and some resiny hop aroma. While rich and sweet, this beer finishes fresh and should be thirst-quenching and moreish. Examples made with American hops are also made but are typically labelled as such.

India pale ale (IPA)

See 'Hoppy ale styles' on pages 36–37.

Mild ale

Mild ale is a typically brown, lower-alcohol (3–3.5% ABV), full-flavoured, slightly sweeter beer. It has traditionally been a worker's beer brewed to be drunk in quantity. It typically has nutty chocolate flavours, often accompanied by liquorice and roast notes.

Brown ale

These beers originate in the north of England, are around 5% ABV, and are typically dry and brown (although there are sweeter styles). They have little bitterness or hop aroma, but do carry rich, round chocolate, hazelnut, fruit and roasted malt flavours. While there are few examples of this style brewed in New Zealand, it is a precursor to the more popular American brown ale style.

Old Ale

These are strong, darkish beers that are aged, typically in wooden vats, before being bottled and sold. They are around 7% ABV and relatively sweet (although over time this residual sweetness can ferment out until the beer is dry), with rich fruitiness and an almost port-like alcoholic and oxidative character. Some traditional examples of this style have some acidity from *Brettanomyces*.

Barley wine
Essentially, barley wine has become a catch-all for strong, malty beers (over 10% ABV) that otherwise defy classification (as a double or imperial IPA, for example), and are named for both their similar alcohol levels to wine and their similar, intensely complex flavours – not to mention their capacity for cellar-ageing (and are thus often vintage-dated). These beers range from relatively pale to extremely dark, but share a full body, a high level of malt sweetness, vinous and sometimes oxidative characters and, typically, but not always, low hop bitterness and aroma. American-brewed (and American-inspired barley wines) are significantly more hoppy than English examples.

Scotch ale
Also described as 'wee heavy', Scotch ales are rich reddish-brown beers with a sweet malt character and roasted malt and caramel notes, and are typically brewed between 7% and 9% ABV. While not traditional, many Scotch ales are now brewed with a small percentage of peat-smoked (or other smoked) malt, giving these beers a similar smokiness to Scotch whisky.

Irish red ale
Usually between 4% and 5% ABV, these beers are typically a vibrant red colour, ranging from dark copper to mahogany. With their distinctive toffee-like sweetness and roasted malt character, they have low bitterness and hop aroma but are often extremely dry.

Hoppy ale styles

While I have described these beers as 'hoppy ale styles' they could also be referred to as 'American ale styles'. They grew out of a micro-brewing revolution that started on the west coast of the US in the 1970s and 1980s, and featured beers that were generously hopped with local varieties. The style has since spread throughout both the rest of the US and the world.

With the importance of hop cultivation to the New Zealand beer industry, many local examples of these styles are now hopped predominantly with New Zealand-grown hops, which give very different flavour and aroma profiles from the pine, orange and grapefruit notes typical of American hop varieties; hops from Continental Europe, the UK, Australia and Japan (among other regions) are also often used. I have thus used the term hoppy ale styles to distinguish between hoppy beers and those that feature American hop varieties.

It should be noted that many of these styles evolved out of traditional English styles and others still – Belgian IPA, for instance – represent a second evolution, combining American styles with the aromatic yeast strains to create hybrid styles.

New Zealand/Kiwi/Aotearoa

Rather than a style category of their own, these terms indicate that beers belonging to another style category are hopped with New Zealand-grown hops, giving them a uniquely Kiwi flavour profile.

Golden ale

Much like the English golden ale style (see page 34), these beers are typically light- to medium-bodied beers with a golden hue. Unlike the English style, however, these beers have a more assertive hop character, usually from American or New Zealand hops. The term sparkling ale is used almost interchangeably with golden ale by some breweries.

American wheat ales and Pacific ales

American wheat ales refers to beers that have been brewed with a proportion of wheat malt, or unmalted wheat, but which are hopped in a similar way to a pale ale style. They are fermented with British or American ale yeasts that don't give the wide variety of flavours German or Belgian yeast strains achieve. These beers are pale with some cloudiness; they have a distinctively wheaten element to them, but are also relatively bitter and have aromatic hop characters.

Recently, there has been an emergence of New Zealand- and Australian-hopped golden ales with a small proportion of wheat malt. The archetypal beer in this style is Stone & Wood's Pacific Ale. These beers have especially vibrant tropical hop flavours, including passion fruit, papaya and pineapple.

India pale ale (IPA)

This was originally a high-strength pale beer that was generously hopped in order to survive shipping over the Equator between Britain and India. While it originates in the UK, since the 1980s it has become the de facto style for craft breweries the world over, starting with brewers in Washington's Yakima Valley (a notable hop-producing region) using locally grown hops. This style of beer, typified by the citrus and pine flavours of Chinook and Cascade hops, spread down the American west coast and eventually across the country and around the world, re-establishing IPA as a popular style.

IPAs take on the characteristics of the hop varieties with which they are brewed and, given this, those brewed with American hops (which is common) are distinctly different to those brewed with New Zealand or Australian hops. When a beer is described as an English IPA, this usually indicates both that English hops have been used and that the malt base of the beer is more pronounced than American styles.

IPAs should range from around 6.5% to 7.5% ABV and vary in colour from gold to copper. While they have sweet malt notes due to their strength (which are more emphasised in English-inspired examples), they should finish dry. Their defining characteristic is their persistent, focused bitterness combined with vibrant hop aroma and flavours.

Pale ale/American pale ale (APA)

This was one of the first 'Americanised' styles of beer to establish itself. These beers were originally based on English pale ales (see page 34) and bitters, but hopped with American rather than traditional English hops. They are higher in alcohol than these beers, though, with 5% to 6% ABV. Unlike IPAs, which should have a solid backbone of malt, these beers are about hops, hops and more hops. Light, crisp and refreshing, they are often bracingly bitter and with a panoply of US hop character: pine, orange and grapefruit. There are a growing number of New Zealand pale ales, hopped with citrus, tropical fruit and grassy New Zealand hop varieties.

Double/imperial IPA

These beers are stronger, hoppier takes on the IPA. They range from 8% up to around 14% ABV; stronger beers again are often described as 'triple' and even 'quadruple'. Due to the amount of malt sugar needed to produce these beers, they are often considerably richer and sweeter than IPAs, with a distinct honeyed sweetness. The bitterness of these beers can be extreme, and this is usually accompanied by vibrant hop character.

Session IPA/session pale ale

Technically, the term 'session' refers to any beer with a moderate amount of alcohol that can be drunk continually over a long period of time – i.e. a session. Session IPAs and pale ales are beers brewed to emulate the aggressive bitterness and vibrant hop character of these beer styles but at a lower strength of between 2.5% and 4.6% ABV. They are pale, light-bodied and often extremely dry. Because of this final fact, these beers are often criticised for their lack of balance, with an aggressive amount of hops overlayed onto a relatively light frame of malt.

Belgian IPA

These beers are brewed as traditional IPAs but are fermented with Belgian yeast strains, giving them a rich, intense, secondary aromatic character driven by fermentation esters.

Wild/Brett/farmhouse IPA

Also known simply as American wild ale, these beers are fermented with either commercial strains of the yeast *Brettanomyces* or inoculated with wild yeasts floating around in the air. The presence of wild yeasts in these beers often translates to a sour note. Where this is the case, and in order to soften the acidity and achieve balance, they are often aged before release, meaning they sometimes have less dominant hop characters than other styles.

Amber ales and red ales

Amber ales are typically brewed with darker malts than pale ales and IPAs, and are therefore richer and maltier, with toffee and caramel notes. The more dominant malt profile has less dominant hop characters but is still distinctively hoppy.

American brown ale

This style arose from American craft brewers seeking to replicate the brown ales of the north of England. Typically, these beers are bitter and heavily hopped, although many examples are also flavoured with coffee and nuts.

American strong ale

This is a catch-all for strong (over 7% ABV), heavily hopped beers that don't readily fall into any of the previous categories. These beers are big, malty and hoppy. Stone's Arrogant Bastard is one of the best-known examples of the style.

Belgian/French ales

Belgium, which is roughly the size of the lower North Island, has more than 300 breweries and a myriad of beer styles. We have dealt with lager and wheat beers, so this section will deal exclusively with the ales of Belgium (and to some extent northern France and the Netherlands). Unlike the traditional ale styles of England and the US, whose flavour relies predominantly on the interplay between malt and hops, the ales of Belgium (and, in fact, Belgian ales brewed elsewhere) rely more heavily on the variety of flavours created by yeast strains, often unique to individual breweries, during fermentation. Likewise, in contrast to most other families of beer, many of these styles are subtly flavoured with fruit, herbs and other ingredients.

Trappist beer

While not a style, but a family of beers in multiple styles, Trappist beer must be brewed by one of 10 Trappist monasteries, six of which are in Belgium. There are a further two on the Dutch side of the border, between the Netherlands and Belgium, and one each in the US and Austria (although until 2012 only the six Belgian breweries and the Dutch De Koningshoeven, brewing under the La Trappe name, existed). Trappist beers are all brewed according to strict rules. While not an indication of quality in and of itself, the consistent high quality of these beers has meant the term Trappist is widely regarded as the pinnacle of Belgian brewing. Other than the beers from the Westvleteren brewery and those from recently founded breweries, Trappist beers are widely available in New Zealand.

Belgian blonde/golden ales

Also referred as pale or blonde ales, these beers are among the lightest in colour of the Belgian ales and usually have an alcohol content between 6% and 8% ABV. The moderate to high level of alcohol is often well hidden by the light body and dry mouthfeel, resulting in a deceptively 'drinkable' beer. Typically, these beers have caramel, light malt notes, and some subtle noble hop character with a rich, spicy note derived from fermentation. While there are countless examples of this style, the most widely recognised is Duvel.

Farmhouse ales

Comprised predominantly of the French bière de garde and Belgian saisons (but also including other similar beers), these are group of beers traditionally brewed at a higher strength and designed to be kept and drunk throughout summer, when it was difficult to brew without modern refrigeration – in practice, they were often kept much longer than this. While these beers are not considered 'sour', some acidity can be present. Bières de garde range from 5% to 8% ABV and are typically gold to red in colour, with a dominant malt profile and subtle hop character. These beers are rich without being sweet, and often have an earthy, yeast-derived flavour due to the presence of *Brettanomyces* yeast. Saison beers have a similar range in colour and alcohol, but rather than having a malty sweetness are typically highly attenuated and dry. While they can have some *Brett* flavour, they also have a characteristic black-pepper spice element and are sometimes flavoured with speciality ingredients.

Belgian brown ales

This is a wide range of beers tied together by their colour, which ranges from copper to extremely dark. They usually have a dominant malt profile with some sweetness, a rich, creamy body, and flavours that include toffee, black bread and roasted malt, accentuated by subtle spicy yeast aromas. These beers tend to range between 5% and 7% ABV but can have a higher alcohol content. Like Belgian blonde ales, they can be deceptively drinkable, with their complexity and texture masking high alcohol levels.

Dubbel

Usually produced by a Trappist or abbey brewery (or by brewers inspired by these styles), dubbels share their colour palette with Belgian brown ales. However, rather than malt, their colour is derived from the use of dark candi sugar.[21] This gives the beers an almost vinous raisin character, which can be intensified by the fruit esters produced by the yeast.

Tripel

Tripel is a style of strong golden ale that is associated with Trappist and abbey brewers and was first brewed in the 1930s, originally by secular breweries and later by Westmalle. These beers are brewed with an amount of brewer's sugar that raises the alcohol level without affecting body. They have a complex flavour with subtle hop characteristics, light malt notes and spicy aromas that range from clove and burnt orange to banana and vanilla. Tripels are relatively dry and effervescent, and produce a mousse-like head. Despite being between 7% and 10% ABV, they should be extremely balanced and drinkable…too drinkable.

Quadrupel

The weakest of the Trappist and abbey quadrupels start at around 9% ABV and increase from there. They range in colour and style but typically have intense aromas of dried and fresh fruit: dates, raisins, figs, grapes and plums, with a distinctively vinous character and overt yeast ester notes. Unlike the other styles of Trappist beer, these beers usually show sweet malt character and have noticeable alcoholic notes.

Flanders red and brown ales

With their bracing acidity, the sour beers of Flanders are among the most distinctive beer styles in the world. Both the red and brown ales are extremely complex, with malt sweetness, flavours from oak-ageing and sharp acidity from unique yeast strains coming into play – they sometimes even have a hint of acetic acid character. These beers are typically made by blending young and older beers to get the desired balance.

Black beer

The very descriptive term 'black beer' refers to several families of beer, both lagers and ales, that have a dark brown to black colour due to their use of black malt, roasted malt or roasted barley, which also impart a distinct bitterness and astringency. At first it seems like a relatively homogenous group of beers, but in fact they can range from delicate to extremely powerful, and from silky sweet to coarse and bitter. More than any other style, black beers can be flavoured with all manner of other ingredients, but especially other 'dark' flavours: nuts, dried fruit, chocolate, coffee, oak and even other spirits like bourbon (from barrel-ageing).

Schwarzbier

Literally translated as 'black beer', schwarzbier is a German style of dark lager that is the softest, most subtle of the black beer styles, at around 5% ABV, and has a light to medium body and moderate bitterness. These beers typically have a sweet malt characteristic and bittersweet notes of dark chocolate, coffee and vanilla.

Black IPA

This is an assertively hopped, bitter and intensely aromatic style of black beer that originated in the US, probably Vermont. Its name is oxymoronic, but that's what you get when you let an east coaster brew hoppy beer.[22] Other descriptors, like American black ale, India black ale and Cascadian dark ale are often used. Especially where American hops are used, these beers can have a distinctive chocolate/citrus character. They are typically between 6% and 8% ABV but double/imperial and higher strength versions are not unknown.

Porter

Porter is the precursor style to stout (the earliest stouts, including Guinness, were originally referred to as stout porters). These beers are brewed with a base of pale malt, with the addition of black, chocolate or smoked brown malt, giving the beers rich chocolate, coffee and nutty characters. They have a firm bitterness. Those hopped with American varieties of hops are common and usually described as American porters.

Imperial or double porters are regularly brewed by micro-brewers as a base beer for many flavourings, especially sweet spices such as vanilla, but also coffee and chocolate.

Stout

Rather than being an individual style, stout is better described as a family of beers. These beers derive their unique flavour, raspy bitterness and dryness from the use of roasted barley and other roasted grains, and have flavours that are often described as black coffee, dark chocolate and molasses-like malt notes. The flavours of hops are generally subdued by the character of the roasted malts and, as such, while bitter, stouts typically do not have vibrant hop aromas (an exception is American-style stouts).

Beers simply described as stout range from 4% to 7% ABV and are extremely dark, often jet black. As above, they have a distinctive raspy bitterness from roasted grains and usually have dark and burnt notes. While not always described as such, American stouts are very similar other than their aggressive hopping, which adds more bitterness and some hop aromas (especially pine and citrus).

Irish dry stouts

Epitomised by Guinness, these beers are around 4% ABV and are the lightest and driest of the stout family. They are often lightly carbonated and thus are creamy (a trait that can be intensified by pouring over nitrogen).

Milk stouts

Also known as sweet stouts, these are typically lower in alcohol (around 4% ABV) and are sweetened by the addition of lactose, a milk sugar that is unfermentable by the yeasts used in beer production. Because of this, they are sweeter and creamier than other stouts. Flavours of milky coffee and milk chocolate are more common and often intensified by the use of these ingredients as flavourings.

Oatmeal stouts

Oatmeal can also be added to the mash when making a stout, resulting in the creatively named oatmeal stout. These beers are incredibly smooth as the oatmeal increases their body and creaminess.

Imperial stout

From the late 1700s, porter brewers regularly produced stronger versions of their beer, which are still today described as Baltic porters – these beers grew in popularity and eventually made their way to the court of Catherine the Great. There they became stronger again, and thus the moniker Russian imperial stout was used (the Russian has since been dropped by most, but not all, brewers). Since the 1980s, this style has become more and more popular among craft brewers and today refers to a stout between 7% and 12% ABV. A sweet, dark fruit and port-like character, from the amount of malt used, is balanced by high levels of roasted barley and hops. Imperial stout has been embraced by extreme brewers who seek to push flavour and alcohol even higher and regularly do things like adding coffee, chocolate, vanilla and dark fruits, as well as ageing the beers for long periods in oak barrels before sale.

41

Other weird and wonderful beer styles

These are beers that fall outside the traditional families of beer styles already outlined. They include beers made with adjuncts, beers flavoured with fruit, spice and smoke, and beers that are aged in barrels. Many of these styles and techniques are used in conjunction with one or more established styles. For example, smoked beers can be made in almost every style imaginable.

Rye beer

Rye beer refers to any beer brewed with whole grains, processed flakes or rye malt as a proportion of the grain bill. Traditional to some styles like German roggenbier, rye is now used in almost every style of beer but especially red ales and IPAs. Ryes impart a spicy, complex depth to beer and soften the mouthfeel of a beer, making it smoother and rounder. Rye has a naturally red hue, so often adds this colour to beer brewed with it.

Pumpkin ale

As a vegetable, pumpkin is rich in fermentable sugars – it was originally used by English settlers in America to boost the alcoholic strength of their beers. Today, either raw or roasted pumpkin (sometimes even the 'juice' thereof) is added to the boil or fermenter. There are a few New Zealand examples of pumpkin beer, and also of kumara beers made in a similar style. In the US, pumpkin beers are often produced for Halloween, aong with the addition of 'pumpkin pie spices' – cinnamon, nutmeg, ginger, allspice and others.

Honey beer

Honey can be added either prior to fermentation to add its distinctive flavour as well as roundness to a beer or, as in the case of most mass-market honey beers, to pasteurised beer after fermentation to give it sweetness as well. Different varieties of honey all add their own character to beer.

Fruit beer

Many beer styles can be flavoured with fruit. The most common are wheat beer and sour styles, but the flavouring of black beers with berries and stone fruit like plums and cherries is becoming more common.

Fruit can be added both before and after fermentation. Typically, it is the more serious producers who add fruit before fermentation, creating a more integrated, complex fruit character. More commercial styles will have fruit added to pasteurised beer so it sweetens as well as flavours it. These beers are typically (and cynically) marketed toward women.

Coffee, tea and chocolate beer

All three of these ingredients can be used to flavour beer. The unique flavours of each add an extra layer of depth to a beer, often accentuating another character, such as coffee or chocolate flavours in black beer or, as in the case of beers brewed with Earl Grey tea, the citrusy floral characters of some hop varieties. All three ingredients will also add caffeine, and usually extra bitterness, to a beer.

Spiced beer

Beer can be flavoured with almost any imaginable spice or herb, though some are much more common than others. Each spice adds a distinctive aromatic quality and many also add secondary characters, such as bitterness and warmth. As with fruit beer, almost every beer style can be flavoured, although there are some styles that are most often adapted, especially wheat beer styles, Belgian ale styles and lightly hopped brown and amber ales.

Many beers are brewed using ingredients native to a brewing region; in New Zealand, for example, the Mussel Inn brews their Captain Cooker with manuka tips and has licensed its brewing around the world. Of the many spices regularly used, vanilla is common, especially in high-alcohol dark beers. Chillies (in various forms, from fresh through to smoked chipotle) are used in a variety of beer styles, from pale lager to imperial stouts, and coriander is a traditional ingredient in Belgian witbier. As well as herbs and spices, tree bark, leaf tips, flowers and even nuts and nut extracts are all often used and regarded in the same way as better-known herbs and spices.

Gruit

Gruit ales are brewed without hops but instead use other spices, herbs and ingredients to bitter and preserve the beer. These beers tend to be much sweeter than hopped beer as their ingredients are usually much less bitter than hops.

Smoked beer

While some malt varieties have a smoke-like character, many brewers like to impart a deeper, more distinct smoke character through the use of smoked malt (and other ingredients). Beech is one of the most traditional woods used, notably in the traditional rauchbier (smoked beer) of Bamburg, Germany. Fruit woods tend to impart sweeter smoke flavours, whereas botanicals like manuka impart a uniquely spicy smoke.

Barrel-aged beer

While many traditional beer styles (such as lambics and other sour beers) are brewed in barrels, many modern brewers use barrel-ageing to add more depth and complexity to their beers, and to smooth the high levels of alcohol in some stronger styles.

Beer aged in a barrel will take on several characteristics, notably the wood flavours and tannin from the barrel, and sometimes flavour from whatever was originally held inside the barrel (new barrels are seldom used for beer). Wine barrels are most often made from French oak and impart a more subtle character, finer tannins and fruit characters; those made for spirits (especially bourbon and Scotch whisky) are usually American oak and give more vanillin character and rougher tannins.

Homebrewer Rory Sarten and friends at home in Wellington

Cider and perry

While this book will not cover cider and perry in detail, it makes sense to include some information about them. In the past 18 months, craft cider has taken on a life of its own in New Zealand. Unlike the recent trend among corporate breweries of 'craft washing' (pretending to be craft), corporate cider producers are tending to court the 'alcopop' market with very sweet, artificially flavoured ciders.

Cider producers

Zeffer (Auckland)

Zeffer are a specialist cider producer with a range of offerings. They make excellent green apple, red apple and pear ciders, all around 5% ABV, as well as ciders flavoured with hops or citrus. They also make Slack Ma Girdle, one of the best examples of a more serious cider made in New Zealand. It is rich and complex, with taut tannins and brisk acidity, while delicious on release; it also ages very well.

Hallertau (Auckland)

Hallertau makes one cider that it sells alongside its core range of beer – it is light and fresh, with a hint of funk.

Good George (Waikato)

Hamilton's Good George brewery makes three ciders, all based on Granny Smith apples. The standard cider is crisp, refreshing and vinous; Doris Plum Cider is brewed with Black Doris plums, as well as apples, and has a fuller palate and plum notes; and their Drop Hop Cider is hopped, which creates super-bright tropical fruit aromatics. The Drop Hop won Champion Cider at the 2013 Brewers Guild Awards.

Three Wise Birds (Hawke's Bay)

This is a new Hawke's Bay firm established by third-generation apple growers, with three ciders on the market. All bone-dry, they range in alcohol level and complexity: Bach Life is the lightest at around 6% ABV and has Granny Smith notes and prominent vinous quality; Acoustic Collection is around 9% ABV, and has wild and savoury flavours

balanced by crunchy acidity; and Moulin Rouge is an 11% ABV, intensely rich, single-variety cider.

Paynter's Cider (Hawke's Bay)

Established by fifth-generation apple grower Paul Paynter, Paynter's make two ciders, all from specially grown cider apples. Their first release was awarded the 2014 Fruit Wine and Cider Makers Association Best Cider Award and balances tannin, acidity and a hint of sweetness with intense cooked apple and wild notes. They also make a drier version of the same cider.

Edgebrook Cider (Hawke's Bay)

Produced in Hawke's Bay, Edgebrook's range of excellent ciders straddle the boundary between traditional and modern styles. Their Festive Cider has more emphasis on a hint of ripe apple sweetness balanced by acidity, whereas the Village Cider has more tannin structure and grip. If you are visiting Hawke's Bay, make sure to check them out at the weekly farmers' market in Hastings.

St Andrews (Hawke's Bay)

Now packaged in handy 250ml bottles, as well as 750ml bottles, St Andrews is an excellent example of the commercial New Zealand style made with Granny Smith apples that balances acidity, sweetness, vibrant apple notes and a bright crunch.

Peckham's (Nelson)

Peckham's brew traditional English-style ciders, often with a Kiwi twist. All of their products are excellent, but I am especially fond of their Moutere Cider, their Cardamon Cider and their Pommeau, which is a blend of apple brandy and cider apple juice.

Rochdale (Nelson)

Rochdale ciders are produced by the McCashin family, originally of Mac's fame but now brewing beer under the Stoke label. All made in an approachable style, they include apple and pear ciders as well as several flavoured varieties.

Townshend (Nelson)

As well as producing traditional English-style beers (among other things), Martin Townshend occasionally produces traditional English-style cider using apples from around Nelson.

Sprig & Fern (Nelson)

While Sprig & Fern produce a delicious regular cider, from local apples, they also make the absolutely delicious Berry Cider, produced with blackberries, strawberries and blackcurrants – a real stunner that puts other berry-flavoured ciders to shame.

Mussel Inn (Tasman)

Mussel Inn produces Apple Roughy, which is a rustic, dry cider that weighs in at 4% ABV and is made with Granny Smith, Sturmer Pippins and 'other random fruit from around the hood'. They also produce the 100% feijoa cider, Freckled Frog.

KJD Eve's NV (Canterbury)

This is a delicious medium-dry cider made by master brewer Kirsten Taylor. Bursting with fresh apple, it is balanced and drinkable.

Scoundrels and Rogues (Canterbury)

This is a rich, intense and strong (8.5% ABV) cider, with high residual sugar counterpointed by high levels of acidity. It is a little bit wild, with earthy/funky notes.

Camla Farm (Canterbury)

Camla Farm produces single-variety apple juices. Their cider is made with traditional varieties and typically has a wild fruity element (almost tasting like feijoa, although it is 100% apple juice), and is bone-dry.

Other things you need to know about beer

Buying beer

Depending on your tastes, budget and inclination (do you want to try as many beers as humanly possible in your lifetime? Would you prefer to drink just a handful of favourites? Or, more likely, are you somewhere in between?), there are a couple of strategies for buying the best possible beer for you.

Cultivate a relationship

I would certainly recommend cultivating a relationship with a knowledgeable beer merchant and/or bartender. There are excellent beer outlets all over New Zealand (see the 'New Zealand beer destinations' section); while independently owned outlets usually have either more choice or a more finely curated selection, don't overlook the chains such as Liquorland and Super Liquor, especially in small towns where there are not as many other outlets. Similarly, some supermarkets like the New World, Fresh Choice and Pak'n Save chains are locally owned and operated, and thus can stock different, more interesting beers than a chain like Countdown, which buys collectively.

If you like an outlet's beer selection just ask for 'whoever buys your beer' and start up a conversation. Most beer professionals love talking about beer (especially those in smaller towns with fewer beer lovers to talk to) – start by asking them what they think is good and telling them the sorts of beers you like. Once you have a relationship going, keep buying from them and even, if possible, share interesting beers with them (going on holiday? Bring back a regional speciality beer). Many of these beer retailers and bars will have clubs or tasting groups (either formal or informal), which will allow you to try far more beers than any sane budget would typically allow for.

Buy fresh

All too often I talk to a beer lover who has sworn off a particular beer or producer because they did not enjoy a particular hyped-up beer they had finally tried. Nine times out of 10, however, the brewer was not at fault; it was simply that the beer picked had passed its best, either through poor shipping or storage or simply age. While the saying 'fresh is best' is often bandied around, it isn't always the case

in the beer world (see the next section on cellaring beer). It's more often true than not, though, especially when it comes to light-bodied and hoppy beers, both of which can deteriorate pretty quickly. It's relatively easy to get fresh domestic beer, especially for high-volume beers. Nevertheless, it pays to check the drink-by dates on beers or check with the bar staff or retailer before purchasing.

For imported beers, the story is a bit different – poor storage and handling in the international supply chain can mean beers well within their drink-by dates can be far from enjoyable. I would recommend looking at who imported the beer and how it is stored before buying. Beer Force, Beertique and Beer Without Borders are all excellent importers, and their name on a bottle of beer will usually mean you are drinking it in the best possible condition. Likewise for all beers, other than the strongest dark beers and Belgian ales, buy only beer that has been stored/displayed in cool places, especially if it has (or looks like it has) been sitting there for any length of time.

The grey market

Some brewers actively discourage or prohibit the export of their beer. Others export but the demand for their beers internationally is such that their production levels cannot satisfy the market. Grey market importers are those who import and distribute beers without the official blessing of a brewery, sometimes against the wishes of that brewery or in competition with the legitimate importers of a beer. More often than not, these beers are not imported in the best of conditions (i.e. they are not shipped and stored cold) and, as a result, quality can be marginal. While I'm going to say 'don't buy these beers', sometimes these importers are the only way to get hold of a particular beer you may desperately want to try. I would, however, urge caution, especially for lighter and extremely hoppy beers as these are the most likely to suffer from poor handling. It is also important to be aware that by supporting these importers you make it harder for licensed importers with higher overheads and margins to do business and, as a result, you, the beer lover, will lose out in the long term.

47

Cellaring beer

While lighter beers, especially those with high levels of aromatic hops, are best consumed fresh, many other styles, especially rich, strong, malty beers, can last and even improve with time. Among the various styles that can age well are Belgian abbey ales, imperial stouts and porters, barley wines and wild ales, but, that said, most beers that are vintage-dated can be cellared.

Among my favourite New Zealand beers to cellar are:

* Yeastie Boys His Majesty and Her Majesty
* 8 Wired iStout (and other 8 Wired imperial stouts)
* Twisted Hop Enigma barley wine and Nokabollakov imperial stout
* Invercargill Brewery Smokin' Bishop
* Renaissance Stonecutter Scotch Ale
* Epic Epicurean Coffee & Fig Oatmeal Stout
* Ben Middlemiss Nota Bene
* Hallertau Funkonnay and Porter Noir
* Emerson's JP

If you can afford it, try to buy at least six bottles of any beer you want to keep for a long period of time. Drink one every year or so until it either tastes so good you can't stop drinking it or it tastes worse than it did last time, in which case it is time to drink up what you have left. If you get to the end of the stash and a beer is consistently getting better over time, it is time to buy more (say a dozen) of the most recent vintage.

Once you have found a collection of beers you like, it is very rewarding to buy these beers every year, as being able to open several different vintages of the same beer and taste them (vertical tasting), drink them or serve them together as part of a meal can be both one of the most enjoyable and the most interesting beer experiences you can have. If possible, buy big bottles (such as 750ml bottles) – these tend to age slower and therefore last longer than 330ml bottles. Because of this, many beers that are suited to cellaring are made only in larger formats.

Any potential beer cellar needs to be cold, dark and relatively free from vibration. This could be a wooden box under stairs or in a cellar. Specially designed wine cellar units are becoming cheaper and are just as good for wine as they are for beer. Aside from beers stoppered with natural corks, try to keep beer bottles upright as this will prevent the tops from rusting and will make the beers easier to serve – most beers will throw some sediment as they age. Try not to disturb cellared beers by moving them too much before you serve them. Likewise, pour slowly and steadily, and do not hesitate to pour them into a jug or decanter before you pour them into glasses.

Serving beer

So you've gone out and bought a mixed case of excellent fresh New Zealand beers and want to share them with friends. Do you want to make the most of them? Of course you do!

A well-served beer can elevate a fantastically made beer to a sublime experience; conversely, serving it poorly can make the same beer taste dull and off-kilter. The right time, place and temperature can even make a boring beer an enjoyable sensory experience, although unfortunately it will never fix a faulty or unbalanced beer. And, of course, there is little better than a well-brewed, cold pale lager after physical work on a hot day. While the time and place are important factors, these are a little hard to measure and control, whereas storage, serving temperature and glassware can be taken into account much more easily. Please note, when it comes to temperature and glassware, I am only making suggestions based on industry consensus about how beers are best enjoyed. If you like lukewarm pale lager or ice-cold imperial stout drunk straight out of the bottle, don't let me or anyone else tell you better. It's your beer, so drink it how you most enjoy it.

Storage

If you are buying beer to drink (rather than to keep), it pays to drink it as soon as possible (fresh is best), but this is especially true of beer bought in riggers and/or growlers (bottles filled from taps) rather than pre-filled bottles or cans. Beer stored like the former will deteriorate quickly and I would suggest drinking these within a couple of days. Bottled beer and cans can be kept for a much longer period if stored in cool conditions out of the light.

Temperature

The temperature at which a beer is served can make or break it. In general, I would recommend erring on the side of too cold, as beer will naturally warm in the glass – once it is poured, it is much easier to warm up than cool it down. For instance, I prefer drinking most beer styles slightly cooler than is commonly recommended, but that's just me. Below is a list of the temperature different

beer styles are best served at; a good rule of thumb is that the richer and more alcoholic a beer, the warmer you can serve it.

Very cold: 0–4°C

Served this cold, beers are masked of much of their flavour characters, especially malt, hop and yeast ester characters. As such, this serving temperature is suited only to the most bland beer styles, like pale lagers.

Cold: 4–7°C

Most light- to medium-bodied beers between 4% and 5% ABV are best served cold. This includes most styles of lager produced by craft breweries, including premium lagers, Pilsners, Vienna lager and schwarzbier; light-bodied ale styles, such as blonde and golden ales; and most wheat beer styles, including Belgian wit, hefe and kristalweizen, lambic beers and Berliner weisse.

Cool: 8–10°C

Many, if not most, beer styles are most enjoyable served cool; this includes everything other than the strongest Belgian ales, most stouts, amber and red ales and most hoppy ale styles, from APAs through to American IPAs.

Cellar temperature: 10–14°C

This is the traditional serving temperature of most British ales, such as bitters, brown ales and porters. It is also suitable for hoppy beers with a strong malt profile, such as British IPAs, American brown ales and hoppy porters. Malty, higher-alcohol lagers and speciality ales, such as Scotch ale, smoked ales and many barrel-aged beers, can also be served at cellar temperature.

Warm: 14–16°C

Some of the richest beer styles are best served warm. These include barley wines, Belgian quads, imperial stouts and double IPAs, as well as doppelbocks and eisbocks. Even then, other than in the cold winter months, I would normally serve these beer styles at cellar temperature and allow them to warm.

Glassware

There is a wide variety of glassware in which beer can be served, and while it is possible to get extremely technical when it comes to glassware, with special glasses created for certain beer styles, it doesn't need to be complicated. At home, for instance, my favourite beer glass is not a beer glass but a stemless wine glass. As a rule, I would recommend at least one good stemmed beer glass, like the TeKu glass or Spiegelau Beer Classics Tulip, to make the most out of almost every beer style. Failing this, a large wine glass will do. Below are some of the most common beer glasses and the types of beer they are best suited to.

The Boston

The Boston has fast become the default glass of craft beer bars the world over. At 473ml, the Boston holds an 'American pint' and allows for some head. With straight sides, it is a rather neutral vessel for beer, and lacking a bowl allows much of the aroma to escape (this is less of an issue for beers that are not highly aromatic, especially lagers and traditional British styles). I am a huge fan of the mini-Boston (384ml) glasses used by many beer bars and festivals, as these make excellent tasting/judging glasses for almost every beer style.

The imperial pint

With a volume of 568ml (and room for head), imperial pint glasses are used almost exclusively for British ale (but also other beers in British pubs). Unlike the Boston, they typically have some sort of curve, which allows for a smoother drinking experience, and come in a variety of styles, one of the most common being the nonic pint, with a small curve coming out from the glass near the top. Due to their large size, these glasses are not ideal for strong beers.

Mugs

Mugs can come in many shapes and sizes, but by definition have a handle, with the most common being the dimpled pint seen in many a traditional pub. Steins and tankards are similar and are used for particular styles such as Oktoberfest and English bitters.

Pilsner Glass

Pilsner glasses come in a variety of forms but are usually tall, slim and heavy-footed (sometimes with a stem). They maximise the freshness of lighter lager beers, as the name might imply, and are also used by most European lager brewers.

Weissbier glass

With a capacity of just over 500ml, and a tall, curvaceous shape, these glasses are designed to showcase German wheat beer styles at their best. Because of their volume they can also accommodate a whole bottle – being able to pour out the bottle, including the yeast, in one pour is important to the whole experience of drinking some of these beers.

Stange and Willi Becher glasses

These are the standard pub glasses used in Germany and are appropriate for many beer styles, especially lager. The stange is tall and cylindrical, whereas the Willi Becher flares into a subtle tulip at the top of the glass.

Stemmed beer glass/cognac balloon

Similar to a wine glass, these glasses have a large, often ballooned, bowl that traps the aroma of various beer styles, particularly beers with a strong hop character or estery aromas. Because these glasses are best filled part way rather than to the brim, they are ideal for stronger beers. For the very strongest beers, many beer lovers will use the similarly shaped cognac balloon.

Specialist glasses

As craft beer has grown in popularity, there has been an emergence of specialist glasses designed by brewers and other experts.

Spiegelau glasses

Since it produced its IPA glass in early 2013, Spiegelau has released new glasses annually, specially designed for particular beer styles. The company has worked in collaboration with a number of notable breweries, including Sierra Nevada, Dogfish Head and Rogue. These glasses have received a lot of buzz and have had both supporters and detractors in the industry. They are designed to heighten the experience of drinking particular beers, and while they work admirably, they also affect some of the other characters of a beer. The IPA glass, for instance, intensifies the hop aroma of beers, but in doing this it softens the carbonation, which means that some beers taste much sweeter.

I would definitely recommend trying Spiegelau glasses (there are a handful of craft beer bars around New Zealand that stock them – start with these if you don't want to shell out for a set). If you like the effect they have on beer, buy a set and keep using them; if you don't, well, don't.

TeKu glass

Designed by Italian brewer Teo Musso and sensory analyst and beer expert Kuaska (real name Lorenzo Dabove), this glass is produced by German glass manufacturer Rastal, which also specialises in creating custom glassware for particular beers and breweries. The TeKu is billed as 'The Best Beer Glass in the World' and is ideal for every style of beer. It has been adopted by a number of the world's best brewers: Lost Abbey, Mikkeller, Three Floyds, Brew Dog and Firestone Walker, among others. TeKu glasses are excellent, and are particularly well suited to strong beer styles.

Spiegelau stout glass.

TeKu glass.

Spiegelau IPA glass.

Matching beer and food

Before we get on and discuss the specifics of what goes with that, there is one golden rule of matching beer and food:

> Drink the beers you like
> with the food you like!

We all taste things differently and have different biases towards different beers, beer styles and foods. While I believe that matching beer and food can be taken just as seriously as matching food and wine, we can learn from the wine world's mistakes of rigidly enforcing arbitrary rules about what goes with what. Good beer goes with good food and, most importantly, balanced beer goes with balanced food. Don't worry about what I or any other experts, brewers, friends or whomever might say. If you enjoy stout with ceviche or witbier with rib-eye, drink it, eat it, enjoy it. If you enjoy a match, go for it and don't let anyone else tell you that you are wrong!

Forget about flavour

This may sound counterintuitive when discussing food and beer, but matching flavours is actually the least important and sometimes the last thing you're looking to do. When you try to match specific flavours, a match will often come off as forced and will fail to hit the mark. Think more about the textures, tastes (bitter, sweet, sour, salty, hot and umami) and intensity of the beer in combination with the food.

It's all in the sauce

When it comes to matching beer and food, think about how a dish is being served. All too often when looking at a match we jump right to the main feature of a dish – the protein. While not completely a blank slate, the protein (let's say a steak) is the bass line – meaningless without treble and vocals. What is it being served with? A steak served with creamy mushroom sauce is likely to match better to a darker, roastier beer than one with a refreshing chimichurri. Think about whether a dish is being served with side dishes and other

accompaniments, and how these will change the textures and sensations.

Match a beer to the dish, not the dish to a beer

As a sommelier and now a drinks writer, I've attended more than my fair share of wine dinners and now, more recently, beer dinners. Many of these fall flat as chefs and sommeliers try to craft dishes around the particular flavours of a beer or wine and get it wrong, especially when their preconceptions about what a particular wine or beer is supposed to taste like gets in the way. So if so many professionals get it wrong, as an amateur, why go to all the bother? Think about the dish you want to cook, then think about what beers might go with it. Buy and drink one or more of those beers. Don't try to be too smart.

Taste and reseason

Just before you serve anything, ever, taste it and reseason. If you are matching it with a beer, taste it, taste the beer and then reseason. Does it need salt, pepper, or a splash of acid (lemon juice or vinegar) or heat? A little correction before a dish is served can make the difference between a mediocre and an amazing match. Chefs often criticise home cooks for underseasoning their food and most people read this as 'add more salt'. But a splash of acidity can work wonders, especially on richer dishes.

What grows together goes together

This is an adage from the wine world that is just as true when it comes to beer and food. Most of the time, beers from particular regions (this is especially so of older beer styles) go well with foods from that region. This is particularly true of beer and cheese combinations.

Match intensity

The easiest way to miss the mark with a beer and food match is to misalign the intensity of beer and food. If you have a light, delicate dish, regardless of ingredients, and you match it to a powerful beer, the dish will be steamrolled. Some ingredients are naturally lower or higher on the intensity scale, but most vary depending on how they are cooked. Salmon, for instance, can range from delicate (served raw) to extremely intense (hot-smoked). Likewise, some beer styles are bigger than others, but there are subtle stouts out there just as there are big, robust Pilsners.

Think about the match

This, too, seems self-explanatory, but think about how you might want the beer and food to inter-play. Generally, there are five different ways to go about this. As we run through them they become harder to pull off but, if successful, more and more rewarding.

Contrast/Cut

This is simple and effective. Look at the dish's most dominant taste or feature and aim to balance it with a characteristic from a beer. If a dish is extremely rich, you could balance it by contrasting either a sour or bitter beer to cut through the richness. A sweet dish can be counterpointed by a bitter beer, while something extremely spicy can be softened by a beer with a sweet body of malt. Match an extremely bitter IPA to slow-cooked pork belly and you will know what I mean: the bitterness of the beer cuts against the richness of the meat, providing overall balance.

Combine

Rather than looking at the beer and food as two separate components offsetting each other, this tactic treats the combination of food and beer as one, ideally seamless, whole. When this goes well it can really pop. Essentially, you are combining elements in the food with complementary but different elements in the beer. One example of this is combining a roasty stout with a chocolate dessert to create a mocha effect.

Weave

This sort of match balances the combination of complementary components with those that offset each other. This can be hard to pull off but it works spectacularly well. One example is match-ing a big, rich, roasty black beer with slow-cooked meat. The sweetness of the beer and meat, as well as the intensity of the beer, match each other, while the bitterness of the malt and hops provides balance to the sweetness.

Match

Sometimes you can create a lovely depth or inten-sity by combining similar components in a beer. For example: sweetness – barley wine with a plum pudding; bitterness – asparagus, endive and other bitter greens will taste sweeter when matched with a slightly more bitter beer; a textural component like creaminess – stout poured off nitro with a chocolate mousse.

Do something crazy!

Sometimes combinations just work. I have no idea why stout works well with oysters but they do (so well, in fact, that people even make oyster stouts).

Beer tasting

There is no doubt that drinking beer is an amazingly fun experience. That said, sometimes even more pleasure (not to mention intellectual stimulation) can be derived from tasting multiple beers. This is very important both at festivals (where, if you are like me, you will want to try beers you have never tried before) and at formal beer tastings, where you may be tasting several beers of one style, or from one producer or, if you are extremely lucky (or patient), a vertical – several different vintages of the same beer.

So how should you taste beer? While the verb 'taste' implies that you will use only one of your senses, in actual fact you will be using all five: taste and smell obviously, but also feel, sight and sound.[23]

Step one: Inspect

Once a beer is poured, examine it. What colour is it? What colour is the head? Is it cloudy or crystal clear? How vigorous is the carbonation? All of these things will tell an expert taster something about the beer they are drinking, but it is important, even for those of you who are just beginning, as it will help you get into a more thoughtful tasting mindset.

Step two: Smell

Bring the glass up to your nose and inhale deeply. The smell of a beer will tell you a lot about it, but it will also prime your palate and intensify your tasting experience. When smelling a beer, try to isolate the aromas in it, as this will help you describe it. Just as important as the aromas are their intensity and how they interplay – for example, an IPA will have a pronounced hop character, some malt notes, as well as some subtle character from the yeast. The other smells to watch out for are anything that could have been used to flavour the beer and any beer faults.

Rather than simply trying to pinpoint individual flavours and aromas, it can help to cast your net wide and gradually narrow in on the exact words you are looking for. If you are looking to describe a hop character, for instance, start by asking whether it is fruity, floral, spicy or earthy. If it is fruity, then what family of fruits could it be evoking? Citrus? Tropical? Stone fruit? If citrus, then what sort of citrus? Lemon? Lime? Grapefruit? Orange?

Once you have pinpointed the exact flavour you are looking for, you can have a think about what hop variety (or other ingredient) might then have that character. If you have decided the beer has a pronounced grapefruit character, then you can safely suggest that it might have been hopped with Cascade, a hop that produces that sort of character.

While some people are naturally more sensitive than others, this is a technique that can be learnt, so buy some beer and get practising.[24]

Step three: Taste, feel and think

Once you have smelt the beer, now is the time to taste! Take a small amount into your mouth (no big gulps or you won't be able to retaste) and then swirl it around to let it touch all parts of your mouth. Think about the various flavours and about how the beer feels in your mouth.

There are six main flavour groups: sweet, salty, bitter, spicy, sour and umami. All of these come into play when tasting beer, but the most common are sweet (from the malt) and bitter (from the hops). Ask yourself questions like: How do these interact? Is the beer sweet to begin with and becoming bitter over time, or is there a burst of bitterness at the start followed by a more mellow taste?

Think about how the aroma of the beer might have changed since you first smelled it. The interaction between the flavours of the beer can change the aroma, maybe making parts of it more subtle and others more noticeable. Perhaps you are drinking a golden ale; what was a subtle hay-like malt aroma on pouring can, with the influence of the sweetness of the malt, transform into something more like freshly baked bread.

Step four: Talk (or write)

If you are tasting in a group, the most experienced tasters will usually go first. If you know what you want to say, feel free to chip in politely with your thoughts. Remember, everyone's palate is different and what you experience is personal. Don't let anyone tell you that a flavour you might pick up is wrong.

This said, if you are drawing conclusions about a beer (whether it has been infected, what hop varieties are used, etc.), listen to those with more experience. This is how you learn and how you will get better and more knowledgeable. It is not uncommon to pick up on a character in a beer and then incorrectly ascribe it to something. If you get something (factually) wrong about a beer, don't be embarrassed. Just ask those with more knowledge to describe it better for you, so that if you come across it again you are more likely to identify it.

If you are in a group and don't know what to say, don't hesitate simply to say nothing. After you have tasted the beer, look at it thoughtfully, resmell and nod (you can also punctuate this with a thoughtful sigh or 'hmmm'). If this is done with enough confidence and gravitas, you will look like the most knowledgeable person in the room.[25]

When tasting, it pays to keep some sort of a diary or record. This could be in a book or digital format such as a website or app like Untapped, RateBeer.com or BeerAdvocate.com. It will allow you to go back to beers you have tasted to see what you thought of them, and will show you how your tasting skills are advancing (I cringe when I read old reviews I have written, especially online, but am also proud of myself for how far I have come).

Jules van Cruysen at The Malthouse, Wellington.

Beer festivals

There are a number of regular beer events hosted in New Zealand every year. Here are some of the biggest. In addition to these there are a plethora of smaller local events and one-off events held by beer bars and breweries.

Beervana

Beervana is New Zealand's largest and premier beer event. Held in Wellington's Westpac Stadium, the 2014 event showcased over 250 beers from 85 breweries (with 25 of these being international breweries, many not otherwise available in New Zealand). Beervana also has some of the best festival food on offer, with many of Wellington's best restaurants showcasing their fare. Held annually in August around Wellington on a Plate, this event is not to be missed. Aside from Beervana itself, the week before this event is usually packed with various beer events, from product launches to dinners and more.

Dunedin Craft Beer and Food Festival

Celebrating a range of Kiwi and international beers but with an emphasis on the beers of Otago, this festival is normally held in early October.

Marchfest

Nelson/Tasman is New Zealand's premier hop-growing region and has more breweries per capita than any other part of the country. Marchfest is the annual Nelson event that celebrates the beers of Nelson and Marlborough (as well as a couple of others), and showcases a number of exclusive festival beers. There is also a variety of events, such as a craft beer lunch, seminars and brewing demonstrations, as well as live music. Unlike many of the other beer festivals, Marchfest is child-friendly, boasting an environment where 'responsible drinking and responsible parenting go hand-in-hand'.

Great Australasian Beer SpecTAPular

GABS is being held in NZ for the first time in June 2016. Previously held only in Melbourne and Sydney each year, the festival has earned its place as a landmark event attended by many NZ beer lovers and breweries. GABS showcases over 250 beers from 150 breweries, of which 120 are only available at, or debut at, the event. This is sure to be one of the most important dates in any beer lover's calendar.

Great Kiwi Beer Festival

A large outdoor festival held at Hagley Park in the middle of Christchurch, the Great Kiwi Beer Festival is an excellent event with something for everyone: from the enthusiastic drinker through to the die-hard craft beer connoisseur. As well as a large number of breweries showcasing their beers, there is also live music, beer and food seminars, and excellent food.

Greater Wellington Brewday

Held in Martinborough around February, this event celebrates the beers and brewers of Wellington City, the Hutt Valley, Kapiti Coast and Wairarapa.

Pacific Beer Expo

Held over Labour Weekend by beer bars Hashigo Zake and Golding's Free Dive, and speciality beer importers Beer Without Borders, the Pacific Beer Expo showcases the best beers and brewers of the Pacific Rim, including New Zealand, Australia, Japan, California and Oregon.

SOBA City of Ales

Held in July, City of Ales is SOBA's Auckland festival and features North Island breweries. Like its sister Winter Ale Festival, it showcases around 30 beers, many of which are brewed exclusively for the festival and many others of which are not otherwise available in Auckland.

SOBA Winter Ale Festival

Held in Wellington, this is one of the most fun festivals of the year. Attended by around 30 breweries, almost all offering rich, round, warming ales, the SOBA Winter Ale Festival allows a group of enthusiastic tasters to taste every beer on offer, so it is ideal for completionists.

SOCIETY OF BEER ADVOCATES (SOBA)
Beer for the right reasons

The Society of Beer Advocates (SOBA) is an independent, consumer-led, not-for-profit society of beer lovers that is dedicated to 'promoting a wider availability of better quality beer'. To achieve their mission, they engage in a number of activities in order to benefit the consumer.

Advocacy
Whenever beer is in the media, SOBA will be there to provide a balanced consumer voice. Recently, for example, they have spoken out on issues such as proposed legislation preventing beers from being labelled as gluten-free, on campaigns that target beer drinkers (over those who drink other forms of alcohol) and on liquor licensing. They typically take a commonsense approach to issues and promote responsible drinking rather than being apologists for the booze industry (whom they are also quick to criticise).

Education
SOBA engage in various educational activities, such as helping to fund a guidebook to New Zealand craft beer (see what I did there). They also have a number of excellent online resources for beer lovers and publish an excellent quarterly magazine, *In Pursuit of Hoppiness.*

Events
SOBA host regular events up and down the country. These cover everything from beer dinners and visits to local breweries to trips to various parts of New Zealand to visit brewers. Every year they hold the National Homebrew Competition, New Zealand's premier homebrew competition and one that has launched the careers of several brewers. They also hold the City of Ales festival in Auckland, the Winter Ales Festival in Wellington and, in 2015, the inaugural Mountain Ales Festival in Taranaki.

Recognition
SOBA hold annual awards to celebrate the best of the New Zealand beer industry. As well as brewers, they also champion the best retailers, bars and restaurants in each region, which in turn encourages other businesses to up their game. In addition, many craft beer businesses offer discounts to SOBA members.

If you like the look of what SOBA do and want to join, go to www.soba.org.nz

Brewery profiles and beer notes

Notes from the author

This section includes information on 140 breweries and tasting notes for over 400 of the beers they produce. All of these beers have been tasted in the year to 31 March 2015. To disclaim, I have paid for about 20% of these beers; the rest have been contributed by the breweries (and sometimes as samples over a bar). If a beer was bottled, where possible I have tasted it out of the bottle as this is how the majority of you will be drinking it. As a rule, I taste out of a large stemless wine glass, a Spiegelau beer tulip or a TeKu glass. I have tasted approximately 25% of these beers at the brewery.

For some of the smaller and emerging breweries, I have not been able to include every beer they have listed as a 'year-round beer', simply because many have not been brewed yet or, as Greig McGill, owner of Brewaucracy, puts it: 'Currently we can be said to have three year-round beers, though due to production schedule limitations, most of the time there's only one out at a time!' There are some beers from well-established breweries that also fall into this category, especially those that are heavily hopped using a hop variety with extremely limited supply. I have written about these beers but I have included tasting notes only if I have been able to taste them.

While I had originally intended to provide notes on regular seasonal beers as well, I have decided against this. First, it would have taken up an extra 50 pages, making the book unwieldy, but I also decided this would take too much focus away from the profiles on the brewers, breweries and brewing companies. These profiles are far more important than tasting notes on individual beers, and there are other places where you can get this information.

Throughout these notes, I occasionally refer to the beer rating and information website RateBeer.com. I have used this as a resource – all of the RateBeer.com scores are correct as of 31 March 2015. The reason for this is that while mobile apps like Untapped now have more users, and include far more beers and breweries, RateBeer.com requires beer reviewers to add a considered review and rate beer against several specific criteria rather than a nebulous mark out of five. The website is also used internationally and is better able to incorporate international feedback on our beers. Most importantly, it benchmarks beers against others in their style and overall rating, so is able to provide a percentile ranking. A score above 95 in style or overall rating is significant and indicates that a beer is truly one of the best in the world. Because beers are not judged 'to style', as they are in beer competitions, this provides another perspective on beers that bend traditional style guidelines. One of the flaws of this system, however, is that raters often show a strong preference for certain styles – big, strong and hoppy (imperial IPAs, imperial stouts, Belgian quads, etc.). As a result, some marvellous beers (and entire beer styles) can be overlooked.

In addition to the breweries listed that were in existence as of 1 January 2015, I am also aware of the following brewers that have since entered the market:

BEffect, Wanaka
Catlins Brewery, Deep South
Coolship Brewing, Nelson
Crate Brewery, London (run by Kiwis, and now also brewing in New Zealand for the local market)
Godsown, Hawke's Bay
Hop Hustlers, Wellington
The Laboratory Brewpub, Lincoln
Rough Hands, Nelson
Sneaky Brewing, Hawke's Bay
Victoria Store Brewery, Clyde
Webb Street Brewery, Wellington

That brings the total up to around 150 breweries. I'm sure there are some I've missed – if this is the case, please get in touch and I will make sure they are included in the app.

8 Wired Brewing Co.

Brewery
Established: 2009
Location: Warkworth
Owner and brewer: Søren Eriksen

8 Wired was founded by Danish import Søren Eriksen, who started working as an assistant brewer at Renaissance in 2008, leaving his job as a biochemist but funding himself by his professional poker playing – he won the New Zealand Poker Championships in 2009 and 2010, reaping $160,000 over these two events. (Eriksen would be listed in the top 12 New Zealand players but he is listed as a Danish player.) In late 2009, he released two beers: first Rewired and then Hopwired, both brewed out of Renaissance. In 2011, he won Champion Brewery at the Brewers Guild Awards; the same year, he also started brewing out of Steam in Auckland. By early 2014, Eriksen was brewing 8 Wired beers at three different breweries – Renaissance in Marlborough, Stainless Brewing in Christchurch, and Steam in Auckland – which he describes as a 'logistical nightmare', noting that he did not become a brewer to move beer around the country.

Eriksen commissioned his new Warkworth brewery in early 2015. As well as having a home for his own beer, he will be brewing beer under contract for Behemoth Brewing Company. That said, he does not intend to spend all of his time brewing other people's beers: 'I don't want to deal with multiple customers.' However, he is working with some established international breweries – when asked if these include a certain Danish gypsy brewer, he only says: 'Possibly... nothing official yet.' 8 Wired has had tremendous international success, being the only brewery not only in New Zealand but the entire southern hemisphere to be listed on RateBeer.com's 100 Best Breweries in the world, a position it has maintained for the past four years. Eriksen's iStout is rated as the top beer in New Zealand and, at the time of writing, the only Kiwi beer to be rated in the 100th percentile – that is, better than 99.5% of beers listed on the RateBeer.com site. In fact, all of Eriksen's year-round beers are in the 90th percentile for both style and overall rating.

When asked about his brewing style, Eriksen acknowledges that he has never really thought about it. However, he believes that it is important to 'maximise flavour'. As well as pioneering the New Zealand IPA genre with 8 Wired and helping to cement New Zealand's craft beer reputation internationally with beers like iStout, Eriksen has the largest (by far) barrel programme in New Zealand, with over 200 barrels, each containing about 225L of beer. His wild and sour beers are also among the country's best.

Now that Eriksen has his own brewery and bottling line, he has a lot more flexibility – previously he had to bottle about 8000L of beer at a time; now he can 'just make a small batch of something crazy'. Joining his highly regarded Feijoa Sour will be a Sauvignon Blanc Sour, made with wine that's been contaminated by *Brettanomyces*.

Unlike the majority of New Zealand brews, or the majority of beers full stop, most 8 Wired beer is sold internationally rather than in the domestic market, with Australia and the US being Eriksen's two top markets; the Asian market is also growing quickly. 8 Wired has engaged in a number of collaboration beers, both in New Zealand and internationally with breweries like Nøgne Ø and BrewDog. To celebrate 8 Wired moving on from Renaissance, the two came together to brew Wirecutter, which combines the highest-regarded 8 Wired and Renaissance beers, Hopwired and Stonecutter, in the form of a massively hopped Scotch ale.

Semiconductor (Session IPA)
4.4% ABV

Lovely firm body of malt with clean bitterness and vibrant, aromatic hop notes of peach, grass and lemon. Very integrated and an excellent example of the session IPA genre.

Hopwired (NZ IPA)
8% ABV

When Hopwired first burst onto the market, it virtually created a new style, the New Zealand IPA (although brewers in the US and UK had made New Zealand-hopped IPAs already). It is a distinctive beer, bursting with Sauvin hop character – passion fruit, gooseberry, citrus and cut grass. These aromas are overlaid onto a medium-weight malt body; not light, but not heavy and sweet either. One of New Zealand's most distinctively Kiwi beers and one that craft beer nuts fawn over.

Saison Sauvin
7% ABV

Heady and aromatic, this beer's white pepper and clove spices and pear drop esters from saison yeast meld seamlessly with the passion fruit, cut grass and gooseberry hop notes coming from the Nelson Sauvin. These beautiful aromatics are laid onto a body of giving malt with a hint of sweetness.

C4 Double Coffee Brown Ale
8% ABV

A luscious, big round beer with smoky coffee and intense milk chocolate notes. Aromatic hop notes meld with the coffee aromatics to create a long finish.

Big Smoke (smoked porter)
6.2% ABV

Brewed with traditional Bamberg smoked malt, this beer has a very beechy smoke profile, adding a high note to the intense chocolate notes of the porter. It finishes with a long, focused bitterness.

Tall Poppy (American red ale)
7% ABV

A big, thick red IPA with intense resinous pine and grapefruit pith notes from the US hops, overlaid on a body of rich biscuity caramel.

Super Conductor (double IPA)
8.88%

A very refined double IPA; sure, it is hugely hoppy, but it is very balanced, integrated and drinkable. Both citrusy US hop character and more floral Kiwi hop notes come together seamlessly over a body of light malt.

iStout (imperial stout)
10% ABV

Dark, intense and absolutely delicious. This is a thick, rich but very balanced imperial stout – there is too much going on to describe in a few lines but if you haven't tried it make sure you do. It also tastes *amazing* poured over good vanilla-bean ice cream.

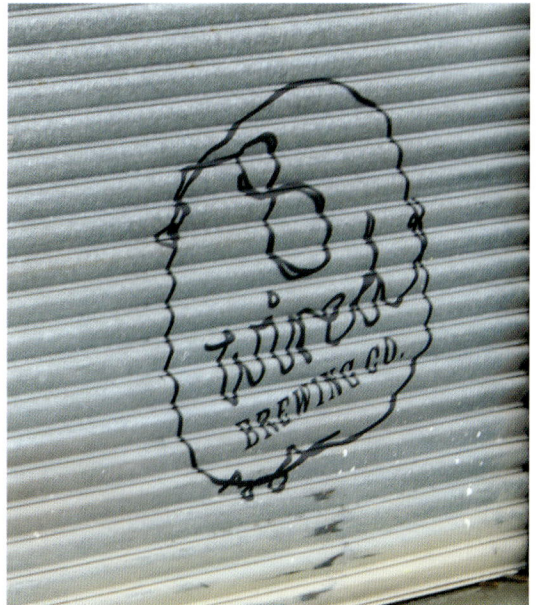

Altitude Brewing Studios

Contract brewery
Established: 2013
Location: Queenstown
Owner and brewer: Eliott Menzies

Eliott Menzies established Altitude Brewing to 'educate Queenstowners in proper beer'. In addition, the passionate conservationist and outdoorsman donates 5% of the profits from two of his beers, The Posturing Professional and the Mischievous Kea, to Search and Rescue NZ and the Kea Conservation Trust, respectively. As he builds his brand, he intends to work more with similiar charities and would ideally like to brew collaboration beers with them, with some of the proceeds being donated.

In 2015, Menzies intends to open a brewery shop and increase production.

Goldpanners Profit Golden Lager
4.4% ABV

A vibrantly hopped lager with clean, focused bitterness overlaid on a body of soft golden malt.

Posturing Professional Alpine Ale (NZ pale ale)
5% ABV

Resinous hops dominate this beer, giving it a luscious marmalade note that is balanced by firm, almost astringent, bitterness.

Mischievous Kea (IPA)
5.5% ABV

Luscious but balanced with pine, grapefruit and cutting bitterness overlaid on generous malt with warm bready notes.

Bach Brewing

Contract brewery
Established: 2013
Location: Auckland
Owner: Craig Cooper

Craig Cooper has been employed in almost every aspect of the beer and liquor industries, both in New Zealand and abroad. He has worked in sales and marketing at Lion and Independent Liquor, as well as for brewing and spirits giants internationally. He co-owned the seminal (for me, anyway) Limburg Brewery in Hawke's Bay, which was set up by Chris O'Leary of Emerson's, and works as a brewing and business consultant.

Cooper's beers are extremely approachable, and Bach is a brewery I'd recommend to those starting out on their craft beer adventure. The beers all have a lightness, freshness and excellent hop definition without intense bitterness.

All Day Ale (session IPA)
3.7% ABV

Really soft orange blossom hop notes combine with a deftly crafted body of malt to create a clean, focused, easy-drinking golden bitter. Lovely.

Beachstone (NZ Pilsner)
4.8% ABV

Light and bright with zippy Kiwi hop character: gooseberry, passion fruit and cut grass. A delicious, extremely aromatic Kiwi lager.

Driftwood (session IPA)
5% ABV

Bright with a spicy, grassy and herbal hop aroma. There are some luscious peach and apricot notes on the mid-palate – a nice interplay between hop and malt. Round and rich body with a short finish.

Kingtide (IPA)
7% ABV

Kingtide combines the pine and citrus notes of US hops with the passionfruit character and floral notes of New Zealand hops. The malt bill is rich and there is some sweetness on the palate, but overall the beer is focused and long.

Duskrider (American red ale)
6% ABV

Billed as a red IPA, this has a ruby colour that is lighter in body for the style, very much in keeping with the house style. Long and fresh, it has a clean but not aggressive bitterness and zesty hop aroma.

Bannockburn Brewing Co.

Brewery
Established: 2013
Location: Bannockburn
Brewer: Jody Pagey

Located in Bannockburn, arguably the most well-regarded region for Pinot Noir production in Central Otago, if not New Zealand, Bannockburn Brewing Co. are elusive – they have a Facebook page but no website and brew out of the same site as Terra Sancta Winery, with their brewer also being the winemaker.

The beer is fermented in Pinot Noir barrels, which lends it a rather dominant red berry note. The beers I have tasted have also been quite funky, with strong wild yeast notes taking over the beer and muting the hop character (the beer boasts an IBU of over 100).

Killarabbit Double IPA
(7.2% ABV)

This double IPA has very plump red fruit on the nose with some herbal notes. The palate is full and creamy; lots of funky ester character and muted hop notes leave this beer partway between an IPA and a Belgian tripel.

Bays Brewery

Brewery
Established: 1993
Location: Nelson
Brewer: Peter McGrath

Bays is the epitome of the regional brewery: independently owned and one that has fought the big boys over taps since day one. As a result, they produce the holy trilogy of Kiwi beers: a gold, an amber and a dark lager. While commercial, they exemplify the style and are extremely enjoyable.

Bays also produce a handful of beers especially for restaurant and bar customers in the Nelson region. Of these, the doppelbock is both the most enjoyable and the truest to style.

Bays Gold (premium lager)
4.2% ABV

An excellent, focused lager with a lovely richness of malt in the mid-palate and a soft bitterness.

Bays Draught (NZ draught)
4% ABV

Malty and rich, with some sweetness, this beer is clean and focused, with a hint of bitterness.

Bays Dark (black lager)
4% ABV

Clean, focused and well made, Bays Dark has coffee and cocoa notes.

Baylands Brewery

Brewery
Established: 2011
Location: Petone, Wellington
Owners: Aidan Styles,
Nikki Carmichael and Steve Young
Lead brewer: Aidan Styles

Originally started in the Styles' garage in Newlands on a 300L brew kit, Baylands released their first commercial beer at Golding's Free Dive in May 2013. In late 2014 they upgraded to a 1400L brewery and moved into larger commercial premises in Petone.

Baylands has won several important awards in its short history, including the People's Choice at the Malthouse West Coast IPA Challenge in 2013 and 2014, and People's Choice at the 2014 SOBA Winter Ale Festival.

The brewery site is also home to Baylands brewing supply store. This has a colourful history, having been established and run originally by Yeastie Boy's Stu McKinlay and then sold to Joe Wood of Liberty Brewing.

Baylands have become notable for using rye malt – to date five beers have incorporated the ingredient, including several of their core range. Brewer Aidan Styles believes that rye can add a variety of characters to a beer, from the more typical spiciness to the subtle rye notes achieved by using chocolate rye malt and cararye. He describes his philosophy as 'wing it!' and 'hops, lots of hops'. That said, despite some of their beers' weight they are always designed to be drinkable, 'so that you can have more than one glass'.

Miss Demeanour (golden ale)
3.5% ABV

With vibrant notes of passion fruit, this golden ale has beautiful floral top notes overlaid on a body of light malt. Crisp and refreshing.

4B (best bitter)
4.5% ABV

Available on hand-pull and keg, this is a nutty, approachable English bitter style with long, focused bitterness and malty richness.

Woodrow's Veto (IPA)
7% ABV

Hopped heavily with US hops, this is a long, fresh, lighter-styled IPA with grapefruit pith, pine resin and a rich stone-fruit note.

Rock Solid (NZ pale ale)
5.8% ABV

This is a light-bodied pale ale that just bursts with intensely scented tropical and floral aromas, backed up by gooseberry and papaya fruit character. On the finish, the beer reminds me of lemonade fruit: bright and zesty with a hint of sweetness.

Enforcer (black IPA)
6% ABV

This beer is one of my favourite black IPAs, a style that I love. It has a solid body of malt with chocolate and cola notes, and a long, refreshing bone of bitterness running through it. On the finish it bursts with orange and pine aroma. Enforcer is especially enjoyable served on hand-pull.

Beer Baroness

Contract brewery
Established: 2013
Location: Christchurch
Owner and brewer: Ava Wilson

Aside from being the 'Beer Baroness', Ava Wilson also manages Pomeroy's on Kilmore, one of Christchurch's best pubs. In 2013, the pub established its own brewery, Four Avenues. It was at this time that Wilson decided to brew beer under her own label as well. 'It wasn't a question of why, it was why not!'

Having brewed for only a short while, she describes her style as fluid and states that she is 'here to learn'. This said, her first few beers have been received extremely well by the industry and Wilson is planning to start releasing bottled beer soon. To improve her skills, she has collaborated with Luke Nicholas of Epic and Joe Wood of Liberty.

Wilson has also been a campaigner for recognition and support of women in the brewing industry, and helped to establish the Pink Boots Society here in New Zealand. Beyond those listed below, she has brewed two other beers: Unite, a pale ale brewed for International Women's Collaboration Brew Day (7 March), which about 70 other female brewers participated in; and Unite 2.0, an American stout brewed to celebrate the launch of Pink Boots in New Zealand, which was brewed with Jayne Lewis of Two Birds (Australia) and Denise Ratfield of Latitude 33 (US). Unite 2.0 was one my top 10 pints of 2014.

First Lady (APA)
5.8% ABV

A lovely APA with a slightly richer malt profile than most beers within this style. It has a focused, long bitterness with peachy/marmalade top notes and a subtle floral finish.

Lady Danger (American red ale)
6.5% ABV

Originally brewed in collaboration with Epic, Lady Danger is a big, thick, resinous IPA that balances aromatic and searingly bitter hopping with luscious red malt.

Ava Wilson aka the Beer Baroness.

Behemoth Brewing Company

Contract brewery
Established: June 2013
Location: Auckland
Owner and brewer: Andrew Childs

At 1.98m tall, Andrew Childs is one of the giants of the brewing industry, if only physically. He fell in love with beer at 11 (don't worry, Health Promotion Agency, he was only collecting beer glasses back then) and started homebrewing in his 20s. A lawyer by training, he quit his job in the public sector to work behind the bar at Wellington's Fork & Brewer, taking a 60% pay cut in the process, before securing a job selling homebrew supplies for Mangrove Jack's in Auckland.

In 2012, Childs won 'Wellington in a Pint', a homebrewing competition to create the most 'Wellington' beer possible – his contribution was called the Celia Wade-Brown Ale (named after the current mayor, a self-proclaimed beer lover). Celia Wade-Brown Ale was also the first beer he brewed under his Behemoth label.

While he may tower over his competition, Childs is also notorious for lowering the tone, sometimes to the point of silliness. On his blog, *Buzz and Hum*, the Wellington beer and music blogger Scott Anderson described him as having 'the rude and robust humour of an entire classroom of fourteen-year-old school boys'. To illustrate, when I asked Childs to sum up his brewing philosophy in 10 words, he said, 'Make bigger-tasting beer to drink. Yum. Purple Monkey Dishwasher.'

When brewing, he tries to make as 'hoppier a beer as possible without making them unbalanced', and 'late-hopped and dry-hopped', acknowledging that they are on the drier side of the spectrum, something more traditional brewers often criticise.

At the 2014 Brewers Guild Awards, Childs took out golds for his two, at the time, flagship beers: Chur and 'Murica, both names evocative of the more macho sides of New Zealand and the US (Chur is hopped with New Zealand hops, and 'Murica with US ones). He also won the trophy for best festival beer with Brave Bikkie Brown Ale (inspired by Anzac biscuits).

In the two years he has been brewing, Childs has been prolific, with 24 different beers listed in total on Untapped, in addition to the three available year-round. He has collaborated on various pale ale styles with The Twisted Hop, Mike's, Weezledog and Black Sands, and has also made a variety of milk stouts, often flavoured with ingredients such as hazelnuts, coffee and chilli.

As a rule, Behemoth's beers are big on flavour without being heavy or high in alcohol.

'Murica (APA)
6% ABV

Vibrantly hoppy, with pine and orange zest aromatics, this beer is full of burnt orange and caramel malt character. To compensate for the sweetness on the palate, it has a very long, bitter finish. 'Murica won gold at the 2014 Brewers Guild Awards.

Chur (NZ pale ale)
6% ABV

An extremely well-balanced, New Zealand-hopped pale ale, Chur is vibrantly hopped with tropical fruit and cut grass notes. It has a solid body of malt, some of which gives sweetness, and has firm bitterness without this being overpowering. Chur won gold at the 2014 Brewers Guild Awards.

Hopped Up on Pils (Pilsner)
5% ABV

A hoppy Pilsner, this beer is light in body and colour, with soft, grassy, floral hop character notes of passion fruit and other tropical fruits. Fresh, long and focused.

Ben Middlemiss Brewing Company

Contract brewery
Established: 2006
Location: Auckland
Owner and brewer: Ben Middlemiss

Ben Middlemiss is deeply entrenched in the history of craft beer in New Zealand. He began his brewing career at the now defunct Marlborough Brewery before brewing beer for the Cock and Bull Tavern chain (now Steam Brewing). In 1997, he and Keith Galbraith formed Australis Brewing and produced three notable beers: Benediction, Romanov and Hodgson. All were featured as the finest examples of their style and the top 500 beers in the world in Michael Jackson's *Great Beer Guide*, and, in fact, Australis was one of only three New Zealand brewers to have beers mentioned (the other two were Richard Emerson and Roger Pink).

Middlemiss created his own brand to 'expand on already established excellence... while striving for authenticity'. Originally inspired by the 'masterful beers of the Belgian abbeys and the wonderful British ales', he also takes inspiration from the American, and now Kiwi, craft brewing movements.

Among his most recent achievements, Middlemiss cites winning a gold medal at the 2013 World Beer Cup in Dublin for his abbey ale Nota Bene, and a silver at the Alltech Commonwealth Beer Cup in 2014 (his was one of only 87 out of over 1000 that won a medal). He is currently looking at brewing 'involvements' in the US and UK.

Middlemiss has two beers that are available in bottle: Nota Bene (which he also makes a vintage example of), a *Brettanomyces*-infected abbey beer; and Hodgson, a traditional IPA. As well as these, he has a number of beers available only on tap: Sawn-Off, Lunatic Soup, Puddy Muddles and White Lady. The beers never fail to excite.

Nota Bene (Belgian strong ale)
8.7%

A strong, hoppy Belgian-style beer, conditioned with *Brettanomyces*. Full and nutty, with sweet raisiny notes and a lot of funk from the *Brett*, which also leaves a long, dry finish. This is an exciting take on Belgian tradition and a very enjoyable beer.

Big Growler

Contract brewery
Established: 2014
Location: Petone
Owner and brewer: Garth Edwards

Driven by a love of beer, home brewer Garth Edwards wanted more than just his mates to try his beers. Inspired by English beers, especially Fuller's, he set out to re-create those styles with a Kiwi twist.

At this stage, Big Growler has released only a handful of one-off beers, including The Bitter Ex (APA), The Whinging Pom (an ESB, not to be confused with the Behemoth/Mike's Hoppy Wheat Ale collaboration) and Mrs Palmer's Porter (flavoured with raspberry and chocolate).

Black Dog Brewing Co.

Brewpub
Established: 2011
Location: Wellington
Owner: Dominion Breweries
Brewers: Dale Cooper, Darren Lovell
and Simon Edward

Created by DB as a craft offering, Black Dog was established in 2011 and began by selling beer via DB-tied pubs and bars, as well as their own brewbar, just off Courtenay Place in downtown Wellington.

Brewer Dale Cooper describes the Black Dog style as, 'a traditional mix of styles from UK and Germany combined with the new world'. Their core beers are approachable takes on US styles, and are available on tap in most DB-tied establishments and bottled; their Pango Kuri ('Black Dog' in Maori) is an American stout and is exceptional. Due to increasing demand, the core beers are now brewed off site, with the small brewpub brewery being used for seasonals. The latter are, without exception, exceedingly good; my favourites are the Berliner weiss and Clifford, a red ale named after the Scholastic Books character.

Bite (hoppy Pilsner)
5.5% ABV

Hopped with Sauvin and Motueka, this is an incredibly aromatic Pilsner with lemongrass, gooseberry and floral notes, and clean, focused bitterness.

Kiwi Unleashed (APA)
6% ABV

Formerly called Unleashed, Kiwi Unleashed is an APA with lovely malt sweetness, and a long line of bitterness that brings together the malt weight and the lemony, grassy hop notes.

Golden Lab (golden ale)
4.5% ABV

A simple golden ale with giving malt and lemon-drop hop notes.

Chomp (New Zealand pale ale)
4.75% ABV

Chomp is a really enjoyable beer, if a bit rich and full in the malt department to be a NZ pale ale. It has a luscious biscuity malt weight with clean bitterness and a hint of grapefruit hop aromatics.

Selection of malts at Baylands Brewery, Petone.

Black Sands Brewing Company

Brewery
Established: 2013
Location: Kelson, Auckland
Director: Ian Hebblethwaite

Ian Hebblewaithe describes the commissioning of his brewery as the 'natural and inevitable outcome of an unrestrained home brewing obsession combined with an accommodating partner'. Inspired mainly by the west coast IPA style of the USA, he describes his beers as, 'handmade ales brewed old school', eschewing 'fancy, non-traditional ingredients'.

Bloom Theory and Envirospecific Brewing

Brewery
Established: 2012
Location: Whanganui
Owners and brewers:
James Chatterton and
Michael Cheyne

James Chatterton and Michael Cheyne of Bloom Theory travel to interesting locations with a portable brewkit. There they brew beers inspired by the location using a recipe but adapted on the fly with foraged, begged or borrowed ingredients. They then return to home base to scale these up. Their travels are videoed and can be watched at thebloomtheory.co.nz. They also produce an amber ale, which is available at the Whanganui farmers' market.

Boundary Road Brewery

Brewery
Established: 1987
Location: Auckland
Owner: Asahi Holdings (Australia)
Pty Limited
Brew master: Trevor Rollinson

Having brewed beer since 1987 (mostly rather bland, cheap industrial lager), Independent Liquor launched the Boundary Road Brewery brand in 2011 after its acquisition by Asahi. With strong ties to the liquor and RTD market, the company's launch of Boundary Road Brewery marked the emergence of another major player (alongside Lion and DB) in the New Zealand beer industry.

The growing demand for craft offerings and the fact mainstream publicans now have more than two options has meant more guest taps and bottled craft offerings in all pubs. It has also forced Lion and DB to concentrate on craft offerings as well as improving the quality and range of brands like Mac's and Monteith's.

The Boundary Road beers are approachable takes on already established craft beer styles, and some are excellent. To date, the brewery has had 23 beers on the market, with 13 currently available. Master brewer Trevor Rollinson describes their output as 'pretty prolific', and while they are yet to produce seasonal beers (these are on the agenda), their philosophy has been one of testing and reacting to the market: 'If a brew doesn't get a strong consumer uptake, we will replace it.'

Boundary Road also import a number of international brands, including Sam Adams, Asahi and Budvar, but also, for a time, Brew Dog from Scotland, a match that due to Brew Dog's politics and outspoken attacks on large corporate breweries (including those that Boundary Road also import into New Zealand) seemed doomed to fail. In addition, Boundary Road produce a range of volume beers, including NZ Pure, Wild Buck, Haagen, Ranfurly and New Zealand Lager.

The Chosen One (golden lager)
5% ABV

Simple, effervescent lager with a hint of funky hop notes.

Bouncing Czech (Pilsner lager)
5.2% ABV

Refreshing golden lager with long, persistent bitterness.

Flying Fortress (NZ pale ale)
4.6% ABV

A pale ale with very sweet caramel notes with a hint of vanilla and sherbet tropical hop notes.

Mumbo Jumbo (IPA)
5.2% ABV

A light-bodied malt with subdued aromatics, though what it lacks here it makes up for in long, firm bitterness. Simple but, considering the price, excellent value.

18th Amendment (APA)
6% ABV

Lots of sticky, orange marmalade US hop notes come forward at the start. However, these fade after taking a sip. Lovely smooth malt, although it comes across as unbalanced; lacks aromatics or bitterness in the finish.

Steam Brewing Company, Auckland.

Stolen Base American (double IPA)
8% ABV

Like the APA, this starts with a huge burst of burnt orange but has more follow-through, with taut bitterness against the rich malt. It is enjoyable but lacks refinement.

Jack the Sipper (London porter)
5.6% ABV

Boasts soft toasty notes and an iron-like richness. However, this beer does not have either the sharpness of a traditional London porter or the hop vibrancy of a new world one, leaving it a bit hollow.

Arabica Dabra Coffee Oatmeal Stout
6.5% ABV

A vibrant espresso note on the nose and a smoky, earthy body are brought into balance by a hint of sharpness. Full and rich.

Chocolate Moose (chocolate porter)
4.5% ABV

With banana bread on the nose and a hint of iron (not uncommon for dark beers), this beer is light in colour for a porter, and thin with little depth of flavour. What there is, is a huge, sweet, chocolate note that mingles with the savoury elements from the malt to create a mocha quality. It does exactly what it says on the bottle.

Brauhaus Frings

Brewpub
Established: 2003
Location: Whangarei
Owners: Leon Inder and
Warren Curren

Established by Denis Frings, this eponymously named brewpub serves as a live music venue and beer garden. Current owners Leon Inder and Warren Curren have three core beers, available only at the brewpub, and also make regular seasonal beers.

Brave Brewing

Brewery
Established: 2014
Location: Hastings
Owner and brewer: Matt Smith

After travelling, then living in Auckland for a decade, Matt Smith moved back to Hawke's Bay with his wife Gemma in 2013. Having become 'obsessed' with craft beer, he decided the burgeoning market of Hawke's Bay would be a good place to settle down and 'have a crack at running a brewery'. The Champion Brewer award at the 2013 SOBA National Home Brew Competition gave him enough confidence that his plan was a winner.

Smith currently brews American- and Belgian-style beers in a 300L kit in his converted garage. His first two beers, Extra Pale Ale and Farmhouse Ale, are crisp, balanced and refreshing. Like many regional brewers, his number one focus is establishing his local market, meaning consumers will get to drink his beer 'as fresh as possible'. He intends to grow his brewery into a brewpub, but figures that 'starting small whilst keeping a day job would be a sensible stepping stone'.

Aside from selling through a variety of local outlets, Smith has a pop-up 'bar' at the Hastings Farmers' Market, held every Sunday morning at the Hawke's Bay Showgrounds – if you are in the bay, check it out!

Extra Pale Ale (APA)
5.7% ABV

A crisp, refreshing pale ale with vibrant but not overpowering orange zest and pine aromatics, and a clean bitterness. It is broad for the style with a soft, sweet malt body.

Farmhouse Ale
5.3% ABV

Bone-dry, incredibly spicy and with a hint of tartness, this beer is packed with white pepper and lemony citrus zest notes. An approachable saison with wheaten elements.

Matt and Gemma Smith of Brave Brewing.

Brew Moon

Brewpub
Established: 2002
Location: Amberley, North Canterbury
Owners and brewers: Belinda Gould
and Kieran McCauley

Having lived in California in the 1990s, Belinda Gould and Kieran McCauley 'got a taste for good craft beer'. When they relocated to Amberley, where Belinda was a winemaker, they discovered there weren't many craft breweries around, so decided to establish one.

Until recently, they have brewed out of a café site (which they originally owned) just south of Amberley, but are about to move into a larger brewery in 'downtown' Amberley (a town of about 1600 people).

Brew Moon strive to make 'interesting and balanced ales' that are sustainably produced. They describe their style as 'fairly hoppy' and 'fruity and yeasty', acknowledging that they tend to ferment their ales at higher temperatures.

I find the beers of Brew Moon universally drinkable and balanced. They are not over-the-top beers that get media headlines and outrageously high ratings on beer websites, but they are strong, consistent performers. Writing his yearly round-up of top beers and brewers for 2014, beer writer and bartender Dylan Jauslin said of Brew Moon's flagship Hophead: 'This year the single pint of beer that I enjoyed the most also happens to be the beer I enjoyed the most consistently. And that beer is... drumroll... Brew Moon Hophead IPA. This is without a doubt one of the best, yet possibly one of the least celebrated beers of New Zealand.'

Hophead IPA (NZ pale ale)
5% ABV

Billed as an IPA, at only 5% this beer is better described as a New Zealand pale ale. It has a generous malt body with some burnt caramel notes, vibrant grassy hopping and a long, dry, bitter finish.

Amberley Pale Ale (session pale ale)
4% ABV

Light-bodied but very aromatic, this session ale has lemon and orange zest and juicy pineapple notes.

Luna Wit (spiced witbier)
5% ABV

Luna Wit has orange sherbet on the nose, with a luscious round palate combining Belgian yeast notes and cream wheaten character. There is some very subtle acidity ,with dusty coriander and complex spice notes.

Olé Molé (spiced beer)
5% ABV

This is one of the most rich, complex and enjoyable spiced beers I know. With a full, caramelly malt base, it is inspired by Mexican moles, which, done well, are exceptional but are often too sweet. Layers of cocoa, cinnamon, coriander and cumin are present, as is a hint of lime. These build up, interplay and culminate in a finish dominated by the warm fire of chipotle peppers.

Dark Side (of the Moon) (stout)
6% ABV

One of my favourite New Zealand stouts, this is a big, rich, roasty beer that is creamy and full. It is big and complex without being overly alcoholic.

Brew Mountain

Brewery
Established: 2014
Location: New Plymouth
Owners: Liam Tranter,
Shannon and Kelly Ryan
Brewers: Liam Tranter and
Shannon Ryan

Brew Mountain was established when New Plymouth GP Liam Tranter and real estate agent Shannon Ryan were able to borrow a 300L brewkit no longer needed by Joseph Wood, who had recently relocated his brewery to Auckland. They teamed up with Shannon's brother Kelly, an already established and well-regarded brewer, who was on sabbatical in New Plymouth following the death of his and Shannon's father, Olympian boxer Pat Ryan.

Named in honour of their father, the first beer they brewed was Pale Pat Supreme, an APA that straddles the Pacific using US and New Zealand hops. Influenced by the 'big hoppy beers' brewed by Epic and Liberty, the Brew Mountain beers are hoppy without being over the top; they are exceptionally drinkable and have a subtlety and depth that held my attention as I tasted.

The brewery was established with the idea of brewing a handful of 'flavour-filled beers that everyone can drink' and purchase from local outlets. However, the success of Pale Pat and the demand for bottled product now means that the beer is brewed under contract at the Beer Fountain, part-owned by Joseph Wood.

Blondini (golden ale)
4.2% ABV

Blondini has vibrant passion fruit, guava tropical hop notes, and lovely fresh-baked bread notes of malt and yeast. Focused bitterness and bursts of aroma come through on the finish in this tightly wound and focused beer.

Pale Pat Supreme (APA)
4.6% ABV

Hopped with US and New Zealand hops, the Pale Pat Supreme has a light, biscuit, sweet malt body, a vibrant hop aroma and a very clean bitterness. Very refreshing, it is a wonderfully balanced, hop-forward, light-bodied APA. Bottles of this beer are brewed under contract at the Beer Fountain in Auckland.

Bright Eyes (IPA)
6.1% ABV

Characterised by pine hop notes with some grapefruit pith and a biscuity malt profile balanced by long bitterness the whole way through. An excellent, understated IPA that is very drinkable.

Magmatude (American Red Ale)
4.2% ABV

Smooth and round with nice depth, Magmatude has some smokiness and good length. It bursts with hop aroma but the bitterness is in balance. Very smooth and drinkable.

Brewaucracy

Contract brewery
Established: 2011
Location: Hamilton
Owners and brewers: Greig McGill
and Phil Murray

Encouraged to scale up from a homebrewed batch of his pumpkin beer, Punkin' Image Ltd, by Joseph Wood of Liberty Brewing, beer geek and homebrew enthusiast Greig McGill formed Brewaucracy with his business partner Phil Murray. They currently brew their beers at the Shunters Yard brewery in Matangi, close to Hamilton.

Greig is passionate about 'overlooked or taken-for-granted' styles of New Zealand beer and has deep respect for the Kiwi craft brewers who have brought New Zealand to where we are today: Stu and Sam of the Yeastie Boys, the 'Three Kings' (Richard Emerson, Carl Vasta and Luke Nicolas), and those who paved the way for the above, notably Ben Middlemiss

and Keith Galbraith. Currently, Brewaucracy has a core range of three beers: Bean Counter, In Triplicate and Smoko, although they have recently acquired a small stock of barrels from Graeme Mahy's now defunct 666 Brewing company (Mahy has recently returned to Australia to take on the head brewer role at Murray's Brewing Company – a business he helped establish). Because they have their beer brewed under contract, McGill acknowledges that 'we never seem to have enough beer', although rectifying this is high on his list of priorities for 2015 and beyond.

Totara Brewing hop farm in Wai-iti Valley, Nelson.

Brothers Beer and Brothers Brewery

Brewpub
Established: 2011
Location: Auckland CBD (Brothers
Beer) and Mt Eden (Brothers Brewery)
Owners: Anthony Brown and Andrew
Larson

Brothers Beer have quickly become the centre of the Auckland brewing industry, both geographically and spiritually. They are a brewpub, retail outlet, contract brewery and more. In late 2015, they are going to be opening a larger, second location, Brothers Brewery in Mt Eden.

Brothers currently make two regularly available beers: a lager and a pale ale. Once the Mt Eden Brewery facility is open, these core beers will be brewed here, leaving space at the smaller Brothers Beer facility for more experimental beers. In addition to these beers, the brewpub serves a plethora of regularly changing beers from other breweries, both in bottle and on 18 taps.

Lager
5% ABV

A light, bright lager with rich barley notes and a fruity, flowery hop character.

Auckland Pale Ale (NZ pale ale)
5.3% ABV

With a rich body of sweet malt and an aroma akin to walking in a hay field on a hot summer's day, this is an approachable New Zealand pale ale with vibrant floral aromas on the finish.

Cassels & Sons Brewery

Brewpub
Established: 2009
Location: Woolston, Christchurch
Owner: the Cassels family
Brewer: Zac Cassels

Alasdair Cassels, along with his son Zac and son-in-law Joe Shanks, established the brewery in 2009 in order to supply beer to bars and restaurants around Christchurch. The brewery is on the site now occupied by the beautifully appointed Tannery complex (which has been owned by the family since 1994). Following the February 2011 earth-quakes, the industrial buildings on the site were rendered uninhabitable, and work quickly began on rebuilding The Brewery, the brewpub where the Cassels beers are made. This was opened only four months after the quakes and remains a highlight of the ever-expanding Christchurch beer industry.

The Tannery complex is a Victorian-inspired indoor arcade with boutique retail outlets, including an excellent deli and bottle store, as well as Gustav's, the Cassels' more formal restaurant and wine bar.

The Cassels' beers are unmistakably British. Specialising in cask-conditioned ales, they are, with the exception of the occasional seasonal that purposefully pushes the boundaries, true to style, being focused and long. Of these, my favourite is their Milk Stout, which is one of the best examples of the style brewed in New Zealand. In addition to cask-conditioned beers, there are a number of other beers, including a lager, a Pilsner and an exceptional dunkel. As well as the brewery and restaurant at the Tannery, the Cassels also have a brewbar on Madras Street in the Christchurch CBD.

One P.A. (APA)
6% ABV

A celebration of a single hop (NZ Cascade), this beer has intense grassy and burnt orange notes with long, persistent bitterness.

Lager
4.8% ABV

A clean, fresh, focused, simple pale lager. Very enjoyable and very balanced.

Pilsner
4.8% ABV

A vibrantly hopped Pilsner with grassy hop notes over a body of honeyed malt. Has a long, bitter finish.

Best Bitter
4.3% ABV

Served cask-conditioned at the brewery or from a bag on hand-pull, this is a medium-dark bitter with nutty notes and tremendous complexity and malt depth. Finishes long and bitter.

The Alchemist (APA)
4.6% ABV

Rich, complex caramel and biscuit malt notes make way for herbal aromatic hops. This APA is full for the style but extremely rewarding. Served cask-conditioned or from a bag on hand-pull.

Dunkel
5.6% ABV

A rich, full, dark lager with a round, fulsome malt weight and notes of burnt caramel and a hint of roasted coffee, this has a long, dry finish, which combines the bitterness of hops and roasted barley.

Milk Stout
5.2% ABV

One of my partner Lauren's favourite beers and winner of the trophy for Cask Conditioned Ales at the 2011 Brewers Guild Awards, this is intensely rich and creamy (without being heavy), with flavours of milk chocolate and burnt toast.

Choice Bros

Contract brewery
Established: 2012
Located: Wellington
Owner: Michael Pullin,
Iona Calderwood and Kerry Gray
Brewer: Kerry Gray

After homebrewing for many years, Kerry Gray began bringing his beers into the craft beer bars he frequented in order to get more feedback. Buoyed by the warm reception and inspired by the likes of other 'contract-only' breweries, such as Yeastie Boys and Danish gypsy brewer Mikkeller, he decided that he would try his hand at brewing commercially.

Gray describes his beers as 'risky, experimental, original' and, with out-there ingredients such as peanut butter and bacon, I cannot disagree. Because there are already so many amazing, world-class beers on the market, he believes that it is his job to try something different, asking whether there is any point in brewing a beer when you can already buy a great example of the style?

Gray's focus for 2015 is to cement his core range of beers, which will become more readily available, both on tap and in the bottle, as well as to showcase his more 'unique and interesting' brews at beer festivals. He is also planning on establishing a physical brewery and tasting room in Wellington by early 2016.

His three core beers will be: Modern Love – an excellent hoppy beer that he describes as a 'new world ale'; Serious Moonlight – a spiced imperial stout; and On the Brain – an English rye ale with peanut butter and raspberries.

In addition, Gray will be releasing a series of beers called Culture Vulture, made with yeasts harvested from bottle-conditioned beers; and Hand Pulled Pork, a bacon beer brewed with 'meat in every part of the brew process' for International Bacon Day. He has already brewed collaboration beers with Craftwork and NineBarnyardOwls.

Coromandel Brewing Company

Brewpub
Established: 2008
Location: Hahei, Coromandel
Owner and brewer: Neil Vowels

With experience brewing in the UK, Neil Vowels established the Coromandel Brewing Company in his Matarangi garage in 2008, making it the only brewery on the Coromandel Peninsula at the time. Since then, he has opened a brewpub, The Pour House, in Hahei.

Crafty Trout Brewing Company

Brewpub
Established: 2012
Located: Taupo
Owner: Rebecca Draper-Kidd
Brewer: Anton Romrier

Looking over Lake Taupo, Crafty Trout was established by Anton Romrier, of Austrian descent. Romrier's grandfather was also a brewer, and he has tried to create beers that are inspired by his Austrian heritage.

Using the first SmartBrew system, designed by Brian Watson of Hamilton's Good George (and chief judge of the New Zealand International Beer Awards), Romrier uses wort made at Good George and ferments batches of the various beers as needed.

In order to get more depth and complexity into his beers, he ages the wort in large bladders, designed to store apple juice before it is fermented into cider.

Above the brewery, Crafty Trout also has a Bier Kafe that serves everything from pizzas and platters through to traditional Austrian specialities; it also has a beautiful view of the lake.

Hook Vienna Amber (Vienna lager)
4.5% ABV

Inspired by the beers of Romrier's family brewpub in Austria, this is a beautifully coloured copper lager with rich biscuit and caramel notes from the malt and a refreshing bitterness.

Spinnaker (hefe weizen)
6.8% ABV

Not a traditional hefe, as it is spiced with coriander, orange and pink grapefruit, this beer has a pink tinge and bursts with citrus notes that are intensified by the Galaxy hops. It has a rich mouthfeel from the fermentation esters.

Anton Romrier at The Crafty Trout.

Line Taupo Pale Ale (herb/fruit pale ale)
4.2% ABV

This is a light, refreshing pale ale with clean bitterness. The added lemon zest and thyme give the beer a herbal, citrus note.

Sinker Porter
7.5% ABV

To me, this is the most enjoyable beer in the range. A lighter example of the porter style, it has some old ale tart notes, these complementing the almost coffee-like bitterness from the roasted malt.

Downrigger Imperial Pale Ale (American strong ale)
11.9% ABV

This interesting beer is a blend of a 10% ABV lager and a 6% ale. Big and malty, it has a rich, warming sweetness and some alcoholic notes. There is some bitterness and hop character, but not enough to balance the beer's cloying finish.

Craftwork

Brewery
Established: 2014
Located: Oamaru
Owners and brewers: Michael O'Brien
and Lee-Ann Scotti

With just a 50L production, Craftwork is certainly one of New Zealand's smallest and most idiosyncratic commercial breweries. In fact, they describe their own brewery as 'ludicrously uneconomic'. Specialising in Belgian-inspired ales, they have a range of beers, including several variations on saison, such as those flavoured with citrus, pear, anise and even Christmas spices (this beer, intriguingly, is called Poodlefaker), and a Flanders red ale called Red Bonnet. They also brew a grisette, a historical Belgian-style beer named after the female workers for whom it was brewed, a Belgian strong ale and an IPA.

Having tried only a handful of the beers, I have found them to be singular. While they are flavoured, this adds only a subtle complexity over and above that of the base beer. They are intense, powerful, complex and amazingly enjoyable.

Croucher Brewing Co.

Brewery
Established: 2004
Location: Rotorua
Owners: Paul Croucher and
Nigel Gregory
Brewer: Paul Croucher

Croucher was established by Paul Croucher and Nigel Gregory 'in the midst of a dual mid-life crisis'. While many breweries have been similarly inspired, the pair were uniquely suited to the brewing industry, with Croucher having a PhD in chemistry and Gregory being an experienced marketer and business development manager.

While they established the brewery in 2004, they did not produce any beer until 2006 and managed to win a bronze medal for their pale ale at the Brew New Zealand Awards that year. To Croucher, particularly, this reinforced his decision to start a brewery.

Croucher's brewing draws on his scientific background. However, his philosophy is simple: 'scrimp on kit, never ingredients'. He has been at the forefront of several major style trends since the brewery was established – his Pilsner was among the first to be hopped liberally with New Zealand hops, and he was among the first New Zealand brewers to make a black IPA. Most notable, though, is his 'smallest' beer – Lowrider, a 2.7% ABV pale ale with amazing hop aroma and intense flavour concentration.

While hoppy pale ales may be the signature beer of most breweries, Croucher's has been their show-stopping Pilsner. It won Champion International Lager at the Brew New Zealand Awards in 2010, and Champion Pilsner at the Australian International Beer Awards in 2012. As of February 2015, this beer was also in the 97th percentile by style on RateBeer.com.

Due to increased demand, in late 2014 they moved into a bigger brewery, which will allow them to increase production of all of their beers but also to produce more seasonal and one-off beers. Having been under so much pressure in terms of both production and space, Croucher intends to play a fuller part in the 'craft beer revolution, both at home and abroad', beginning with collaboration beers in their new brewery, which they believe will help them keep 'growing our skills and keeping us motivated'.

Croucher Brewing Co. also own two craft beerpubs called Brew, one in Rotorua and one in Tauranga. Each pub has around a dozen taps, half of them serving Croucher beers and the rest serving craft beers from other New Zealand and international breweries.

Pilsner
5% ABV

With a subtle aroma of lemon blossom and passion fruit, this beer has a lovely, rich mid-palate with luscious golden malt. It finishes with long, refreshing bitterness.

Lowrider (Session IPA)
2.7% ABV

Almost technically a 'light' beer, Lowrider has vibrant hop flavour – citrus flowers, passion fruit and guava, overlaid onto a body of light, dusty malt. Because of the low alcohol and high hops, this beer is extremely dry. For me, it's not an issue – this is a delicious beer that can be drunk in situations where you might think twice about ordering another alcoholic drink. This beer won Runner-up to Best Beer at the SOBA Beer Awards 2013 and a gold medal at the Brew New Zealand Awards in 2013.

Pale Ale (APA)
5% ABV

Orange-hued and with subtle hop notes: passion fruit, guava and lychee, as well as pine. With some sweet malt notes to provide balance to the bitterness, this beer is very precise and focused, with a long, dry finish and lingering bitterness.

ANZUS (IPA)
7% ABV

A blend of Australian, New Zealand and US hops, this IPA has an extremely well-integrated hop component with no individual character sticking out. Lemon and fir are the dominant notes. It is long, focused and refreshing.

Patriot (black IPA)
5.5% ABV

This beer bursts with intense chocolate-orange aroma, like a Jaffa that isn't sweet. This is backed up by pine-needle notes. Palate-wise, it is smooth and creamy without being heavy. Its long bitterness keeps you coming back for more.

Dale's Brewing Co.

Contract brewery
Established: 2011
Location: Nelson
Owner and brewer: Dale Holland

Dale Holland describes himself as 'self-taught' when it comes to brewing. In 2010, he won Champion Brewer at the SOBA National Homebrew Competition, so he decided to turn his passion into a business and began brewing the recipes he'd perfected at home.

Holland is most passionate about beers that balance malt and yeast character, and lists his favourite New Zealand brewers as Richard Emerson and Martin Townshend, both masters of this. His favourite beer is the eccentric sour Belgian red ale Duchesse de Bourgogne. Rather than brewing Pilsners and pale ales, two of the more common styles on the market, Holland prefers to focus on beer styles that have few New Zealand examples; his Belgian Pale Ale in particular is highly regarded, but he also brews other neglected styles.

Belgian Pale Ale
5.4% ABV

This beer epitomises the genre – vibrant fruity hop notes combine with funky Belgian ester characters and lovely rich malt to create a flavour explosion.

American Amber Ale
5.4% ABV

A balance of nutty, caramel malt and a hint of fruity ale yeast are set against a clean, long bitterness with pithy orange, ripe apricots and pine notes.

Extra Special Bitter
5.6% ABV

Rich and warming, with a distinct malt character and a hint of toffee, this beer has focused bitterness through the mid-palate and a burst of citrus blossom hop notes on the finish.

Doppelbock
7.5% ABV

A lovely, rich copper colour combines with dark bready notes, luscious sweet caramel and a hint of roastiness that gives grip to the finish. Towards the end, the citrusy hop notes get in the way of the lovely malt character.

Hop pellets.

DB Breweries

Brewery
Established: 1929
Locations: Waitemata, Mangatainoka,
Timaru and Greymouth
Owner: Heineken Asia Pacific

The Waitemata Brewery opened under protest from both the prohibition lobby and the established breweries of the day. It was established by William Coutts but soon became Dominion Breweries when Coutts went into partnership with Henry Kelliher, with Coutts brewing and Kelliher running the business. From day one, Coutts's son Morton was deeply involved in the brewing business and applied rigorous scientific study to the brewing method, developing, among other things, the process of continuous fermentation – this would go on to change much of the commercial brewing industry, in both New Zealand and around the world. Over this time, Morton Coutts won numerous international brewing awards.

The company grew, taking over a number of breweries, such as the Mangatainoka Brewery (now Tui), as well as building others, like the Washdyke (now DB Draught) in Timaru. While DB has taken over a handful of breweries in its lifespan, it is much less the product of mergers and acquisitions than Lion is.

DB had been listed on the stock exchange since 1930. But in 1981, Brierley Investments acquired a significant stake of the business and in 1987 Magnum Corporation (controlled by Brierley) bought out DB shareholders in a share swap (they sold their DB shares for Magnum ones). In 1991, Asia Pacific Breweries (now Heineken Asia Pacific) took a 54% stake in Magnum, with Magnum becoming the DB Group and the brewery being renamed DB rather than Dominion Breweries. Between 1994 and 2000, Asia Pacific Breweries took over DB entirely by buying out individual investors and by investing more into the business.

Export Gold (pale lager)
4% ABV

A clean, simple lager.

DB Draught
4% ABV

A simple amber lager with some malt definition but very little of anything else.

Tui (NZ draught)
4% ABV

Billed as an 'East India Pale Ale', this does not even vaguely resemble an IPA, nor is it even a ale. It is, in fact, a smooth, malty New Zealand draught with virtually no hop character.

Double Brown (NZ draught)
4% ABV

A darker, sweeter beer than Tui or DB Draught, but still very simple and lacking character.

Dr Hops

Contract brewery
Established: 2012
Location: Cromwell
Owner and brewer: Nicky Claridge

More of a brand than an actual brewing business, Dr Hops has a fun steampunk aesthetic that is exemplified by the moustachioed chap on the label and bottle text on the World Pale Ale, currently the sole beer in the range: 'Ladies and Gents... We present to you the first official brew from the mysterious impresario... Dr Wiley Hops. Born the love child of Daddy Longlegs, the infamous high stilt walker, and his ravishing gypsy wives, his formative years were spent travelling the globe amongst his family of side show freaks and outcasts.'

In reality, Dr Hops is a woman – wine logistics professional Nicky Claridge, who has the beer brewed under contract at Invercargill Brewery.

World Pale Ale (APA)
5.6% ABV

Called 'World Pale Ale' because it incorporates hops from the US, New Zealand, England and Germany, this is an understated APA that is approachable and extremely drinkable. It has rich malt notes, with citrus and herb, and a subtle floral top notes.

Dead Good Beer

Contract brewery
Established: 2010
Location: Nelson
Owners: Mic Dover and Eelco Boswijk

Describing themselves as a 'virtual brewery' and steadfastly 'anti-fashion' when it comes to style, the Dead Good Beer owners also own Nelson pub The Free House. While they no longer produce bottled beers, they occasionally produce an IPA that is served exclusively in the pub. Each year they also produce a festival beer for Nelson's Marchfest.

Bottling line at McCashin's Brewery, Nelson.

Deep Creek Brewing

Brewpub
Established: 2010
Location: Browns Bay, North Auckland
(brewpub), and Silverdale (brewery)
Directors: Paul Brown and
Jarred MacLachlan
Brewer: Hamish Ward

Located on Auckland's North Shore, Deep Creek was established as a brewpub but has since grown to include two more pubs: Coast in Orewa and Cove on Waiheke Island. Originally, all of the beer was brewed at the Browns Bay site; however, as demand for the beers has grown since 2012, Deep Creek have brewed their core range of beers at their brewery in Silverdale, with the smaller batches and seasonal beers brewed at Browns Bay.

Stylistically, the beers are quite rich and malt-focused compared to many similar examples of the styles brewed here in New Zealand. While they have relatively high residual sweetness, the high levels of hops used provide balance through aroma, especially quite floral elements and bitterness.

Undercurrent (NZ Pilsner)
5% ABV

With sweet malt notes, firm bitterness and fruity citrus and floral hop aromas, this is a long, focused Kiwi Pilsner.

Lotus (session pale ale)
4.5% ABV

This beer has a very rich malty body for the style, but a bright orange, peach and extremely floral (almost too floral) hop character.

309 (NZ pale ale)
5% ABV

309 has a balanced body with light biscuity notes and long bitterness. It bursts with vibrant Kiwi hop character – citrus and floral elements abound.

The Leprechaun's Belle (Irish red ale)
4.6% ABV

One of the few true examples of this style brewed in New Zealand, this is a rich copper colour, with creamy warm caramel malt and fine roasty elements.

The Dusty Gringo (American brown ale)
6.8% ABV

A rich, full-flavoured malty ale with some sweetness; it has a long, intense bitterness with bright aromatics coming from US and New Zealand hops.

Pontoon in a Monsoon (IPA)
6.9% ABV

An IPA with very rich and malty with caramel notes, and vibrant crushed orange hop character with a hint of pine needle. While it contains New Zealand as well as US hops, it is very much in the west coast IPA style.

Dominatrix (double IPA)
7.3% ABV

Very sweet, almost to the point of cloying, this beer has vibrant sherbet orange, tropical fruit and sweet floral notes.

Emerson's Brewing Company

Brewery
Established: 1992
Location: Dunedin
Owner: Lion
Founder: Richard Emerson

Colloquially known as Emerson's Brewery (or just plain Emerson's), this brewery was established by Richard Emerson with the help of family and friends in 1992. Its first beer, London Porter (still part of the core range) was released in 1993.

Richard Emerson is unarguably one of the stalwarts of the craft beer industry in New Zealand, with Yeastie Boys' Stu McKinlay describing him as his 'brewing hero'. He started out as a food technologist and this (along with his grandfather's homebrew – the first beer he drank) kindled his passion for beer. After travelling and working as a brewer overseas, he returned to his native Dunedin, where he was disappointed at the lack of quality and choice for beer drinkers compared with other parts of the world. He started brewing on a small scale and soon scaled up to a commercial brewery.

Over its 23-year history, Emerson's has had to move to larger sites four times, with the final move being to a large Anzac Avenue site, which will be completed in early 2016. This will also have guest facilities and a tasting room.

All of Emerson's core range of beers are regarded as among the finest examples of their styles, with two beers, Bookbinder and Pilsner, being the most lauded. Originally an organic Pilsner using Gladfield organic malt (very uncommon at the time), the Pilsner burst with the beautiful floral aromas of New Zealand hops. This beer, when it was retired in 2011, was the highest rated Pilsner on RateBeer.com. It was retired as the supply of malt could not keep up with demand for the beer. As of March 2015, the current version of the beer is rated in the 99th percentile for the style on RateBeer.com.

Bookbinder also uses Kiwi hops in an unusual way. A 3.7% bitter, this remains one of New Zealand's most sessionable beers and is regarded as one of the finest examples of the genre, being rated in the 100th percentile for style.

Like these beers, many of Emerson's seasonal and brewer's reserve beers have also come to define their respective styles, especially in New Zealand. JP, a vintage Belgian ale that changes every year (and is always one of the most anticipated seasonal releases), is brewed in honour of Jean-Pierre Dufour, a University of Otago academic who specialised in yeasts and who was one of Richard Emerson's brewing mentors.

Pilsner
4.9% ABV

A lithe, focused Kiwi Pilsner with a lovely rich golden body of malt, beautiful citrus and floral aromatics, and clean, long bitterness.

Bookbinder (bitter)
3.7% ABV

What do you get when you brew a classic English bitter with Kiwi hops? Booky! Notes of toasted hazel-nuts, a hint of caramel, citrus blossom hop notes, with the most important ingredient for the style – subtle bitterness – bringing it all together.

1812 (pale ale)
5% ABV

Lovely, vibrant, tropical fruit hop notes just burst out of the glass: pineapple, guava and mango, with just a hint of citrus that brings the soft malt base into focus. A complete beer.

London Porter
5% ABV

Lovely rich, layered, dark malts combine with a hint of spicy English hop notes, as this beer unfurls with notes of liquorice and a hint of burnt toast. A lovely beer that is lovelier still on hand-pump.

Epic Brewing Company

Contract brewer
Established: 2006
Location: Auckland
Owner and brewer: Luke Nicholas

Luke Nicholas established Epic Brewing in 2006 while he was brewer for Steam Brewing, launching his first and flagship beer, Epic Pale Ale, that year. Its label made a bold statement: 'IT JUST TASTES BIGGER' – I cannot think of a better way to describe the brewery, the beers or Nicholas himself. Nicholas is often referred to (and even refers to himself) as the 'Impish Brewer' – his personality is as big and brash as his beers, and he is both liked and loathed for his cheeky, mischievous nature. He has no qualms, for instance, bursting into the Malthouse in Wellington during beer events and attacking the stereo, which he quaintly describes on his blog luke.co.nz as giving 'some attention to the playlist'. Nicholas launched the brewery as he was unable to find 'a hoppy style pale ale that [he] wanted to drink', and notes that on launch, Epic Pale Ale was 'by far the most hoppy beer on the market'.

Epic specialises in hop-forward pale ales that are inspired by the best beers from the west coast of the US (Nicholas cites Sierra Nevada Pale Ale as an inspiration). The beers are in high demand, not only for their hoppiness but for their balance. Even his biggest, strongest beers have amazing drinkability, a freshness and lightness that belie their high alcohol content. The Epic Pale Ale went on to win Supreme Champion Beer at the New Zealand International Beer Awards the year it was launched and is probably the most recognised individual craft beer in the New Zealand market.

In addition to Epic's hoppy pale ales, the other staple beer Nicholas brews is simply titled 'Lager' and is exactly that – a hoppy, refreshing golden lager that Nicholas describes as a 'sleeper of a beer that is finally being discovered for the great beer that it is'. He has also brewed an imperial version of this beer, aptly titled Larger.

Nicholas was also one of the first Kiwi brewers to collaborate with high-profile international breweries. He first brewed his Epic Pale Ale at Everards Brewery, Leicester, in 2009 for the JD Weatherspoons International Real Ale Festival, and also brewed an imperial IPA, Halcyon, at Thornbridge Brewery on the same trip. In 2010, he teamed up again with Kelly Ryan to make Epic Thornbridge Stout, and later that year collaborated with Sam Caligione from Dogfish Head on Portamarillo, which was featured on the Discovery Channel show *Brew Masters*. In early 2011, he teamed up again with Ryan (who formally joined the Epic team for a spell) and made Mash Up, a New Zealand pale ale in 'collaboration' with a further 43 other New Zealand breweries – it was documented in the as-yet unfinished web series nzcraftbeer.tv. Nicholas believes collaborations are becoming commonplace and they 'should only happen if there is a natural synergy where both brewers coming together can actually make a beer that neither would ever make themselves', and that beer brewed this way can be 'unique and amazing'.

Nicholas recently created a range of one-off beers called the One Trick Pony series. These are single-hop beers, brewed using new and/or experimental hops that, according to him, means they 'probably [haven't] been used before in New Zealand'. The beers are all 6% pale ales, brewed according to the same recipe with the only difference being the hop variety used. He has so far made this beer with Mosiac and Comet hop varieties and the Zythos hop blend.

Lager
5% ABV

This is a refreshingly crisp lager with a broad body of dry golden malt, bright bitterness and extremely vibrant hop aromatics.

Pale Ale (APA)
5.4% ABV

Probably the single-most recognisable New Zealand craft beer – an incredibly focused, refreshing, light-bodied, US-styled pale ale bursting with grapefruit, lychee and apricot flavours. As of May 2014, it was in the 97th percentile for its style and in the 99th percentile of all beers on RateBeer.com.

Armageddon IPA
6.66% ABV

Twice crowned BrewNZ Best in Class (2009 and 2011), this beer, like Epic Pale Ale, is an incredibly focused and light-bodied beer for its style. It is brewed exclusively with US hops, and has a clean bitterness that cuts against the sweetness of the malt and bursts with vibrant pine resin, grapefruit and orange zest hop aromatics. As of May 2014, it was in the 98th percentile both for its style and overall rating on RateBeer.com.

Eruption Brewing

Brewery
Established: 2012
Location: Lyttelton
Owners: Steve Leftly, Shaun Crossan
and Matthew Tyson

Steve Leftly describes the trio who own Eruption Brewing as 'new world ale fanatics' who decided to create a range of beers in order to see if they would work in the market. After initial testing, they decided to build a small brewery in Lyttelton in 2012.

Inspired by the richer beers coming out of Oregon (as opposed to the offerings of most Californian breweries), Eruption Brewing uses only New Zealand hops and malt to interpret these styles, with the end result being, according to Leftly, 'great Kiwi-flavoured ales'.

In 2015, they are scaling up from a one-barrel kit (about 120L) to a 10-barrel kit (you do the maths) and are opening a brewbar on the main street of Lyttelton.

Fat Monk Brewing Co.

Brewery
Established: 2013
Location: Hastings
Owner and brewer: Dermot Haworth

In order to add depth and a point of difference to his family's winery, Abbey Cellars, as well as to occupy himself over winter, Dermot Haworth decided that in addition to wine there would be value in offering 'great beer on tap', as well as rigger sales. Rather than buy in beer from another producer, he decided to make it himself.

Inspired by great hoppy beers of the US, Haworth describes his style as 'American–Kiwi fusion' but, aside from his hoppy pale ales, he also makes traditional English and Belgian styles.

He has recently undertaken his first collaboration, with Kawerau-based Mata Brewery, making a wheat IPA flavoured with mango. To Haworth, this is an opportunity to learn from 'another brewery that is good at something else', and, with the combined sales, social media and distribution power, to 'take bigger risks and push the boundaries'.

Bottling line at Kereru Brewery, Upper Hutt.

Fiasco Brewing Company

Contract brewery
Established: 2013
Location: Christchurch
Owners and brewers: Jason Waring
and Corey Dorset

Jason Waring and Corey Dorset admit that the idea to create Fiasco Brewing came about, like many endeavours, when they 'got drunk... and thought it would be a great idea'. As for the beers, they are mostly inspired by the hop-forward beers of the west coast of the US, although Waring and Dorset are inspired by 'anything that pushes the boundaries or is slightly left field and interesting'.

While the Fiasco beers available 'change with the seasons', they are working at creating a range of five bottled beers. They also look forward to creating collaboration beers with other brewers, but note themselves that 'no one is crazy enough to work with us'.

Among their achievements to date is their black IPA Double DeckYa, which won People's Choice at Beervana in 2014.

Fitzpatrick's Brewing Company

Brewery
Established: 2012
Location: Tauranga
Owners: Craig and Catherine Fitzpatrick
Brewer: Craig Fitzpatrick

Craig and Catherine Fitzpatrick moved from Wellington to Tauranga in 2003. A homebrewer since he was 16, Craig rediscovered craft beer while working in IT in Wellington. The couple bought a lifestyle block, and when the time came to build a new shed it was important that it had space for a small brewery.

Inspired by the brewing traditions of England and by Kiwi takes on them, such as Emerson's Bookbinder, Craig describes his brewing philosophy as 'locally brewed, locally fresh', stressing how disappointing it was not being able to buy local beer.

The Fitzpatrick's beers are quite traditional, with full malt profiles and hopping providing balance, freshness and length.

Pale Ale
5.3% ABV

Zippy herbal hop notes burst from the glass and then give way to a lovely biscuity malt, before being brought back into focus by intense bitterness and another burst of herbal hops. Long and refined.

IPA
6.3% ABV

A classic English-style IPA with lovely rich caramel malt and spicy, floral aromatic hops overlaid on a base of long, persistent bitterness.

Oatmeal Stout
5.1% ABV

A stout with lovely deep coffee aromas and a creamy smoothness coming from the judicious use of oatmeal, which, combined with hops and roast barley, gives cut and freshness through the back of the palate.

Mash tun at Galbraith's Alehouse, Auckland.

Fork & Brewer (and Fork Brewing)

Brewpub
Established: 2006
Location: Wellington
Owners: Sean Murrie, Dion Page, Ari Roskam, Colin Mallon and Neil Miller
Brewer: Kelly Ryan

Building on the success of his beer bar The Malthouse, and Tuatara Brewery, which he helped to establish with brewer Carl Vasta, Sean Murrie teamed up with Malthouse manager and others in the industry to start the Fork & Brewer, a true brewpub.

Currently, the brewery is run by Kelly Ryan, who took over from Lester Dunn in mid-2014. Dunn had established the recipes and while Ryan has tweaked them, overall, the brewery's philosophy of creating balanced, drinkable beers (especially in their core range) has remained.

The brewery has a handful of regular beers but also brews a large number of seasonal, one-off and collaboration beers, so much so that almost every time you walk up those steps (the bar and brewery are on the first storey of the building) it feels like there is something new to try.

Bohemian Hipster (Pilsner)
5% ABV

A Pilsner with a hint of dry-hopped aromatics, lovely full golden malt with clean bitterness and a citrusy lemonade-like finish.

Low Blow (session IPA)
4.7% ABV

Balancing Kiwi and US hops, this is a one–two of gooseberry and grapefruit overlaid on a light but present body of malt.

Welterweight IPA (session IPA)
4.5% ABV

While lighter in alcohol than Low Blow, this IPA is slightly more malty and sweet, with stonefruit and sweet ripe orange notes.

Base Jumper (APA)
6.3% ABV

A big, resinous APA with intense pine notes, orange and beautiful tropical flowers. Despite its high hopping, bitterness is there but is not overpowering.

Founders Brewery

Brewery
Established: 1999
Location: Nelson
Owners: Independent Liquor (the brand) and the Duncan family (the brewery and café at Founders Heritage Park)

The history of the Duncan family and that of the Nelson beer industry are deeply entwined, with founding father Joseph Dodson arriving in Nelson in 1854 and quickly buying a stake in a local brewery (before becoming mayor in 1874). The family became the Duncans when Henry, Joseph's grandson to his daughter Mary-Anne, joined his grandfather and uncle in the brewing business. Since 1854, there has always been a member of the family in the brewing industry.

The brewery as we know it was established in 1999 when Nelson City Council took over Founders Heritage Park and wanted to feature traditional businesses that reflected the city's history. Needless to say, a small brewery manned by a family with over 150 years of brewing in their blood fitted the bill.

In 2012, the brand was sold to Independent Liquor, who have removed some of the best beers – Long Black and Red Head – and replaced them with well-made, relatively true-to-style beers as a premium craft offering, as compared to their Boundary Road brand. The physical brewery and café at Founders Heritage Park in Nelson remain in the hands of the Duncan family.

1946 (Pilsner)
5% ABV

A very enjoyable, focused Pilsner; not overly serious but it offers excellent value for money and has lovely golden malt and floral top notes.

1981 (pale ale)
5.2% ABV

A clean, light APA with orange and grapefruit notes that are true to style. Simple but, like the Pilsner, it offers excellent value for money.

2009 (IPA)
5.3% ABV

A richer, fuller beer with a more biscuity malt depth. Unlike the other two beers in the range, 2009 does not have the hop level to balance it, resulting in a beer that is a little too sweet.

Pomeroy's Brewing formerly Four Avenues Brewing

Brewery
Established: 2012
Location: Christchurch
Owners: Steve Pomeroy and Ava Wilson
Brewer: Nathan Crabe

Four Avenues is the brewing arm of the Christchurch free house Pomeroy's. Located in the same building, the brewery (Stainless Brewing Limited, which also has BeerNZ, a beer distributor, as a shareholder) was actually set up as a contract facility in order to help Christchurch-based brewers brew their beers.

Because of demand (they are booked up about four months in advance), they are scaling up and moving to the adjacent warehouse. There they will also be working with a contract bottler to provide those services as well.

The beers are brewed by Nathan Crabbe who, having brewed them for the pub, has designed them to be approachable and to 'cater for a wide range of beer drinkers'.

Half Nelson (bitter)
3.8% ABV

A light, fresh and hoppy example of an entry-level bitter. Golden with a creamy texture and lovely malt character to counterpoint the hops.

Opposition (amber ale)
4.8% ABV

A lighter, drier American amber with some praline notes and a hint of roastiness for complexity. Bright US hops give an aromatic lift.

Standing Room Only (porter)
5% ABV

A very full UK-style porter with bitter coffee notes and a hint of tartness to add freshness.

Funk Estate

Contract brewery
Established: 2012
Location: Wellington
Owners: Shigeo (Shiggy) Takagi,
Jordan Evison and Dylan Shearer
Production director: Shigeo Takagi

Funk Estate was launched in 2012 with much aplomb at Hashigo Zake, where production director Shiggy worked as a bartender. They managed to sell 250L of their Funk'nstein black IPA within a little over three hours – this remains a record for the craft beer bar.

Funk Estate's owners, a trio of craft beer lovers, came together over a joint hunger (or should I say thirst) to 'contribute our own special something to the growing industry'. They believe in 'experimenting with unusual techniques, ingredients and flavours' in order to make beers that stand out from the crowd, eschewing the traditional style guidelines.

Despite this, they have been relatively successful at the Brewers Guild Awards since their launch in 2012, and were also voted People's Choice at Beervana that year.

Parleyer (Pilsner)
4.2% ABV

A Pilsner with an amazingly vibrant nose and beautiful fruity hop top notes. A lovely rich body of golden malt fills the palate but remains crisp, combining with floral hop notes and long bitterness.

OH LORDY! (NZ pale ale)
5.5% ABV

A vibrantly hopped New Zealand pale ale with grassy passion fruit and lemon hop notes overlaid on a body of light but mouth-filling malt.

So'phisticuffs (IPA)
6.5% ABV

This is a sophisticated IPA, with excellent integration between the white peach stonefruit hop element and sweet, soft malt. The finish is long, bitter and intense, but leaves you wanting more.

Civic Square, Wellington – a city with one of New Zealand's most developed beer cultures.

Galbraith's Alehouse

Brewpub
Established: 1994
Location: Auckland
Owner: Keith Galbraith

Having worked at a high level in the New Zealand wine industry for most of his career, Keith Galbraith established his eponymous brewpub in 1994, cobbling together his brewery from dairy and other equipment because, at the time, Lion and DB would not sell decommissioned brewery equipment inside New Zealand.

Galbraith admits to not trying to make New Zealand beers, but 'classic old world beers using authentic ingredients'. To this end, he sources and imports malt and whole hops himself, being the only brewery to have a MAF licence to do so. Galbraith believes this gives his beer a unique high note that does not come through with beers made using hop pellets. Likewise, he has also collected a selection of yeasts, each suited to a particular beer, and orders his cultures, as needed, from White Labs in San Diego, where he spends a significant amount of his time.

Galbraith's is a real ale brewpub, with around half of the pub's beers being English styles, poured through hand-pumps. If you have not tried beers poured like this or are even the least bit sceptical, Galbraith's is the place to start. Unlike most breweries in New Zealand (with the exception of Townshend, Cassels and The Twisted Hop), these beers are brewed to be served this way and benefit immensely from it. It should also be pointed out that Galbraith's is the only place where many of these beers are served, the pub trucking through 80L barrels of each of the six hand-pulled beers every two days.

As well as the house beers, Galbraith's brew a variety of seasonal pale ales. More recently, they have started to collaborate with some of the best New Zealand brewers, including Emerson's, Liberty, Yeastie Boys and Tuatara on their 'Great Brewers Cask Ale Series'. These are cask-conditioned interpretations of a brewer's flagship beer, with the recipe tweaked to suit pouring via a hand-pump. They release these beers every three months or so. When I visited, they were pouring a cask-conditioned version of Hop Wired, which was delicious, bursting with Nelson Sauvin aromatics but subtly changed (Galbraith admits to using English malt) to be enjoyable at cellar temperature and effervescent rather than fizzy.

In keeping with his traditional style, Galbraith describes his beers as balanced, and while most brewers bandy this term around, it is a fitting description in this case. In his words, 'one ingredient should not overpower the other'. He deftly balances layers of flavour from hops with malt notes and, though individual beers let one or the other of these characteristics sing, they are among the most complete beers available on the New Zealand market.

Bob Hudson's Bitter
3.7% ABV, cask only

A vibrant straw-yellow, this beer bursts with amazingly beautiful floral hop aromas. It has a light but filling body of malt with burnt orange and honeycomb notes. As of February 2015, this beer was listed in the 99th percentile for its style on RateBeer.com.

Bellringers Best Bitter
4.5% ABV, cask only

Darker than the Bob Hudson's, this beer showcases Galbraith's house style of balancing hop and malt characters. Generous burnt caramel and fruit notes are seasoned by high aromatic notes from the whole hops.

Bitter and Twisted ESB
5.3% ABV, cask only

Rich chestnut in colour, this beer has caramel, nutty and rich fruitcake notes; it is generous and round with long, refreshing bitterness.

Grafton Porter
5% ABV, cask only

A lighter style of porter with a hint of smoke, milk chocolate and caramel. Served by hand-pull, it is creamy, long and refreshing.

Munich Style Lager
5.5% ABV

Characterised by notes of warm barley with subtle spicy aromatic hops and clean bitterness, this is a simple but beautifully made lager.

Bohemian Style Pilsner
4.5% ABV

This beer has lovely layered notes of barley, high aromatic floral hop notes and long, focused bitterness. It's simple but has real purity.

Czech Style Pilsner
5.3% ABV

A 'souped up' version of the Bohemian Style Pilsner; it lacks the same prettiness but has taut bitterness and a long focused finish.

Santa Ana (APA)
7.5% ABV

This beer is aptly named after the Santa Ana wind, which Galbraith describes as 'dry and sticky'. Inspired by the famous beers of California's Russian River, this is an APA with pine and grapefruit notes, a long, focused bitterness and a generous base of sweet malt.

Rurik Russian (imperial stout)
7.5% ABV

This imperial stout is made in a very 'English' style, with big, dark, fruity ale ester characters overlaid on a malt base full of dark chocolate and coffee notes. It has just enough bitterness (provided mainly by the roasted barley character) to keep the beer fresh.

Crucifiction Trappist Style Ale (dubbel)
8% ABV

One of Galbraith's seasonal Belgian ales, this dubbel is inspired by Westvleteren 8. This beer is creamy, fruity and full with coffee, coriander and cardamom notes. Rich without being heavy or alcoholic, it is one of the finest Belgian-style beers brewed in New Zealand.

Resurrection Trappist Style Ale (Tripel)
9% ABV

The other of Galbraith's seasonal Belgian ales, Resurrection is copper-coloured with a rich, broad base of malt and candi sugar. It has an intense aromatic spiciness with vanilla notes. Again, it is one of the finest Belgian-style beers brewed here.

Garage Project

Brewery
Established: 2011
Location: Wellington
Founders: Jos Ruffell, Pete and Ian Gillespie
Brewer: Pete Gillespie and Jos Ruffell

Garage Project launched their brewery in 2011 with 24/24 – a project through which they released 24 different beers over 24 weeks at Wellington craft beer bar Hashigo Zake.

Over the four years they have been brewing, 'prolific' would be an understatement: they have 37 beers listed on their website and a whopping 126 on Untapped (some of which are doubles), but even then, Jos Ruffell acknowledges that this does not include the one-off bespoke beers they make for events.

Starting with a 50L brewkit, but since scaling up several times, they are based in a garage on Aro Street in central Wellington. They have been one of New Zealand's (and possibly the world's) most inventive breweries, experimenting with almost any ingredient that comes their way, as well as applying techniques usually associated with the avant-garde food movement to create beer.

Not all of Garage Project's beers have been successes. However, their spirit of ingenuity, their experimentation and their continual questioning of the status quo is to be admired. Just as the culinary world needs progressive chefs, so the brewing world needs Garage Project. Their beers never fail to elicit a response (which ranges from rapture to horror to pious indignation); their philosophy will filter down and gradually change our notions of what is and what isn't beer.

Beer (Pilsner)
4.8% ABV

A beer that does what it says on the tin. It is a clean, focused, Czech-style Pilsner with golden malt and a hint of spicy bitterness.

Pills 'n' Thrills (US Pilsner)
5.5% ABV

My favourite of the Garage Project beers: an intensely grapefruity Pilsner with cutting bitterness.

Hops en Pointe (NZ Pilsner)
6.7% ABV

An extremely dry, tightly carbonated Pilsner bursting with passion fruit and gooseberry.

Hapi Daze (NZ pale ale)
4.6% ABV

Along with Garagista, Hapi Daze is a more recent and more approachable addition to the Garage Project range. It has a lovely soft body of golden malt with vibrant pineapple, passionfruit and lemon blossom hop notes and a long, focused bitter finish.

Garagista (Pacific pale ale)
5.8% ABV

An extremely aromatic, light-bodied pale ale that combines New Zealand (passion fruit), Australian (floral top notes) and US (grapefruit) hop notes in a beer that just bursts out of the glass.

Angry Peaches (IPA)
6.8% ABV

This IPA lives up to its name, with intense Amarillo hop aromas of juicy ripe peach and floral peach fuzz – this character is intensified by a luscious body of malt with a bit of give, then balanced by long, focused bitterness.

Death From Above (IPA)
7.5% ABV

An IPA spiced with mango, chilli, lime and Vietnamese mint. These play second fiddle to the sticky American hops, giving depth and complexity rather than top notes. The beer is long and dry with a hint of heat.

Aro Noir (porter)
7% ABV

A lovely rich, round porter with fruity UK ale yeast notes juxtaposed by vibrant citrusy US hops.

Ghost Brewing Co.

Contract brewery
Established: 2014
Location: Christchurch
Owners: Murray (Muz) Moeller,
Richard and Julian Sinke

The February 2011 earthquakes destroyed much of Christchurch, including popular brewpub Dux de Lux. The Dux has been re-established as Dux Dine, Dux Live and Dux Central. However, while Dux Brewing did brew at Wigram post-earthquake, this ended in mid-2013. Richard Sinke (the primary shareholder in Dux Brewing), with brother Julian and friend Murray Moeller, has established Ghost Brewing Co. The trio are resurrecting the brews of Dux Brewing as well as creating some new beers, and brew out of Three Boys Brewery.

Delicious Pale Ale (NZ pale ale)
4.2% ABV

A Kiwi pale bursting with crisp lime and gooseberry notes, and balanced by rich malt. It lives up to the name.

Giant Brewing

Brewery
Established: 2014
Location: Havelock North
Owners: Chris and Tom Ormond, and
George Mackenzie
Brewer: Chris Ormond

Having developed a reputation for excellent homebrew, Chris Ormond enlisted the help of his brother Tom (who, with his wife, owns Havelock North's Hawthorne Coffee Roastery and Espresso Bar) and his mate George Mackenzie to establish a nano-brewery to service local cafés and bars.

On the release of their first beers at the end of 2014, Ormond describes the Giant beers as true to their name and 'toward the bold end of the spectrum'.

NZPA (NZ pale ale)
5.3% ABV

This is a pale ale that beautifully balances vibrant gooseberry, blackcurrant and freshly mown grass with a body of warm copper-coloured malt. It is richer than is typical of the style but is delicious nonetheless.

Eagle Brewing formerly Golden Eagle Brewery

Brewery
Established: 2010
Location: Christchurch
Owner and brewer: David Gaughan

English expat David Gaughan established his brewery because he missed the traditional real ales of home and wanted to bring a new style of beer into the New Zealand market.

Originally brewing on a small kit in his garage, his first commercial brews hit the market in 2010. In 2012, he travelled back to Rotherham, his home town, to brew a batch of his South Island Pale Ale at Wentworth Brewery, and in 2013 he and Sean Harris of Raindogs Brewing Co. opened their shared brewery and tasting room on Riccarton Road, next to the Volstead Trading Company craft beer bar.

Gaughan describes his beers as 'traditional ales' with a 'modern twist', and his brewing as 'pedantic… meticulous', yet driven by an 'openness to change' and improvement. In addition to his range of beers, he and Harris have in the past brewed regular collaboration beers under the alias 'Eagle vs. Dog', although with the high demand for their beers, the production pressure on both brewers may mean this is a thing of the past.

Old Skool Vienna Lager
4.6% ABV

Lovely caramel malt notes and vibrant vanilla dominate the nose and palate, creating a smooth, creamy, filling, malt-dominant beer.

The Bitter End (Bitter)
4.4% ABV

A lovely, warm body of nutty malt overlaid with British hop varieties give this beer a distinct feel; alongside berry and pithy blackcurrant notes and a spicy, bitter finish.

South Island Pale Ale
5.5% ABV

A tightly wound, focused, dry New Zealand pale ale with zesty gooseberry and nettle hop characters and a long, focused bitterness.

Big Yank (IPA)
7.5% ABV

The nose seduces you with orange zest notes and then the palate punches you in the face with a wall of bitterness. This IPA is totally geared towards the hops but unashamed about it.

Coalface Stout
6.2% ABV

An incredibly rich, intense stout with a sticky, tarry texture and a hint of ashy/burnt coffee notes. This beer is especially enjoyable served via hand-pull.

Golden Bear Brewery

Brewpub
Established: 2008
Location: Mapua, Nelson
Owner and brewer: Jim Matranga

While living in southern California, Jim Matranga became used to extremely flavourful, characterful craft beers. On moving to Nelson, he discovered that, despite the extremely high quality of local ingredients, no one was brewing this kind of hoppy beer. Discovering an abandoned warehouse with a 'for lease' sign virtually falling off the building, he decided that this was where he could build his brewpub. Of the building in the small settlement of Mapua, he says it 'looked like a piece of crap'. Little was he to know that Mapua was to become a buzzing little tourist centre that is still undergoing a considerable amount of growth.

Although Matranga is well known for his California-style pale ales, he creates a variety of beers and admits that each time he brews a beer it changes slightly. He is a fan of experimentation and regularly uses fruits like peach and black-currants. His philosophy is 'make anything, use anything, experiment', and believes that as long as the beers are balanced and fault-free, there is a market for every single one. He describes the blackcurrant beer I tasted when I visited the brewery as 'challenging', but then states, 'if you don't like it, it's really not that important', noting that some customers love his more interesting creations.

For the most part, Matranga's beers are big, rich and full of flavour. He describes them as 'sloppy', lacking the precision and focus of some craft beers. That said, like Matranga, they are generous and big on character.

For those who can't travel to the brewery, where the majority of these beers are served, Matranga also packages his wort for home-brewers. All the hard work is done – all you have to do is add yeast and maybe dry hops, then leave it to ferment and bottle! These are available by mail order from the brewery.

Czech Pils (Pilsner)
5.2% ABV

A soft, floral Pilsner with a broad, sun-kissed New Zealand malt character. Long and bitter on the finish – a very classy example of the style.

American Wheat (wheat ale)
4% ABV

An incredibly simple but enjoyable wheat ale with subtle hop aromatics. Light and fresh.

Nelson Easy (golden ale)
4.5% ABV

A long and refreshing ale with some funky notes – light and bright!

Fat Toad (NZ pale ale)
6% ABV

An extremely aromatic New Zealand pale ale with passion fruit, gooseberry and grass overlaid on a solid body of malt. Its bitterness gives length.

Seismic IPA
7.2% ABV

A sticky west coast-styled IPA. It is light in body with orange, caramel and resinous pine-needle notes. A long, focused beer.

The kitchen pass at Golden Bear Brewery.

WINE:
SAUVIGNON BLANC
PINOT NOIR
RIESLING 9.5% ABV
PINOT GRIS
CHARDONNAY
BUBBLES

BEER:
BOTTLES: 750ML
2013 7.0%

ABV:
ULFS
4.1%
2.45%
NEW!

BEER:
ON TAP:
AMERICAN WHEAT   6.2%
DAILY ALE   7.6%
FAT ROAD   4.2%
SMOKIN OTTER IPA   7.2%
NELSON EASY LAGER   2.0%
SEISMIC IPA   6.1%
BLACKBEARD PORTER   5.8%
CZECH PILS   6.0%
UNDERTONE BLACK CURRANT

CIDER: BLACK CURRANT
5.1%

DUTY MANAGER:
TAIA MARAKI

SOFT:
APPLE JUICE
/ LEMON LIME
GINGER BEER

Good George Brewing

Brewpub
Established: 2012
Location: Hamilton
Brewing director: Brian Watson

Brewing director Brian Watson describes the Good George philosophy simply: 'Creating better moments with great beer.' After years of brewing experience, he came together with a group of friends from hospitality backgrounds, to create a craft beer range and brewpub to show the people of Hamilton and New Zealand how great craft beer can be.

They are named Good George because the brewery and brewpub are located in the former St George's Church, in the industrial suburb of Frankton. In addition to this site, they have Good Neighbour in Rototuna and Little George on Hood Street. Originally planned as a pop-up bar, Little George but soon became a Hamilton institution.

The Good George beers are approachable and full of flavour without being over the top. Their Sparkling Ale, in particular, represents an accessible entry point into the world of craft beer for drinkers of mainstream industrial beers, but still has integrity and character. All of the Good George beers share this – they are easy to drink and approachable while still being complex. I think 'understated' is a good word for them.

Aside from the four core beers, Good George make some excellent seasonal and one-off beers. Their various takes on Berliner weisse and other sour styles have been among the most enjoyable, but they have also had success with big hoppy beers, such as a black IPA.

White Ale (wheat ale)
4.5% ABV

A creamy-textured ale with a distinct wheaten note and chamomile aromatics, making it refreshing and clean. A great beer for those who are interested in wheat beers but do not typically like highly aromatic beers.

Amber Ale
3.7% ABV

Halfway between a bitter and a US amber, this beer has a lovely sweet, toffee-like malt base cut by vibrant marmalade-like hops. Very quaffable.

Sparkling Ale (golden ale)
4.5% ABV

A nose of dry pine needles and fresh grass makes this a lively ale. It has a light golden body of malt, and is very effervescent. The pine character merges with citrus to provide a long, fresh hop character on the finish.

IPA
5.8% ABV

A full and firm IPA with a luscious body of malt; it has some delicious ripe tropical notes and some long, focused bitterness.

Brewing ingredients.

Governor Brewery

Brewery
Established: 2012
Location: Grey Lynn, Auckland
Owner and brewer: Andrew Peacocke

Governor Brewery was named in honour of Sir George Grey, twice governor of New Zealand, thanks to its location in the Auckland suburb of Grey Lynn, itself named after the colonial administrator. Master brewer Andrew Peacocke established his brewery to brew traditionally made German lager according to the Reinheitsgebot (see endnote 19).

Governor Lager
5% ABV

A very pure, focused lager, with a lovely soft, golden malt, subtle hop aromatics and a clean bitterness.

113

Hallertau

Brewery and brewpub
Established: 2005
Location: Riverhead, west Auckland
Owner and head brewer: Steve
Plowman

A geologist by training, Steve Plowman spent 10 years working in Western Australia before he got 'sick of that' and went back to study brewing at university. Helping to establish Margaret River's Colonial Brewery after 18 months, he discovered a site had come up for sale just outside of Riverhead in west Auckland. 'It had everything,' he says of the site – namely a restaurant and a brewery.

Of his brewing philosophy, Plowman describes himself as 'a fanatic... not a purist'. He admits to not following the rules or conventional wisdom when it comes to brewing and will do anything to 'get a beer tasting how I wanna get it', which, in part, pushed him to the limit production-wise.

Enter Joe Wood of Liberty Brewing. In mid-2013, Plowman and Wood started the Beer Fountain. Based at the Hallertau site, the pair (and their families) now co-own the physical brewery, with Wood managing the brewery but Hallertau and Liberty essentially being treated as contract clients (they take others). This has freed up Plowman to work on the beers he chooses, such as a three-way collaboration brew with Masu Restaurant and Baird, a Japanese craft brewery, and MC Slave's Logg Cabin Ale. This is the second collaboration beer he has done with musicians, the first being Beastwars IPA. Of these collaborations, he says they are 'completely fun' because you 'don't have to do anything you'd normally do in terms of what your brand represents... when you get two brands coming together it's often more than the sum of its parts'. As well as collaborations, he and Wood have made a number of beers together – the first was Haterade, a soured IPA, and the most recent is a double oyster stout.

Despite ramping up production, over 80% of Hallertau beer is consumed in Auckland. And while Plowman would like to export, it would compromise his ability to keep supplying the domestic market: 'We want to be a New Zealand brand. We want to get the New Zealand guys sorted out first before we send any overseas.'

Alongside his core beers and the hugely hoppy Maximus, Plowman is a pioneer of sour beers in New Zealand, with two beers currently available – Porter Noir (a *Brettanomyces* porter) and Funkonnay (a strong, soured golden ale) – as well as seasonals and more to come.

#1 Luxe (kolsch)
4.5% ABV

This beer is extremely enjoyable: light and fresh with a long, clean finish, showcasing the fruity passionfruit high notes of New Zealand hops.

#2 Statesman (APA)
5.3% ABV

With a firm, malty backbone and long, focused bitterness, this is a bright, clean APA with orange oil and soft floral notes.

#3 Copper Tart (red ale)
4.2% ABV

This is a clean, focused, rich, malty ale with warm caramel notes and vibrant, spicy, fruity hop character, along with a hint of bitterness from roasted malt.

#4 Deception (schwarzbier)
5.1% ABV

This is one of my favourite dark lagers. Deception is a fitting name – it looks and smells like it is going to be heavy, with lovely mocha notes, but in actuality is light and fresh with a long, spicy, bitter finish.

Minimus (session IPA)
3.8% ABV

Described by Hallertau as a breakfast pale ale, this has lots of resinous citrus and woody hop notes overlaid on a body of light malt. It bursts with aromas of passion fruit and lime zest on the finish.

Maximus (IPA)
5.8% ABV

With funky, dank hop notes, this is a luscious IPA with a creamy texture, a firm body of malt and long, lingering bitterness.

Hancock & Co. Craft Brewing

Contract brewery
Established: 2011
Location: Auckland
Owner: Orah Dom Limited (owned by
the Jakicevich family)

While their labels boast that they were established in 1859 (when the original Hancock's Brewing was established – it eventually became part of Lion), the first beers from Hancock & Co. were released in early 2013. Hancock's is owned by Orah Dom, which in turn is owned by the Jakicevich family, who also own the Hancock liquor distribution business and the wine retail chain Glengarry's, and are the second-largest shareholder of 660 Main Road Stoke, which owns the McCashin's Brewery, including the Stoke brand.

Harrington's

Brewery
Established: 1991
Location: Christchurch
Owner: Harrington family

Harrington's was established in 1991 on the corner of Kilmore Street and Fitzgerald Avenue in Christchurch, the same site now occupied by the Pomeroy's Pub and Four Avenues/Stainless Brewing.

The brewery was originally established because John Harrington, who had been a publican since the 1970s, was sick of the Lion/DB duopoly and the fairly bland brown beer they produced. Harrington wanted to offer beer drinkers of Christchurch a real choice, creating a line of good-value beers brewed 100% from malt.

Since then, Harrington's has expanded dramatically. They now occupy a site on Ferry Street and have six retail outlets throughout Christchurch. In 2015, they are scaling up again to a new brewery in Park House, which will be able to produce 80,000L of beer per week.

In 2012, Harrington's won the Champion Brewery at the Brewers Guild Awards, and they consistently wins medals for many of their beers. Carl Harrington (son of John) describes the brewing philosophy as one of 'consistency, passion and knowledge', noting that their strength is that they enjoy what they do. He doesn't believe they have a 'house style', as the different beers reflect the different brewers' personalities and styles.

Rogue Hop (Pilsner)
5% ABV

Softly floral and aromatic with luscious golden malt, this Pilsner has a clean bitterness and sweet lemon-drop notes on the finish.

East Indies Lager
5% ABV

A bone-dry, malty lager with vibrant citrusy hop notes on the finish.

Strong Pilsner
6.5% ABV

Bursting with greengage plum notes, this is a big, malty beer that remains fresh, even as it warms in the glass.

Ngahere Gold (strong lager)
7.2% ABV

This larger has an amazing, complex nose of rich malt with a hint of estery notes and some aromatic hops. It is a big beer, but is is very enjoyable and the booze is hidden well.

Classy Red (red ale)
5% ABV

A balanced, malty, nutty ale with vibrant citrusy and herbal hop notes. Billed as an ESB, it is actually more of a US red ale.

The Yankdak (APA)
4.7% ABV

Burnt orange and pine define this Simcoe/Amarillo-hopped APA, the hops overlaid on a malt body. The beer is enjoyable if a little clumsy.

IPA
7.4% ABV

This is a big, sweet-malted IPA with some orange and pine notes, as well as long bitterness; this isn't enough to counterpoint the weight of the beer, however, and overall it tastes a little sweet.

Belgian Trappist (tripel)
7% ABV

A rich golden ale with just enough hopping to provide cut, but not quite enough Belgian ester character to give it the depth of flavour it needs. Despite this, it is a very enjoyable, complex, strong golden ale.

Wobbly Boot (porter)
5% ABV

A smoky, dark beer with lovely acidity that marks a traditional porter. Layers of roasted malt and coffee notes make for an enjoyable, complex brew.

Big John Special Reserve (barrel-aged dark beer)
6.5% ABV

Dark, rich malts combine with bourbon and oak to create a beer that is quite dry and slippery, however, it is fairly one-dimensional.

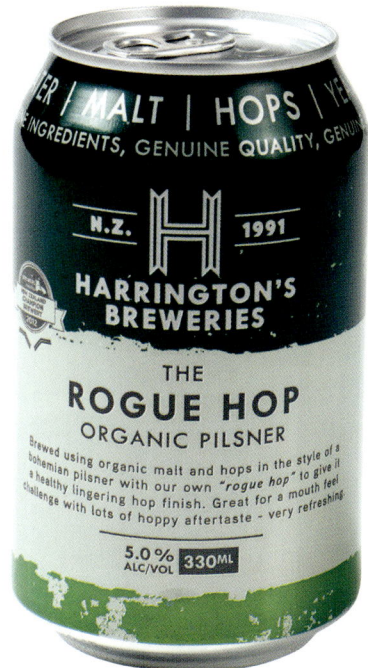

Hawke's Bay Independent Brewery

Brewery
Established: 1995
Location: Meeanee, Napier
Owners: Basil Diack and
Paddy Donovan

A publican, Basil Diack originally established a brewery in Onekawa. As demand from local consumers grew, he then joined forces with Paddy Donovan of the Ballydooly Cider Company and the brewery was moved to Meeanee. At the same time, a tasting room and beer garden, The Filter Room, was built – this has become a haunt for locals and tourists alike.

Hawke's Bay Independent Brewery is a true regional brewery – while the beer is found further afield, the local market is definitely key; they supply pubs and clubs, but also many local wineries.

There are similar beer styles across multiple tiers, designed for different outlets. The beers are sound and enjoyable – the Black Duck in particular is excellent.

Pilsner
5% ABV

Light-bodied, extremely aromatic Kiwi Pilsner with soft floral hop notes and clean bitterness.

Amber Ale
4% ABV

A nutty, slightly oxidised malt body is complemented by lovely marmalade-like hop notes, resulting in a soft, juicy beer.

Special Reserve
5% ABV

A lager flavoured with ginger and honey – clean and dry.

Black Duck
4% ABV

A velvety, soft, smooth black beer with sweet chocolate notes and a toasty bitter finish. Simple but very rewarding, it won gold at the 2014 Brewers Guild Awards.

Herne Brewing Company

Contract brewery
Established: 2013
Location: Tapanui, West Otago
Owner: Tom 'The Pom' Jones

Tom Jones, aka 'Tom the Pom', founded and managed Dunedin's now-defunct organic Green Man Brewery until 2010 (it was put into liquidation in 2014). In 2013, he founded Herne Brewing Company, which currently produces one beer (in stark contrast to Green Man), Tāne. In addition, Jones also runs Crafty Beers.

Tāne (smoked IPA)
5.9% ABV

Rich, smoky barbecue notes characterise this IPA, which has a decidedly meaty tone. Dark amber with burnt caramel notes also come through, making for a very enjoyable beer – but only if you like smoke. Herne's Tāne won a gold medal at the 2014 Brewers Guild Awards.

Hop Baron

Contract brewery
Established: 2013
Location: Christchurch
Owner and brewer: Richmond Tait

Originally created by homebrewers Richmond Tait and two friends (one of whom has since moved to Wanaka to start Beffect Brewing) to supply a friend's wedding, Hop Baron turned into a fully fledged beer label due to demand. Tait describes his brewing philosophy by comparing it to 'good Italian cooking' with 'clean and distinctive tastes... only using a few of the very best ingredients'.

Poolside Pale Ale
5% ABV

A juicy, fruity New Zealand pale ale with pineapple, papaya and passionfruit notes.

Hop Federation

Brewery
Established: 2013
Location: Riwaka
Owner and brewer: Simon Nicholas

In 2013, Simon Nicholas and his wife Nikki took over the Riwaka site, previously inhabited by the Monkey Wizard brewery. Since they started the brewery they have struggled to keep up with the 'crazy' demand for their beer.

To compensate for this, they intend to expand by building a second brewery, having already outgrown their main roadside brewery and tasting room.

Despite their location just around the corner from a number of hop fields, Hop Federation use a blend of US and Kiwi hops for most of their beers. They are hoppy but, as Nicholas puts it, 'not too in your face'.

Golden Ale
4.5% ABV

A light, crisp ale with vibrant, zesty tropical hop notes derived from Nelson Sauvin and Motueka hops.

Pale Ale
5.1% ABV

A light-bodied ale with vibrant gooseberry and passionfruit notes as well as a hint of stone fruit; layers of bitterness tie the beer together.

Red IPA (American red ale)
6.4% ABV

The standout of the range. It has a lovely sweet coppery malt that just jumps with a panoply of US hop character: pine resin, citrus oil and long, cutting bitterness.

American Brown Ale
4.5% ABV

This beer is warm, rich and inviting, with toasty, roasty, milk chocolate malt notes and a creamy body. It has long, refreshing bitterness and vibrant vegetal hop notes. Focused and long.

HOP FEDERATION
GOLDEN

HOP FEDERATION
RED IPA

Hop Invaders

Brewery
Established: 2014
Location: Dunedin
Owners: David Gibson and
Christopher Henderson

Launched in late 2014, Hop Invaders is a new Dunedin brewery that draws on vintage video game imagery. At present, the beers are available only in Dunedin outlets.

Hot Water Brewing Company

Brewery
Established: 2013
Location: Hot Water Beach,
Coromandel Peninsula
Brewer: Dave Kurth

Dave Kurth, previously brewer at the West Coast Brewery, established the Hot Water Brewing Company so he could live in, what is to him, 'one of the best places in New Zealand'.

Kurth brews a range of beers, drawing heavily on the English and American brewing traditions but also influenced by local ingredients such as New Zealand hops. His philosophy is simple: he 'brews the type of beer [he] likes to drink'.

Rather than bottle beer, Kurth is one of a growing number of breweries releasing beer in cans (there are a number of others, like Garage Project, who do both). At the 2014 Brewers Guild Awards, Hot Water Brewing took home three medals, including one for its 2013 Barley Wine.

Golden Steamer (golden ale)
4.5% ABV

A very sessionable golden ale with sweet malt and citrus blossom aromatics.

Kauri Falls Pale Ale
5.2% ABV

Intense grapefruit and pine notes jump out of the can, along with a lovely rich golden malt. Pithy, bitter pink grapefruit shows again on the finish.

About Time IPA
6.5% ABV

An IPA with an intense nose of dank, vegetal hop character, which carries through into the broad palate and finishes with orange sherbet and a hint of marmalade.

Walkers Porter
4.8% ABV

A classic porter with chocolate notes, firm bitterness and a hint of sharpness. Very drinkable.

Invercargill Brewery

Brewery
Established: 1999
Location: Invercargill
Founder and brewer: Steve Nally

Steve Nally completed a degree in chemistry at Canterbury University, which he describes as coming out 'with a degree in beer drinking' as well. After working as a technician, he realised that this was not what he wanted to do with his life, so he 'turned to the only other thing [he] knew'.

Nally describes his brewing philosophy as 'less is more' and his house style as 'classical with flashes of contemporary' – by using Kiwi ingredients and flavours, he 'reinterprets traditional beer styles'. One of the best examples of this is his seasonal beer Smokin' Bishop – this came about when he and his apprentice at the time, Pru Bishop (hence the name), decided to make a rauchbier, a traditional German-style smoked lager. Lacking smoked malt, he teamed up with a local butcher to smoke some Gladfield malt with manuka. It fast became a cult beer, winning a gold medal and trophy at the BrewNZ beer awards in 2007.

Invercargill Brewery doesn't just make its own beer, however. In 2008, Nally was approached by beer lovers Stu McKinlay and Sam Possenniskie to 'make a hoppy porter called Pot Kettle Black'. This was the first commercial batch of Yeastie Boys beer, and since then almost all of the Yeastie Boys' production has been done at Invercargill. Nally has since taken on a number of other contract brewing clients, including those he describes as 'legendary' – including Ben Middlemiss, Pink Elephant and the Mussel Inn. Nally considers the ability to brew these beers 'a total honour and a chance to learn something new'.

Wasp (honey lager)
4.8% ABV

This lager has a nose of golden barley and a subtle, warm honey note. It is dry and very fresh, with lovely, soft malt. Simple but very complete, it is cleansing and long.

Stanley Green (NZ pale ale)
4.7% ABV

With a copper colour, firm maltiness and notes of English toffee, this beer has taut, resiny hop notes and long bitterness but lacks definition.

B.man (NZ Pilsner)
5.2% ABV

With a rich, full, malty body, this beer is big for a Pilsner but very balanced. It has a firm bitterness and beautiful long, aromatic hop notes on the finish.

Pitch Black (stout)
4.5% ABV

A lovely rich, full stout with notes of cocoa, burnt caramel and coffee-like bitterness. A very balanced and complete beer.

Isthmus Brewing

Contract brewer
Established: 2011
Location: North Shore, Auckland
Owners: Hamish Ward and Matt
Littlejohn
Brewer: Hamish Ward

Hamish Ward is the brewer at North Shore brew-pub Deep Creek Brewing as well as running Isthmus with long-time friend and fellow biotech scientist Matt Littlejohn. Isthmus's mission is to create innovative beers. They are brewed at Deep Creek's Silverdale site.

3D IPA
6.6% ABV

This is a US-hopped grapefruit bomb. It has a light but full malt body with extremely long, persistent bitterness.

Pale Ale
5% ABV

This is a light, bright APA with beautifully ripe, plump peach notes and an incredibly floral, rosehip aroma. Very enjoyable and rewarding.

Jabberwocky Brewery

Contract brewery
Established: 2013
Location: Clyde
Owners: Paul Beattie, and Michael
and Ruenell Wing

Jabberwocky is the brainchild of Mike Wing, a Central Otago viticulturalist, his South African wife Ruenell and their business partner Scott Beattie. It is brewed at Wanaka Beerworks (which was recently bought by the same trio). Building on the success of Wanaka Beerworks' old-world-styled beers, Jabberwocky is about exploring modern and new-world styles.

Red Rooster (red ale)
4.6% ABV

Malty and filling, with deep, nutty caramel and a hint of smoke, this beer has a backbone of clean bitterness.

Pale Ale
5.8% ABV

An exceptionally well-made, balanced Kiwi pale ale with passion fruit and guava over a body of sweet malt.

Kaikoura Brewing Company

Brewery
Established: 2012
Location: Kaikoura
Owners: Matt and
Kathlynn Scattergood

One of New Zealand's smallest breweries – its beers are available only in Kaikoura.

Kaimai Brewing Company

Contract brewery
Established: 2009
Location: Auckland
Owner and brewer: Andrew Larsen

Specialising in rye beers, Andrew Larsen (also responsible for the beers at Brothers Beer and Brothers Brewery – where the Kaimai beers are now made) is a flying consultant brewer and owner of Breowan Systems, which helps establish small breweries. Needless to say, his skills keep him extremely busy internationally.

Golden Rye Ale
5.5% ABV

This is a luscious, golden ale with clove and cinnamon spices from the rye malt, and clean lemony and floral hop notes.

Zeelandt Brewery, Napier.

Kereru Brewing Company

Brewery
Established: 2010
Location: Upper Hutt
Owners: Chris Mills and
Natasha Dahlberg

After working in the film industry, Chris Mills and his wife Natasha Dahlberg needed a change of direction, and saw the growth of the craft beer industry, especially of hoppy American styles. They decided to produce a range of 'UK and European beer styles as interpreted exclusively with New Zealand malt, hops and other New Zealand ingredients', with a final goal of creating 'the taste of New Zealand in a beer bottle'.

Starting in their garage but upgrading to a large brewery on Upper Hutt's Maidstone Terrace in late 2013, they have quickly created a name for themselves by brewing beer with 'non-traditional' ingredients, including coconut, seaweed and kumara. These beers all utilise these ingredients in an understated and extremely successful way and, unlike many other brews made with similar ingredients, are in no way gimmicky.

As well as their own beers, Kereru also brew for several brands under contract, producing beers for Funk Estate, Herne and Lord Almighty (among others).

Maidstone Lager
5% ABV

With a lovely rich malty body that is creamy and full, some bitterness and a clean, long profile, this is exactly what I look for in a 5% lager.

Imperial AT-AT Pilsner
11% ABV

Brewed with avowed *Star Wars* fan and 2014 Beer Writer of the Year Neil Miller, this is a giant of a beer, despite its pale complexion. Notes of candied orange and sweet malt are balanced by long, clean bitterness. It's not a 'drink by itself' beer but would be delicious with a stinky, sharp blue cheese.

Big Pigeon Pilsner
5% ABV

Light, lithe and pretty, with lovely soft malt and clean focused bitterness, this Pilsner is more in the bitter Germanic style than the aromatic Czech or international style.

Karengose (Gose)
4% ABV

Wheaten with bristly acidity and a creamy mouthfeel, this beer is a Gose (salt-water ale) with karengo seaweed. These two elements add subtle depth without being overpowering.

Pohutukawa Golden Ale
5% ABV

A lovely refreshing but comforting golden ale with soft aromatic hopping and mellow depth from pohutukawa honey.

Silverstream Pale Ale (session IPA)
3.8% ABV

Rich, creamy malts with some lovely biscuit notes are balanced by a clean pine bitterness and a hint of tropical fruit aromatics.

Hop to It Pale Ale (IPA)
5.9% ABV

A rich, sticky orange marmalade note opens this beer before it gives way to fleshy malt and then long, firm bitterness.

Kumara Brown Ale
5% ABV

Zesty hop notes are overlaid on a malt body, which is reminiscent of brown sugar. The beer is rich and creamy with roasted coffee-bean notes – very earthy and savoury.

Moonless Stout
4.5% ABV

An easy-drinking, almost Irish-style stout with a dry mouthfeel, taut coffee notes and clean, focused bitterness.

Velvet Boot (Belgian tripel)
8.7% ABV

This beer begins with clove and sarsaparilla notes overlaid on fat, sweet malt. It would be the perfect accompaniment to a ripe washed-rind cheese.

Visiting Kereru Brewing with owner Chris Mills.

King Country Brewing Company

Brewpub
Established: 2012
Location: Waitomo

Produced in a SmartBrew system with recipes designed by Brian Watson of Good George, this brewpub's beer is available only on tap in outlets around the King Country.

KJD

Contract brewery
Established: 2009
Location: Christchurch
Owner and brewer: Kirsten Taylor

Kirsten Taylor is a very experienced brewer. Under KJD she releases her own beers and ciders, including the stunning Chocolate Cherry Porter.

Lakeman Brewery

Brewery
Established: 2012
Location: Taupo
Owners: James and Elissa Cooper
Brewer: 'The Lakeman'

Located in Taupo, Lakeman's profile and popularity have grown recently, with the brewery even selling out of beer at Beervana 2014. Their shtick is that the Lakeman (which I imagine is owner James Cooper in a yeti suit; he also turns up to beer launches) brews their beer at more traditional premises after the local iwi stopped him brewing on the shores of his native Lake Taupo. To be honest, I find this brand hype bizarre and in bad taste.

That said, the beers are very enjoyable. They deftly balance malt and hops, and are full and serious while still being approachable.

Pilsner
5.2% ABV

With sweaty passion fruit and tropical flowers, this is a lovely aromatic Pilsner with soft malt and just enough bitterness.

Pale Ale
5.5% ABV

Orange sherbet hop notes are characteristic of this pale ale, with a hint of funk coming through as well. It is luscious on the palate with juicy peach and lemon notes – long and fresh.

Hairy Hop IPA
6.3% ABV

A true-to-style English-influenced IPA with a really lovely body of maple-like malt, a brisk, focused bitterness and a flourish of citrus blossom aromatics.

Laughing Bones Brewing Co.

Contract brewery
Estabished: 2013
Location: Auckland
Owner and brewer: John Morawski

Having sold his brewpub The Brewery Britomart (which has since become Little Empire Brewing), John Morawski wanted to keep brewing. To do this, he contracted space at Brothers Beer in Auckland's City Works Depot.

Morawski's brewing philosophy is simple – if he 'brews good beer... people will drink it'. The beers are approachable but also different.

American Cream Ale
4.5% ABV

This beer reinforces why this style is referred to as cream ale – essentially a golden ale, it incorporates oats at the adjunct, giving the beer effervescent carbonation but a rich, creamy texture. Subtle, aromatic hops round out the beer.

Element5 (NZ pale ale)
5.2% ABV

Softly aromatic with subdued floral notes on the nose, Element5 is light and fresh on the palate with integrated hop aroma and long bitterness.

129

Liberty Brewing Company

Brewery
Established: 2006
Location: Auckland
Owners: Joseph and Christina Wood
Brewer: Joseph Wood

Like most brewers, Joseph Wood started out as a homebrewer. Trying to get the ingredients as cheaply as possible, he looked into the possibility of outcompeting homebrew suppliers – enter Stu McKinlay of Yeastie Boys, who had a similar company but was under more and more pressure to focus on his growing brand. Wood ended up taking over the supply business and decided to build a little brewery in his garage so he could demonstrate beers to his customers 'a try-before-you-buy scheme'. He describes the first beers he brewed commercially as 'really boring stuff', but his fourth beer was a more interesting bottle-conditioned stout, Never Go Black. Thereafter, he released some of his most extreme beers (and that is saying something), with names like High Carb Ale and MMMMoMMftCHv3. Once these beers started coming out, the demand dwindled for the homebrew supplies.

While Liberty beers regularly receive high ratings on Untapped and RateBeer.com, and often clean up at competitions, one of the achievements Wood is most happy about is his 2014 success at the New World Beer and Cider Awards, where he won more medals than any other brewery. This was special because it was also the first time he had entered beer that he had created entirely by himself: 'A lot of times you're entering contract beers and that's sort of, you know... that's somebody else brewing for you.' He acknowledges how important it is for him to get 'those golds for beer we brewed'.

Halo (NZ Pilsner)
5.4% ABV

A lovely focused, subtly aromatic Kiwi Pilsner with gooseberry and passion flower notes.

Oh Brother (APA)
5.1% ABV

Alongside Halo, one of Liberty's 'session beers', this is a softly malted APA with a complex but subdued hop profile of mandarin, citrus blossom and pink grapefruit.

Yakima Monster (APA)
6% ABV

Bursting with aromatic hop notes, white peach, juicy pineapple and guava, with citrus in the background, this beer has a hint of sweetness from the malt but is tied together by pine resin and refined bitterness. As of March 2015, the APA was in the 100th percentile for its style on RateBeer.com.

Yakima Scarlett (American red ale)
6.9% ABV

Rich red malts with notes of toffee blend with grapefruit, passionfruit and guava notes, while the pine resin notes bring the beer together. Bitterness is persistent but not over the top.

Sauvin Bomb (NZ pale ale)
7% ABV

Recently renamed due to a bureaucratic kerfuffle over the term 'Sauvignon', this beer bursts with Nelson Sauvin notes: nettle, passion fruit, gooseberry and lemongrass, coupled with golden malt and long, searing bitterness.

Joseph Wood began brewing for Liberty in New Plymouth, under the shadow of Mt Taranaki.

C!tra (double IPA)
9% ABV

Another celebration of a single hop, this beer bursts with huge juicy lemon and lime notes as well as mango, and with intense bitterness and tree sap notes. Despite its 9% ABV and 99 IBUs, the beer's balance almost defies logic – it is too drinkable.

Darkest Days (oatmeal stout)
6% ABV

Of all the Liberty beers, this is my favourite. It is big without being heavy (or boozy): rich and round with creamy coffee notes and a grippy structure. Darkest Days is so named to celebrate/commiserate the tightening of supply in the international hop market (something Joe Wood has probably contributed to) because these are surely the 'darkest days for hardcore hop heads'.

Lighthouse Brewery

Brewery
Location: Nelson
Established: 1996
Owner and Brewer: Dick Tout

Until 2012, Lighthouse Brewery boasted being the smallest commercial brewery in New Zealand. Tout acknowledges the hobbyist nature of brewing commercially on this scale, saying that the reason he comes to the brewery six days a week is to 'play', and that if he did not own the building, the enterprise would be uneconomic.

Tout creates a range of beers that are true to style, focused and enjoyable without being over the top.

All of the beer he brews is sold within Nelson, either straight from the brewery (where you can do an entire tour of a brewery while sitting down) or in the handful of pubs and restaurants he supplies.

Cheeky Little Lager
4.5% ABV

A simple but well-made lager; round and malty with notes that evoke golden barley fields in the late summer, and a clean, focused bitterness.

Tasman Bay Pils
4.5% ABV

A very aromatic Pilsner: soft, pretty, high hop notes over a body of golden malt, with a long, focused bitterness.

2.9er (bitter)
2.9% ABV

An amazingly flavourful beer for under 3%, and extremely enjoyable. Luscious and rich, it has round malty notes.

Victory (best bitter)
5.5% ABV

Lovely caramel malt notes characterise this long, bitter and very focused beer.

Dick's Dark (bitter)
4.5% ABV

Inspired by the lighter styles of Scotch ale, this is a nutty, slightly smoky beer with some husky cocoa character. Dry but very malt-focused, it has raspy but enjoyable bitterness from roasted barley.

Lion

Brewery
Established: 1861
Location: Auckland
Owner: Kirin Holdings

Lion's roots go back to the Great Northern Brewery, established in 1861, which brewed a beer called Lion and also had one as its logo. Through a series of mergers and acquisitions, the entity became Lion Brewery in 1915, before becoming part of New Zealand Breweries in 1923. New Zealand Breweries changed its name to Lion in 1977 and was merged with L.D. Nathan to become Lion Nathan in 1988. In 2009, Kirin Holdings (owned by the Mitsubishi Group) increased its stake to become the sole shareholder of Lion.

Today, Lion constitutes four main brands: Lion, Speight's, Mac's and Emerson's, as well as imported beers and international beers like Stella Artois, which is brewed under contract. This entry will concentrate only on the Lion brands. These consist of the Steinlager range, Lion Red and Lion Brown, Ice, Crafty Beggars and Rheineck. These are among the most commercial but also widely drunk beers in New Zealand. Other than the Speight's and Emerson's brands, most Lion beers are produced at The Pride in East Tamaki.

Steinlager Pure (premium lager)
5% ABV

The quintessential Kiwi lager, with sweaty, vegetal green-bullet hopping, clean bitterness and some generous golden malt.

Lion Red (pale lager)
4% ABV

A lager with some nice, luscious golden malt but very little character.

Waikato Draught
4% ABV

This beer has sweet malt and some nutty oxidative notes.

Crafty Beggars Pale and Interesting (pale ale)
4% ABV

Despite Lion's commitment to craft brewing (Emerson's) and emerging craft beer drinkers (Mac's), a beer under the Crafty Beggars imprint actively mocks craft beer: 'Someone should make a craft beer you can actually drink.' Its version of one of the most important craft styles, pale ale, is simple and approachable with citrusy hop notes.

Longbeard

Contract brewery
Location: Christchurch
Established: 2013
Brewer and owner: David Reynolds

After 14 years as an architect, David Reynolds was left questioning whether 'anyone actually worked in a job they truly love'. This coincided with his first attempts at homebrewing, 'with a bag of grain, the wrong hops for an IPA and a sachet of the world's worst dried yeast'. While he found the beer horrific (and the kitchen a mess), he had finally found out that he wanted to be a brewer, like his ancestors, who were brewers in Germany.

As for his brewing philosophy, David admits to not having one – he is 'too busy' for a philosophy, concentrating on 'the deeper meaning of my love affair with brewing'.

His beers are simple but lack a bit of definition, especially with regard to hop character and bitterness. The Black Vanilla Porter is the highlight. The current line-up of three beers will be expanded with the addition of a red ale.

Blonde (golden ale)
5% ABV

Copper-hued, this is darker than a golden ale should be. It has very subtle hop notes and caramel malt notes, is very highly carbonated and has some dry hop character on the finish.

Brown (brown ale)
5% ABV

Chestnut-brown, this beer has complex notes of chocolate, coffee, spice, wood and vanilla on the nose. Unfortunately, these don't quite integrate on the palate. Very malty and sweet, it lacks bitterness.

Black (vanilla porter)
5% ABV

With over-the-top vanilla notes overlaid on a rich malty frame and with a ferric aspect to it, this beer is light in body and dry but leaves behind a rich mouth of vanilla.

Lord Almighty

Contract brewery
Established: 2014
Location: Upper Hutt and Bristol, UK
Owners: Daniel Lord and WolfVC
Brewer: Daniel Lord

Working with WolfVC, a UK-based investment company owned by both Kiwis and Brits, Daniel Lord has created Lord Almighty, brewing beers for the UK and the New Zealand markets simultaneously.

Lord Almighty is 'a fictional adventurer loosely based on Danish explorer Peter Freuchen', created to personify brand values. The character is described thus: 'A gnarly giant of a man, who has travelled the world two and a half times in search of the rarest brewing ingredients.' A little more tasteful than the Lakeman, perhaps, but I still find this sort of brand hype difficult, especially when the actual story is just as, if not more, interesting.

Launching in mid-2014, Lord Almighty has since sold over 10,000L of their first beer, Yakima IPA (three times the original goal). A second beer, the 12% Ursus Stout, was released in February 2015, and more are scheduled for release in 2015.

Yakima IPA
5.5% ABV

A lithe, slippery IPA hopped exclusively with Citra. There is just enough malt weight to give balance and depth, but this beer pops with lime zest and orange blossom hop notes.

The view to Wellington harbour from Upper Hutt, one of the homes of Lord Almighty.

Mac's Brewery

Brand
Established: 1981
Location: Auckland and Dunedin (formerly Nelson)
Owner: Lion

Established in 1981 by Terry McCashin (see the Stoke Beer/McCashin's Brewery entry), Mac's was acquired by Lion in 1999. Since then, it has had a number of homes, including Shed 22 on the Wellington waterfront and Canterbury Brewery, which was irreparably damaged by the 2011 earthquakes. Today, it is brewed at the Speight's Brewery in Dunedin and at Lion's The Pride in East Tamaki.

Lion seem genuinely proud of Mac's role as 'craft beer pioneers in New Zealand', and have retooled both the range and the packaging to reflect this. They describe the Mac's range as 'quality, trusted, approachable beers, brewed with creativity and imagination'. Focusing on 'well-known styles', the beers (especially the new releases) achieve their goal of striking a balance between being true to style and not overwhelming less experimental beer consumers.

There are nine Mac's brewbars around the country, which showcase the core Mac's range as well as one-off beers, which are often exciting. In 2015, Mac's resurrected Brewjolais, their much-lauded wet-hop beer, which they had not brewed since the closure of the Shed 22 brewery in late 2009.

Gold (pale lager)
4% ABV

Characterised by generous sweet malts with citrus hop notes and a subdued bitterness. Light and simple but refreshing.

Spring Tide (low-carb lager)
4.5% ABV

Like a doughnut: fleshy around the outside but hollow in the middle. It has some maltiness and hop character but reminds me of artifically sweetened drinks.

Hop Rocker (Pilsner)
5% ABV

An approachable Pilsner with fruity hop notes (a hint of passion fruit and orange) and some clean bitterness.

Great White (Belgian wit)
5% ABV

A slightly tart wheat beer with citrus and a hint of clove esters. Refreshing and true to style.

Sassy Red (amber ale)
4.5% ABV

Luscious copper malt and notes of biscuit and toffee cut by grassy hop notes are the characteristics of this amber ale. Simple but very enjoyable.

Three Wolves Pale Ale
5.1% ABV

A pale ale named Three Wolves for the three hops used: Nelson Sauvin, Simcoe and Amarillo. Some sweet passionfruit, orange zest and herbal notes show through and, though this beer doesn't quite deliver on what it promises, it is very drinkable and excellent value.

Green Beret (IPA)
5.4% ABV

A long, approachable IPA with pine notes. What it lacks in depth it makes up for in price point.

Black (porter)
4.8% ABV

Now described as a porter (that's what the bottle says), this beer used to be a black lager. It is dark and smooth with liquorice notes.

Martinborough Brewery

Brewery
Established: 2013
Location: Martinborough
Owners: Hayden Frew and Stephen
'Fish' Fox

Martinborough Brewery launched in 2013 at the inaugural Greater Wellington Brewday with Black Elixir – their oatmeal stout. While the wine village of Martinborough has been home to breweries before, Hayden Frew and Fish Fox have made a firm commitment to the economy of the village, scaling up from the original 50L nanokit to a 1200L brewkit housed in a specially built brewery and tasting room venue just off the square.

They believe the business is complementary to the region's wine businesses and will satisfy the demand for local beer from thirsty Wellingtonians who weekend in the town.

Vintage Gold (golden ale)
4.5% ABV

Layers of golden malt unfurl in the glass. There is just a hint of hop aromatics, but clean, firm bitterness give the beer sharpness and clarity.

Hop Elixir (IPA)
6.2% ABV

A slight grainy note comes through to begin with and then this is followed by herbal, woodsy hop notes. Bitterness that borders on astringent cuts through the palate. The components come together clumsily.

Foxy Red (red ale)
6.8% ABV

Searingly bitter hops with some orange and pine character are overlaid on caramel malt. Like the IPA, this red ale is too bitter to showcase either lovely malt or hop aromatics.

Black Nectar (oatmeal stout)
5.8% ABV

Lovely and creamy, with the aroma of freshly roasted coffee, this oatmeal stout has a subtle, grainy sharpness that provides freshness and pulls the beer into focus.

Mata Beer/Aotearoa Breweries

Brewery
Established: 2005
Location: Kawerau
Owner: Viitakangas family
Brewer: Tammy Viitakangas

After finding and buying a second-hand brewkit, Tammy Viitakangas enlisted the help of her parents to build Mata Beer and Aotearoa Breweries, as she felt a calling to create her own beer brand and wanted to know whether anyone would buy her beer.

When brewing and creating new recipes, Viitakangas starts with 'a vision in [her] head' of what she wants to create and then sets about figuring out how to achieve this. She also balances the creative side with the technical, describing herself as both a 'fanatical cleaner' and an obsessive note-taker, 'so that when a beer comes out amazing, we can brew it again and again'.

The brewery itself is patched together from three unused storefronts – a dairy, a butchery and a menswear store – but currently Viitakangas is looking to relocate so that they can upgrade the brewery as well as generate more revenue selling beer directly to customers.

Artesian (premium lager)
5% ABV

A lovely smooth lager with subtle spice, honey and crushed grape aromatics.

Hip Hop (NZ Pilsner)
5% ABV

A crisp Pilsner with sweet golden malt and lemon-drop hop notes. It has a long, refreshing bitterness.

Manuka Golden Ale
5% ABV

A smooth, flavourful golden ale with nice bready complexity and a richness and depth from manuka honey.

Wai-Iti Waka (NZ pale ale)
5.5% ABV

Lovely sweet golden malt is complemented by sweet fruit, over-ripe lemons and pineapple with a minty edge.

Tumeke (NZ IPA)
6.5% ABV

With a vibrantly fruity nose of pineapple, peach and lemon, this beer is vibrantly hoppy and has a malt backbone that should balance this. It is enjoyable but finishes a little sweet, lacking a line of bitterness to bring the beer together.

Matawhaka (imperial IPA)
8% ABV

Pine resin and sweet malt come through on the nose. Huge sticky vegetal hops show through on the palate, and are accompanied by rich sweetness and cutting bitterness.

Taking a tour at McCashin's Brewery, Nelson.

Mike's

Brewery
Established: 1989
Location: Urenui, Taranaki
Owner: Ron Trigg

Established by Mike Johnson as Whitecliffs Brewery in 1989, Mike's was bought by Ron Trigg in 2007. When Trigg took over, the beers were also brewed by a Mike — his father.

For the first 15 years of the brewery's history, only one beer was brewed: Mike's Mild. From 2004, Mountain Lager (now Mike's Lager) was introduced by then owners Steve Ekdahl and Sharon Cottam. When Trigg took over in 2007, he gradually introduced more beers into the range, including a hoppy organic Pilsner. Today, there are over 16 beers in the Mike's range (not including X and Y, which are one-off beers that change regularly). At the time of writing, X was a bitter, brewed by Trigg and Johnson to celebrate the 25th anniversary of the brewery. As Johnson's first beer was Mild, Trigg points out, it was only fitting for him to finally make a bitter in the brewery he established.

The brewery was certified organic in 2000 and today Mike's beers are split into two categories: eight beers made with certified organic ingredients; and Mike's Illegitimate Sons range, which are not marketed as organic.

At the time of writing, the site on which the brewery is located was for sale and Trigg intends to move it to a larger site in a city. This is partly due to the costs of running a business in an isolated location (he has to pay the daily courier extra, for instance), and partly to help him build a more viable local market.

Mike's beers have all improved considerably over the last few years. One of Trigg's specialities is black beers, of which he brews five porters and a stout. These are universally rich and robust, but are on the bitter end of the spectrum (including the misleadingly named Chocolate Milk Stout), with intense charcoal-like roastiness. His pale ales tend to be light on malt but burst with hop character. Trigg admits he thinks they are 'unbalanced' but wears it as a badge of pride. I would argue that they have balance but are balanced far more in favour of the hops.

Organic Mild (ale)
4% ABV

A smooth ale with milk chocolate and hazelnut notes. At only 4%, this is a delicious, mild session beer.

Organic Lager
5% ABV

A light, malty lager. Simple but clean, focused and refreshing.

Organic Pilsner
5% ABV

An extremely light-bodied Pilsner with vibrantly aromatic top notes: passion fruit and guava. It has a clean bitterness.

OMPA: Onemorepaleale (APA)
6.3% ABV

Bursting with pink grapefruit and pine resin notes, this is a focused APA with a light body of malt and taut bitterness.

Taranaki India Pale Ale
7% ABV

Hopped with Kiwi varieties, this IPA is big but giving, with pineapple, papaya and rock melon hop notes over the top of sweet malt. Lovely, long bitterness provides focus.

The tasting room at Mike's.

Single American India Pale Ale
7% ABV

With a richer malt body than the Taranaki IPA, this is a tightly wound west coast IPA with passion fruit and guava, along with a pronounced sticky bitterness.

SMASH: Full Nelson IPA
7% ABV

The fourth of Mike's big pale ales, this beer is dry and light-bodied, with crushed gooseberries, lemongrass and passion flower.

THC: Taranaki Cloudy Hefeweizen
5.5% ABV

This is a big, full hefe with over-the-top banana and clove notes and a creamy full finish.

Chocolate Milk Stout
5.5% ABV

Don't let the name deceive you: while this may technically be a milk stout, it has the intensity and bitterness of most American-style stouts. Watch for the long, firm, roasty bitterness, creamy chocolate and coffee notes, and a clean, focused finish.

Robust Imperial Porter
8% ABV

A big, bold, dry porter with ashy, burnt malt notes, softened by fruit character coming from ale yeast.

Vanilla Coffee Porter
8% ABV

A similar beer to the Robust Imperial Porter, but with vanilla providing sweetness and a distinct coffee note; that said, it is still incredibly dark, dry and ashy.

Moa Brewing Company

Brewery
Founded: 2003
Location: Blenheim
Founder: Josh Scott
Brewer: Dave Nicholls

The son of Marlborough wine pioneer Alan Scott, Josh Scott founded Moa after coming back from several years making wine in other parts of the globe. In France, he was introduced to German and Belgian beers, and while working in California he fell in love with 'Americanised craft beer'. First tasting Sierra Nevada Pale Ale, he 'couldn't believe that beer could taste so great'. Alas, when he returned home to New Zealand to take up winemaking in the family business, he could not find any beers as good as those he had tasted abroad, so decided to try applying his winemaking skills to brewing beer.

The first beer that was released was Moa Methode, best described as a Belgian-style Pilsner; Scott applied the *méthode champenoise* technique to making the beer, giving it a distinct estery character, as well as hopping it with New Zealand varieties. Other beers followed suit and a brewery was installed on the current site in 2006. Brewer Dave Nicholls was appointed the following year.

In 2010, Moa received a substantial investment from Geoff Ross's Business Bakery and Pioneer Capital, before being listed on the stock exchange in late 2011. Over this period, the company has had substantial trouble with distribution, resource consent for a new brewery (resulting in them contracting out much of their production to McCashin's) and winning, at significant cost, and then losing a contract to supply Air New Zealand. All of these have resulted in considerable financial woes, with seven-figure losses year on year. Moa recently refocused itself back toward the New Zealand and Australian markets, resulting in more stable sales, and has finally got the go-ahead to build a larger brewery in Marlborough.

Aside from its financial difficulties, Moa has come under criticism for its behaviour in the market. While some of the company's marketing material has been good-natured ('Finally something drinkable from Marlborough'), some has left a sour taste in consumers' mouths, largely their portrayal of women (i.e. their whole IPO document but especially one image of Moa CEO Gareth Hughes standing with a cigar over a model while she balances an ashtray on her head) but also homophobic slurs ('Low Carb Queers') and other insensitive marketing material (like naming a beer 'Black Power').

Despite these setbacks, Moa beers have only got better over the last few years – especially their seasonal and one-off releases. Their sour and barrel-aged beers are the highlights.

Original Lager
5% ABV

Moa's take on the 'green bottle lager' – soft, sweet malt with just enough bitterness and hop aroma to provide focus.

Session Pale Ale
4.7% ABV

An approachable pale ale with some lovely tropical fruit notes overlaid on light, luscious malt. A hint of butteriness is noticeable on the finish.

Methode Pilsner
5% ABV

Named 'Methode' as it is refermented in the bottle using *méthode champenoise* – the Champagne method. To begin with, it has estery notes of clove and banana, before these give way to a more abundant golden barley field character that I associate with Pilsner. It has a rich and creamy texture with a fine bead and long, focused bitterness.

South Pacific IPA
5% ABV

Rich and malty, with a subtle spicy hop aroma, creamy full texture and soft but present bitterness, this is a pale ale rather than an IPA, but nonetheless is still enjoyable.

Southern Alps White IPA
6.4% ABV

One of my favourite Moa beers: grassy hops and juicy passionfruit notes combine with creamy, cloudy wheat malt to create a zippy, dry but full-bodied IPA.

Five Hop English Ale (ESB)
6.2% ABV

Characterised by a lovely, rich body of malt with estery English ale notes, this is one of those beers that you forget about, taste again and go, 'Oh yum, why don't I drink more of this?!' It is rich, filling with layers of flavour and clean bitterness on the finish.

St Josephs Belgian Tripel
9.5% ABV

Light in colour, this tripel has a snow-white head, rich yeast character with cloves and an oily, floral note. Pithy pink grapefruit notes give the beer a lift. At 9.5%, it is full and rich with some residual sweetness, but it remains crisp and extremely drinkable.

Imperial Stout
10.2% ABV

A very balanced big beer with woody, ashy notes coming from time spent in the barrel. It is creamy with a port-like note on the finish.

Monsoon Brewing Company

Contract brewery
Established: 2004
Location: Christchurch
Owner: Kathryn Ward

Monsoon Brewing Company is an export-focused brewing business with listings at some of Australia's, Asia's and the UK's finest gastronomic Asian restaurants.

Monteith's

Brewery
Established: 1868
Location: Greymouth
Owner: DB

Monteith's was established by Stewart Monteith, who took over Reefton's Phoenix Brewery in 1866. In 1927, five West Coast breweries merged to become the Westland Brewing Company, which was managed by William Monteith (Stewart's son); the head office was built on the current Monteith's site in Greymouth.

The Westland Brewing Company was bought by DB in 1969 and became Monteith's in 1990. In 2001, DB rationalised its brewing operations and attempted to shut down the Monteith's brewery, but was forced to reopen days later. While the brewery ticked on between 2001 and 2011, much of the Monteith's beer was brewed by other facilities and a lot of work was put into establishing Monteith's bars. In 2011, DB substantially reinvested into the Greymouth brewery, building a brand-new brewery and guest facilities.

Beer-wise, the core Monteith's beers are sound and enjoyable, especially the black beer. Monteith's own the trademark to the term 'radler' in New Zealand, which upsets many as this is a bona fide style in Germany (Kiwis call this mix of beer and lemonade a 'shandy') – although, being a full-strength beer, Monteith's Radler is not true to its namesake style. With the reinvestment in the Greymouth brewery, Monteith's has created a 'craft' range called the Brewers Series. Some of these are very good but, unlike the craft ranges produced by Lion and Independent Breweries, are often way off the mark style-wise.

Radler
5% ABV

A noticeably sweet lemon- and lime-infused lager with sweet malt notes.

Southern Pale Ale
4.6% ABV

A fruity (citrus and tropical fruits) entry-level example of the New Zealand pale ale genre.

Golden Lager
5% ABV

A sweet, malty lager with some citrusy hop notes and clean bitterness.

Summer Ale
5% ABV

An approachable sweetish lager with ginger notes.

Bohemian Pilsner
5% ABV

Malty and rich for the style, this Pilsner has a clean bitterness and a hint of spicy/floral hop notes.

Original Ale (NZ draught)
4% ABV

A soft, malty beer with nutty notes and some prickly hop bitterness.

Black Beer (schwarzbier/black lager)
5.2% ABV

This is one of the best black lagers in the country, and the hero of the range. Mid-weight, it has liquorice and fruity dark malt notes, but a clean, refreshing finish.

Mount Brewing Co.

Brewpub
Established: 1996
Location: Mt Maunganui
Owner: Glenn Meikle
Brewers: Steve Edkins and
Janine Pharo

Servicing two pubs and a handful of local off-licences, Mount Brewing Co. is a 1000L brewery in Mt Maunganui, Bay of Plenty.

Moutere Brewing

Brewpub
Established: 2011
Location: Upper Moutere, Nelson
Owners: Andrew Cole
and David Watson

The Moutere Inn is one of New Zealand's oldest pubs, established in 1850. Having bought the pub in 2008, owners Andrew Cole and David Watson wanted to create a range of beers similar to those the original inn owners might have enjoyed in their homeland of Germany. Unable to afford the costs of setting up a brewery, they decided to work with West Coast Brewery to create 'classic examples of classic styles'. Moutere Brewing continues this tradition, brewing under contract today.

Sarau Lager (helles)
4.2% ABV

A long, fresh, classically German lager with spicy hop notes. Very complex and long.

1516 Pilsner
5% ABV

This is an extremely aromatic Pilsner with zesty citrus notes and lovely floral aromas. It is long, fresh and clean, with refreshing bitterness.

Neudorf Ale (NZ draught)
4.2% ABV

Described as an altbier, this is most similar to the New Zealand draught style, so I've lumped it in with these. It's an easy-drinking copper-coloured beer; very nutty and creamy, long and clean, with focused bitterness.

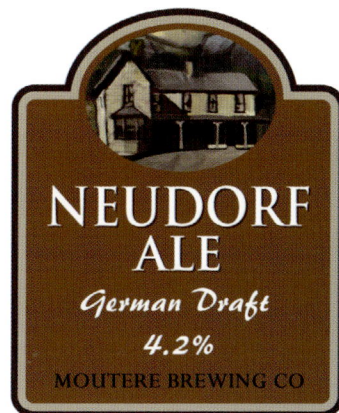

NEUDORF
ALE
German Draft
4.2%
MOUTERE BREWING CO

145

Mussel Inn

Brewpub
Established: 1995
Location: Onekaka, Golden Bay
Owners: Andrew and Jane Dixon
Brewer: Reuben Lee

Opened in 1992, the Mussel Inn is one of the most iconic pubs in the country. Set in isolated Onekaka, two hours' drive from Nelson, it is the kind of place where, once you get there, the stress of the day simply evaporates.

Dixon built the pub from scratch as he wanted to live in the remote community but also had to find something to provide for him and his family. Today, the pub and brewery not only sustain his family but also a host of employees: 'It's nice to be able to create employment.'

About half of the beer Dixon brews is consumed on site, but he says that 'I don't consider us to be a brewery', likening the brewing operation to the kitchen – just one part of a greater whole.

Where many breweries are constrained by tank size and physical space, the factors that constrain the growth of the Mussel Inn are much more organic. Being so isolated means they have to have their own water source, a stream, and they can take only so much water from it before there is a negative effect. They also need to deal with any waste on site. Despite being over the hill from Motueka, Golden Bay is not an ideal place to grow hops. However, Dixon has managed to find some cultivars that work in the climate and has begun growing and kilning his own hops from the 2015 harvest.

Their most famous beer is the Captain Cooker – a 4.4% red ale brewed with manuka tips, inspired by the first beers brewed in New Zealand by explorer James Cook. Dixon created it because there was an abundance of manuka on the property and he 'wanted to create a beer that looked like DB' to appease the drinkers of commercial New Zealand draught beers who criticised him in the early days of the pub. He goes on to say that while 'it looks like an ordinary beer, it does not taste like one'.

Because Captain Cooker is so different, Dixon has been approached several times to export it; the idea of shipping beer in bottles did not 'sit comfortably with our environmental philosophies', so instead he licensed the recipe and it has since been brewed at specialist contract brewer De Proefbrouwerij in Belgium (where the legendary Danish gypsy microbrewery Mikkeller brews much of its beer), at Squatters Brewery in Utah, and at Hawkshead Brewery in the UK's Lake District. Between 2009 and 2012, Dixon also contract-brewed a 5% version of Captain Cooker at Invercargill Brewery to keep up with demand for bottled product. In 2015, he also began brewing Super Swine, a higher-strength version of Captain Cooker.

Aside from its Captain Cooker and other core beers, the Mussel Inn is becoming increasingly recognised as a producer of exciting sour beers.

Golden Goose (lager)
4.4% ABV

A malty, clean, vibrantly hopped lager. Long and refreshing.

Captain Cooker (red ale)
4.4% ABV

Copper-hued malt and spicy, woodsy, herbal notes characterise this very aromatic and intense red ale. It is extremely enjoyable, with warming notes of manuka.

Pale Whale (strong ale)
7% ABV

A big, fat, malty ale with only subtle hop notes. Despite being extremely luscious, it finishes dry, balanced and clean.

The hop garden at the Mussel Inn.

Ninebarnyardowls

Contract brewery
Established: 2014
Location: Wellington
Owner and brewer: Brayden Rawlinson

For Brayden Rawlinson, a glass of Tuatara Ardennes 'expanded [his] mind into a whole word of opportunity', turning him from a Tui drinker to a craft beer advocate. Brewing on a small scale, he focuses on Belgian and French styles, pushing the boundaries with ingredients (at the time of writing, he was working on a collaboration with a Wairarapa winery). He has brewed beers at the pilot brewery at Massey and at Fork & Brewer, and regularly brews at Wellington's Occasional Brewer. Ninebarnyardowls has relocated to Sydney.

Fill-your-own taps at Baylands Brewery, Petone.

North End Brewing

Brewpub
Established: 2013
Location: Waikanae
Founders: Kieran Haslett-Moore, Todd Cameron and Aaron Wagstaff
Brewer: Kieran Haslett-Moore

Kieran Haslett-Moore started off as a cheese professional and avid homebrewer (so avid that he had a 'home pub'), before taking a role as beer specialist at Wellington's Regional Wines and Spirits. Growing his capability as a brewer, he brewed several collaboration beers with Emerson's before starting his own contract brewery, Southstar.

In 2013, Haslett-Moore teamed up with the owners of Long Beach (where he had been a long-time patron) to start work on a physical brewery, on Ngaio Road in Waikanae, which in late 2015 will became a fully operational brewery that will also feature a brewpub and barbecue restaurant. While Haslett-Moore takes inspiration from around the brewing world, he is most inspired by traditional English beers, such as those by Fullers and Timothy Taylor, but also Kiwi interpretations of these styles: Emerson's Bookbinder and Galbraith's Bob Hudson's Bitter.

In light of this inspiration, he has designed his core range of beers with sessionability in mind – 'to be drunk by the flagon or six-pack' – with seasonals being stronger and 'designed more for savouring'.

In keeping with this traditional philosophy, he typically shies away from dry-hopping beer, preferring to use late kettle additions that give 'aroma and resinous flavour over outright backhop bitterness'. That said, while his beers are rooted in the British brewing tradition, he is also open to the use of non-traditional ingredients, such as adjuncts, but only 'for the right reasons'.

In addition to its British-styled beers, North End has begun a barrel programme. While many of these beers are yet to be brewed (let alone released), some will be takes on the various styles of soured Belgian ales.

Pacific Blonde (golden ale)
4.7% ABV

A kolsch-style golden ale that celebrates two Kiwi hops – Pacifica and Pacific Jade – which give the beer a lemon-drop note and a long, dry finish.

Super Alpha (Pacific ale)
5% ABV

A lovely, light, pale ale with the addition of wheat malt. Long and bitter, it has citrus and aromatic East Asian spice notes.

Amber (amber ale)
4.4% ABV

An amber ale that combines the malt weight of an English ale with biscuit malt, caramel and a hint of chocolate, along with a grapefruit marmalade-like US hop character.

Field Way (APA)
5.8% ABV

Like all of North End's beers, this APA is quite complex on the malt front (especially compared to other examples of this style), with biscuity notes and a hint of caramel. The hop profile bursts with lime sherbet with a herbal edge.

ESB
5.8% ABV

A rich beer that balances rich malt flavours with zesty/herbal New Zealand-grown hop varieties. Complex, sweet toffee with a hint of ginger and fruitiness from the English ale yeast combine with mandarin pith notes and a long, dry finish.

Forty South (IPA)
6% ABV

A traditional English IPA with a firm body of biscuity malt, woodsy citrus and bramble hop notes, and long, focused bitterness.

Panhead Custom Ales

Brewery
Established: 2013
Location: Upper Hutt
Owner: Neilson family
Brewer: Michael Neilson

Established by ex-Tuatara brewer Michael Neilson, Panhead describe themselves as 'boutique beer bogans' and are named after Harley-Davidson's unique 'panhead' engine, which appears on their labels.

Launching at Beervana 2013, they soon established a reputation for the quality and drinkability of their first four core beers (Whitewall was introduced to the core range in late 2014). They focused largely on their local Wellington market before beginning to sell their beer further afield.

As well as their core beers, they have an exciting range of seasonals with striking labels designed by Simon Morse, one of New Zealand's best tattoo artists. Panhead used Morse to add interest to their Beervana 2014 stand (although I'm told Morse was tattooing only his current customers). These beers have varied wildly in style but are typically big and either hop- or yeast-driven.

In March 2015, Panhead also brewed beers in collaboration with the *Dominion Post*, to celebrate the newspaper's 150th anniversary, each beer inspired by a historic news story from the paper.

Port Road Pilsner
5.2% ABV

A stunning Pilsner with soft golden malt and aromatic tropical notes, culminating in long, refreshing bitterness.

Whitewall (Pacific ale)
4.3% ABV

A light malt with hay and distinctly wheaten notes, and fruity, citrusy hops that just burst out of the glass. It is light-bodied and dry without that typical yeast fruitiness characteristic of most wheat ales.

Quickchange XPA (pale ale)
4.6% ABV

Although light in body, this pale ale bursts with clean bitterness and tropical hop notes of mango, guava and lychee.

Supercharger APA
5.7% ABV

Fuller than the XPA, Supercharger has intense, resinous lime, orange and subtle citrus blossom notes, along with long, driving bitterness.

Blacktop Oat Stout
5.5% ABV

A rich, smooth, creamy stout with raspy bitterness, dark coffee, vanilla and burnt sugar with a crisp, dry finish.

ParrotDog

Brewery
Established: 2011
Location: Wellington
Owners and brewers: the three Matts
– Warner, Kristofski and Stevens

ParrotDog's first beer, brewed under contract at Mike's in Taranaki, was launched at Beervana in 2011 – it was called BitterBitch and went on to win People's Choice at the event. This reinforced the beliefs of the owners – the three Matts: Warner, Kristofski and Stevens – that they should become full-time brewers. They began work on establishing a physical brewery on Vivian Street, which was commissioned in late 2012.

Since then, ParrotDog has cemented its role in the Wellington and Kiwi beer ecosystems. They don't have a gimmick (not that there is anything wrong with that), but brew sound, focused and flavourful beers that please drinkers and critics alike. At the 2014 Brewers Guild Awards, their Red IPA Bloody Dingo won champion in the US Ale Styles category (one of the most contested categories) and it is also in the 99th percentile for its style on RateBeer.com.

FlaxenFeather (golden ale)
4.7% ABV

The most underrated of the ParrotDog beers – a textural golden ale with a flaxy note (maybe it's just the name that makes me think this) and lovely integrated New Zealand hop notes. A perfect quencher.

DeadCanary (NZ pale ale)
5.3% ABV

With lovely rich malt and fruity hop characters of mandarin and aromatic tropical fruit, this is a balanced, drinkable New Zealand pale.

BitterBitch (IPA)
5.8% ABV

The beer that put ParrotDog on the map! Long, driving bitterness combine with grassy, citrus and pineapple hop notes over a lovely round malt body.

Bloodhound (red ale)
6.3% ABV

Round and full, with luscious red malt and with notes of biscuit, burnt toffee and a hint of espresso, this red ale is characterisded by lovely full fruity hops.

Peak Brewery

Brewery
Established: 2010
Location: Masterton
Owner and brewer: Rhys Morgan

Located just south of Masterton on an organically farmed lifestyle block is Peak Brewery. Here, Rhys Morgan brews traditional German and English beer styles using organic ingredients. They are available at outlets in the Wairarapa and occasionally at specialist beer bars, on tap or in the bottle.

Pink Elephant

Contract brewery
Established: 1990
Location: Blenheim
Brewer and owner: Roger Pink

Roger Pink established his Blenheim brewery in 1990, but more recently he has been brewing his beers under contract at Invercargill Brewery. Alongside Ben Middlemiss and Richard Emerson, he was one of just three New Zealand brewers to have his beers included in Michael Jackson's classic *Great Beer Guide*.

Like Pink himself, the beers are uncompromising and eccentric – big is an understatement. They are takes on traditional English styles and as such are full, intense and malty.

Golden Tusk Special (English strong ale)
7% ABV

With luscious golden malty notes, a brisk bitterness and a long, sweet finish with complex notes of orange marmalade and burnt caramel, this is a big malt-focused but very moreish beer.

Queenstown Brewers

Contract brewer
Established: 2012
Location: Queenstown
Owner and Brewer: John Wallace

John Wallace 'got frustrated with brewing small batches of beer that didn't last long', so decided to start contract brewing on a commercial scale in 2012 and 'hasn't stopped since!'

Brewing British- and American-style beers with New Zealand-grown ingredients, Wallace is most concerned with brewing beers with a 'depth of flavour', something he certainly achieves. In 2016, he intends to expand his core range as well as increasing the availability of his beers.

Steam Brew (California common)
4.9% ABV

A malty, effervescent amber ale with some funk, creamy vanilla and clean, prickly bitterness.

25oz Pilsner
5% ABV

A lovely punchy Sauvignon Blanc-like aroma combines with soft golden malt and very floral aromatics. A very refreshing Kiwi take on Pilsner that is unlike any New Zealand-hopped Pilsner I've tasted.

Wry Red RRR (rye red ale)
6% ABV

Light-bodied for the colour, with grassy, passionfruit and gooseberry notes and a hint of tartness, this beer is very good but totally not what I'd expect from a rye ale.

Dead Snake Porter
4.5% ABV

Lovely liquorice, coffee and other dark malt notes combine for a full, rich, spicy porter with a hint of grain and smoke.

Hop kiln at Totara Brewing, Nelson.

Rain Dogs

Brewery
Established: 2011
Location: Riccarton, Christchurch
Owner and brewer: Sean Harris

Before the February 2011 earthquakes that destroyed much of Christchurch, Sean Harris was head brewer at The Twisted Hop brewpub. Post-quake, he continued to brew for The Twisted Hop (using Three Boys as a base – The Twisted Hop was in the Red Zone) but realised that he 'needed to start my own brand or be out of a job'. He started brewing his beers on a contract basis out of Three Boys but admits that contract brewing 'had its frustrations' – he decided he needed his own brewery. Rather than do this on his own, he teamed up with Golden Eagle Brewery in July 2013 to share a site and equipment. Aside from the beers from Golden Eagle and Rain Dogs, they also make Eagle vs. Dog beers at this site.

Having worked at The Twisted Hop, Harris acknowledges that his brewing is influenced by British techniques, but he believes that his beers also incorporate American influences and, on top of this, he has chosen to brew only with New Zealand ingredients, meaning his beers combine aspects of all three.

Wee Bairn Best Bitter
3.8% ABV

A simple fruity, nutty English bitter. Clean and focused.

Apothecary Amber Ale
4.9% ABV

A light-bodied ale for the style, with creamy vanilla notes, toasted almonds and caramel malt.

Mr Clean Pale Ale
5.2% ABV

Long and rich, without being heavy, this pale ale has a woodsy hop profile and just a hint of smokiness.

Deadwood IPA
6.8% ABV

A long, very 'classic' malt-focused British style with taut bitter pine resin and bright tropical fruit notes, which give lift. It has a driving, focused bitterness.

Shroud Tailor Porter
5.8% ABV

Creamy with some tartness, this porter is very mocha-driven. Although full, it is very fresh and lively.

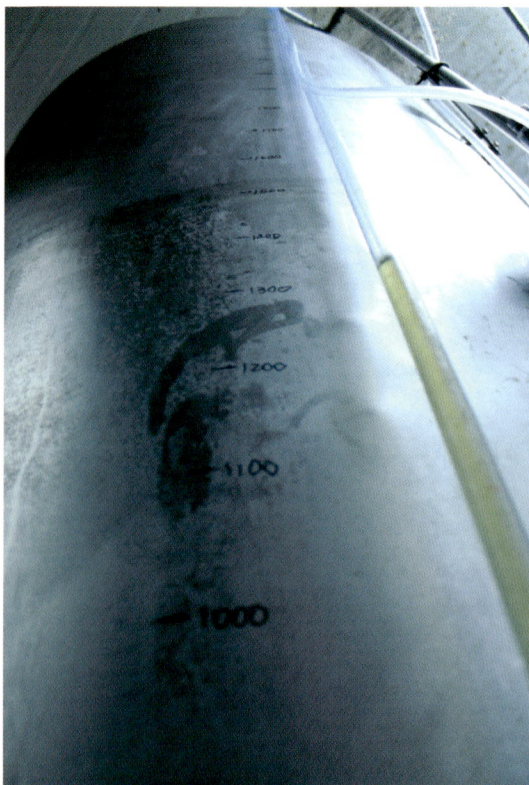

Regent 58

Brewpub
Established: 2012
Location: Carterton
Owners: Gary Fisher and Brent Goble

Based in Carterton, Gary Fisher and Brent Goble brew enjoyable examples of traditional English styles that are available at their brewpub and around the Wairarapa.

Remedy Brewing

Contract brewery
Established: 2013
Location: Wellington
Owners and brewers: Richard Deeble and James King

Winning the Champion Beer award at the 2012 SOBA National Homebrew Competition for their New Zealand pale ale led to the production of a commercial batch of this beer at Hallertau. This spurred on homebrewers Richard Deeble and James King to experiment further by contract brewing commercial batches. Due to their size, they are yet to have a regular line-up of beers, but they are trying to make this happen.

Renaissance Brewing

Brewery
Established: 2006
Location: Marlborough
Founders: Andy Duchars and
Brian Thiel

With Andy Duchars and Brian Thiel both hailing from the craft beer mecca of San Diego, the idea to start Renaissance 'seemed like a good idea at 2 a.m., when sitting in a hot tub'. Based in Marlborough, a region better known for its wine than its beer, they were inspired by the beers of their home town. They have a strong house style that encompasses 'British style, American know-how, [and] Kiwi terroir', the resulting beers being all about 'balance, balance, balance'.

They make four different pale ales, each hopped differently but all with a generous malt weight to balance and showcase the particular hop character. In my mind, their two best beers are their darker ales: Elemental Porter and Stonecutter Scotch Ale. These are rich, malty, full of flavour and deftly balanced, with defined bitterness being a hallmark of both. The beers are regarded as the best examples of their styles, not just in New Zealand but internationally. In January 2015, Elemental Porter was rated the 15th best porter beer in the world in the RateBeer.com RateBeerBest awards.

In 2013 and 2014, Renaissance managed to win the Champion Small International Brewery award at the Australian International Beer Awards, and in 2013 won Champion Brewery at the Brewers Guild Awards. They have also won countless awards for individual beers.

More recently, they have begun producing one-off beers under their Enlightenment range. These are beers not necessarily confined by the rules of style and often do not fit within the strict boundaries of the Renaissance range. Among others they have produced are a number of wheat and rye beers, as well as an American-style pumpkin ale. Personally, I have been extremely impressed by beers from this programme – it is

headed up by Matt Dainty, who replaced Søren Eriksen as assistant brewer in 2012.

In late 2014, Renaissance managed to raise $700,000 using crowd equity-funding platform the Snowball Effect. They were the first business in New Zealand to raise money using this funding model and achieved their target from 300 backers in only a couple of days. As well as equity in the business, Renaissance shareholders will get access to a special batch of beers, made exclusively for them.

Empathy (light beer)
2.5% ABV

Light and fresh, but with full malt and clean, focused hopping, this is a lovely low-alcohol beer.

Clipper (session IPA)
3.7% ABV

Bursting with burnt orange and grapefruit pith, this is a hop bomb with just enough weight to carry the long, sustained bitterness.

Odyssey Wit Beer
5% ABV

A beautifully aromatic wheat beer with banana, citrus and sweaty passion fruit. It is creamy on the palate with clean, drying bitterness, and is quite hoppy for the style, which walks a fine line between working and not, just pulling it off.

Paradox Pilsner
5% ABV

Effervescent and crunchy, with passion fruit and lemon-drop hop notes over a light body of malt, this is a fruity Pilsner with a seamless line of bitterness throughout.

Discovery American Style Pale Ale
4.5% ABV

Resinous notes of grapefruit, gooseberry and earthy spice on the nose characterise this APA. These follow through on the palate and are joined by a more marmalade note with creamy malt and taut, lingering bitterness.

Perfection English Style Pale Ale
5% ABV

This ale has a very integrated nose with lovely hop notes and a hint of berry. It is creamy with a lovely citric note and earthy, savoury woodsy notes. Very moreish.

Voyager (IPA)
6% ABV

Sweaty hop notes jump out of the glass. Layers of hops and malt unfurl, but biscuity notes and grapefruit pith and orange dominate. Neither the weight of the beer nor the bitterness are over the top, but both are very present.

Elemental Porter
6% ABV

Smooth and round this porter has luscious, fruity English ale ester notes. It is dark and intense, with notes of burnt coffee, milk chocolate and taut bitterness. A very complete beer.

Stonecutter Scotch Ale
7% ABV

A full, rich and complex ale with a hint of peat smoke with nutty caramel notes on the nose. On the palate is just a hint of tartness, which gives the beer focus. Layers of smoky toffee, a hint of milk chocolate and spice weave together. For a big beer, it finishes long, dry and clean.

M.P.A. (double IPA)
8.5% ABV

This is a huge Kiwi double IPA. M.P.A. is short for Marlborough pale ale. It is luscious. Personally, I prefer this beer relatively cool, as I find the combination of resinous hops and sweet malt become cloying at the warmer temperatures at which I normally drink a double IPA.

Rocky Knob

Contract brewer
Established: 2013
Location: Mt Maunganui
Owners: Stu and Bron Marshall

Having wanted to be a brewer since high school (his careers counsellor talked him into taking up forestry), Stu Marshall moved with his wife Bron from Nelson to Mt Maunganui and was disappointed that he no longer had access to a wide range of locally brewed craft beer. Frustrated by this, he decided to fire up a long-neglected homebrew kit and began to brew seriously. Converting friends (and friends of friends), he was spending more and more time brewing, until in early 2013 his wife convinced him to go pro (in part so she could get her garage back).

Marshall's philosophy is to 'keep it fun, keep it social' and make beers that are 'big on flavour' but mostly 'sessionable and repeatable'. The three year-round beers are big (all over 6% ABV), but they are extremely drinkable and currently packaged in pre-filled 1.25L riggers, ideal for sharing.

Hop Knob IPA
6% ABV

Very drinkable, this IPA has well-integrated hop and malt character, and a generous pale malt backbone, but finishes dry with some sweetness toward the back of the palate. Fresh blackcurrant-like hop top notes shine through.

Oceanside Amber (amber ale)
6.5% ABV

A rich amber ale with a dusty note and crème caramel-like richness, the caramel from the malt giving a rich creamy texture. Overlaid on this are stonefruit hop notes. This beer is broad and malty but with bright hop notes and a smooth finish.

Snapperhead Imperial IPA
7.4% ABV

Long, smooth and full, this imperial IPA has lemon zest and gooseberry notes coming from the combination of Citra and Nelson Sauvin hops. It is broad and coats the palate nicely, and is sweeter but also lighter on its feet than both the Oceanside or Hop Knob.

Roosters Brewhouse

Brewpub
Established: 1994
Location: Hastings
Owner: Chris and Jill Harrison

Winemakers Chris and Jill Harrison (who also own Beach House Wines in Hawke's Bay) founded Roosters in 1994, at the edge of the Gimblett Gravels wine-growing area. The beers won significant awards in the 1990s and remain approachable and enjoyable. They are available at the brewhouse and at a handful of local bars and pubs.

Sawmill Brewery

Brewery
Established: 2004
Location: Leigh, north of Auckland
Owners: Mike Sutherland and Kirsty McKay
Brewer: Mike Sutherland

The Sawmill Brewery had been operating as 'a hobby brewery' when Mike Sutherland and Kirsty McKay bought it, wanting to produce 'clean, pared-back beer' in the little town of Leigh, just over an hour north of Auckland's CBD.

In their first year, they doubled the production of their brewery, focusing largely on the local Auckland market, which, at the time, Sutherland concedes 'was a city still pretty new to craft'. Having outgrown the brewery, they are opening new premises, which will have a more formal tasting room.

Sutherland describes his brewing style as 'relatively understated', wanting his beer to reflect his 'belief in doing things as well as we possibly can with resourcefulness and creativity'. He believes this ethos is echoed in the history of Leigh, 'from the sawmillers who came here in the 1860s to the community we are part of now'.

Pilsner
4.5% ABV

A stunning example of the Kiwi Pilsner: a light malt body and grassy gooseberry notes.

Crystal Wheat Lager
4.5% ABV

A creamy, fine-textured lager brewed with wheat malt. It has a hint of estery banana and spice, and clean, sweet lemon notes on the finish.

Pale Ale (APA)
4.5% ABV

A vibrant APA with notes of stone fruit, pithy grapefruit and pine resin, and long bitterness.

12 Gauge (imperial pilsner)
6.5% ABV

A big, juicy, luscious lager with lovely full golden malt and vibrant tropical hops: guava, lychee and pineapple.

The Doctor (doppelbock)
6.5% ABV

With lovely rich malt notes, toffee, burnt butter, hazelnuts and sweet stewed fruit, this is an intensely complex, layered beer.

Schippers Beer

Contract brewery
Established: 2011
Location: Auckland
Owner and brewer: Niels Schipper

Niels Schipper established his eponymous brewing company on the back of winning a Moa-sponsored homebrew competition. He says that he moved into brewing full time because the 'discovery of craft beer excited me so much'. He saw it as an opportunity to drink more great beer, meet great people and 'make the world a better place'. Schipper describes his range as malt-focused, English-style beers with a Kiwi twist.

Mistress Pilsner
5% ABV

A German-style Pilsner with a herbal, white pepper-like punch. Clean and refreshing.

Geezer Session IPA
4.6% ABV

Formerly Geezer Golden Ale, this beer has been retooled a little. It has lovely generous golden malt with tropical hops and clean, refreshing bitterness.

Maverick IPA
6.7% ABV

An IPA that is more English in style, counterpointing the bold Chinook hopping. It is characterised by lovely, nutty malt with spruce resin and a hint of marmalade.

Chinook IPA
7.3% ABV

Sticky and resinous, this IPA has bright peach and apricot, along with some lively citrus and pine needle notes. It is on the sweeter side (which is unsurprising given the high ABV) but lacks the weight and intensity to remain balanced. Nonetheless it is enjoyable.

Scotts Brewing Company

Brewery
Established: 2007
Location: Oamaru
Owner and brewer: Philip Scott

Originally brewing gluten-free beers (which they still do), Scotts have recently installed themselves in Oamaru's Victorian precinct and widened their range considerably, now brewing beers with malt as well (despite their brewer being coeliac). Other than the gluten-free pale, which is widely available, the beers are sold on tap (and occasionally in the bottle) in the bottom half of the South Island, and are rich and full-flavoured.

Gluten Free Pale Ale
4.5% ABV

Very fruity, with an aromatic nose and vibrant passion fruit and guava on the palate. It does not have the weight of a malt-driven beer but is extremely drinkable.

Shakespeare Hotel

Brewpub
Established: 1898 (pub),
1986 (brewery)
Location: Auckland
Owner: the McIntyre family

Established in the 100-year-old Shakespeare Hotel, the Shakespeare was New Zealand's first bona fide brewpub. While it produced excellent beers in its day, over the years the quality of both the pub and the beers deteriorated. In 2013, it was bought by Nick McIntyre and his family, and has since undergone substantial refurbishment, with brewing brought back to the site.

Shunters Yard

Brewery
Established: 2006
Location: Matangi, Hamilton
Owner and brewer: Peter McKenzie

Located at Woodside Estate in Matangi, Shunters Yard is a small brewery run by Peter McKenzie. As well as his own beers, McKenzie produces beers for Brewaucracy under contract.

Sparks Brewing

Contract brewery
Established: 2013
Location: Auckland
Brewer and owner: Adam Sparks

Adam Sparks established his eponymous brewery with a little help and a push from his wife; a designer, she 'was instrumental in the process of taking all of my jumbled ideas and giving them some identity and direction'. Sparks describes his philosophy as 'follow your heart, brew what inspires and trust your palate'.

Prospector Farmhouse Ale
4.9% ABV

A luscious combination of malt and rich fruity, spicy yeast ester characteristics. Full and rich but fresh on the palate. Sweet but balanced. A very enjoyable and complete beer.

Frontier Extra Stout
6.2% ABV

A luxuriously rich stout, jet-black with intense ferric notes. Clean, long and bitter.

Speight's Brewery

Brewery
Established: 1876
Location: Dunedin
Owner: Lion

The Speight's Brewery was established by James Speight, Charles Greensale and William Dawson in 1876, and went on to win gold medals at the 1880 Melbourne Exhibition. At this time, their flagship beer was renamed Gold Medal Ale.

In 1923, the brewery became part of New Zealand Breweries, which then became Lion Breweries (see Lion). Since 2001, Speight's has been brewed in Auckland as well as Dunedin to keep up with demand. Over the past few years, Speight's has received serious reinvestment from Lion, including a $40 million redevelopment of the Dunedin brewery site.

In 2012, Speight's launched their Triple Hop Pilsner, which has gone on to win numerous awards, including a gold medal at the 2013 International Brewing Awards (IBA) and a silver at the 2014 World Beer Cup (WBC). Both of these competitions award only individual gold, silver and bronze awards, and in 2013 and 2014 Speight's, along with Mac's and Garage Project, were the first Kiwi breweries to win awards at each. (Mac's Sassy Red won gold at the 2013 IBA and Garage Project's Cockswain's Courage Double Barreled Edition won silver at the 2014 WBC).

Triple Hop Pilsner (pale lager)
4% ABV

Although not a Pilsner, that doesn't stop this beer from being damn good. It has light, golden malt and clean bitterness provides freshness.

Mid Ale (light beer)
2.5% ABV

A light-bodied beer with very sweet barley sugar notes. Simple.

Gold Medal Ale (NZ draught)
4% ABV

I'm not 100% sure what category this beer should be in. It is golden with nice malt character but offers very little else.

Distinction Ale (NZ draught)
4% ABV

Vanilla and caramel on the nose, with syrupy sweet malt notes, characterise this ale.

5 Malt Old Dark (porter)
4% ABV

Vanilla, coffee and sweet dark malt shine through in this porter, which I rate as the best of the bunch.

Sprig & Fern

Brewery
Established: 2006
Location: Nelson
Owners: Ken and Tracy Banner
Brewer: Tracy Banner

Sprig & Fern is a brewery and a chain of independently owned pubs based in Nelson and helmed by Tracy Banner, a brewer with over 30 years' experience in the UK and New Zealand. Banner opened her first tavern in 2006, wanting to offer people something different to the 'bland, mainstream beer' on offer. At the time she was working at the Lion-owned Speight's Brewery in Dunedin, the first female brewer to helm the brewery. Having previously managed the Mac's brewery in Nelson, she returned there in 2008 just before it closed. In May 2009, she bought into Tasman Brewing Company and it became Sprig & Fern.

Banner continues to win multiple awards and acclaim for her beers. They are focused, understated and elegant.

Pilsner
5% ABV

A light, refreshing Pilsner with citrus and passion fruit-like hop notes.

Tasman Reserve Lager (strong lager)
6.5% ABV

Sprig & Fern's second biggest-selling beer. This is a full, luscious lager with clean bitterness, lovely golden malt and a hint of sweetness.

Blonde (golden ale)
5% ABV

Made with a blend of wheat and barley malt, this beer is light and creamy with lemony hop top notes.

Fern Lager (pale lager)
4% ABV

A clean, focused lager with lovely golden malt, present bitterness and citrusy fruit notes.

Fern Draught
4% ABV

One of the better examples of this style: lovely rich caramel malt with fine bitterness and a clean, dry finish.

Best Bitter
5% ABV

Rich maltiness with caramel and biscuit notes, firm bitterness, and lemon-drop and herbal hop notes characterise this beer.

Kiwi Pale Ale
5% ABV

A light, focused Kiwi pale with lemon, gooseberry and passionfruit notes.

IPA
5% ABV

An entry-level English ale (not hoppy or boozy enough to be a true IPA), but delicious and drinkable nonetheless. Woodsy and herbal hop notes are overlaid on rich malt. Full and luscious.

Fern Dark (schwarzbier)
4% ABV

A light, quenching black beer with milk chocolate, toasty coffee and a hint of sweet caramel. The finish is refreshing and dry.

Porter
5% ABV

A rich porter with dark malt notes, fruity ale esters and a lovely creamy texture.

Doppelbock
8% ABV

A lovely rich beer that shows how complex lagers can be: layers and layers of malt richness; caramel, vanilla, milk chocolate and dark dried fruit; all balanced by a long, dry finish.

Scotch Ale
6.5% ABV

Rich ruby in colour , Scotch Ale has sweet malt, notes of toffee and a hint of roasted, smoky malt. There are luscious fruity ale esters and just enough hop bitterness to dry the palate. A big beer but one that is understated and refined.

Sprig & Fern brewer Tracy Banner.

Stacpoole's Brewing Co.

Brewery
Established: 2012
Location: Dunedin
Owner and brewer: Bart Acres

In 2012, homebrewer Bart Acres 'heard about a 300L brewing system that was kicking around Dunedin' and jumped at the chance to buy it. With a passion for the locavore (local food) movement and a background in the biological sciences, he is interested in producing analogue beer for a digital age. 'Apart from a digital thermostat,' he says, 'you won't find a single piece of digital equipment [in the brewery]... we develop our recipes on paper, we regulate mash temperature manually, we use a gas-fired kettle.'

Steam Brewing Company

Brewery
Established: 1995
Location: Otahuhu, Auckland

Despite releasing only one or two of their own beers a year, Steam Brewing Company is one of New Zealand's most important breweries. It has eight client breweries (including Epic, which was established by Steam alumni Luke Nicholas) and until recently brewed beer for the Cock & Bull chain of pubs, which was sold to Simon Gault's Nourish Group in 2012 and now stocks Lion products.

Steve Kermode established the Cock & Bull chain with Ben Middlemiss as head brewer ,and they received numerous awards for their beers, most notably Monks Habit. They set up the business because Kermode believed that what was happening in the wine industry (the growth of small, quality-focused wineries and consumers moving away from volume brands) would be echoed in the beer world.

They decommissioned the original East Tamaki brewery in 2004 as production dictated a move to a bigger site: Auckland Breweries in Otahuhu, where they are currently based.

Steamer Basin

Brewery
Established: 2013
Location: Dunedin
Owners: Karen Gazzard and Paul Kelly

Steamer Basin is a new Dunedin set-up brewing beers in small batches. The beer is currently only available at their tasting room and at selected Otago outlets.

Steam Brewing Company.

Stoke Beer/McCashin's Brewery

Brewery
Established: 2009
Location: Nelson
Owner: McCashin family

In 1999, the McCashin family sold their eponymous brand Mac's to conglomerate Lion, also leasing their Nelson-based brewery and cidery. In 2008, Lion moved brewing from Nelson to Auckland (also closing the Mac's brewery on the Wellington waterfront). This also happened to coincide with the expiry of a 10-year restraint of trade on family patriarch Terry McCashin, so, in 2009, he and his son Dean reopened the family brewery and launched Stoke Beer and sister brand Rochdale Cider.

The key to the Stoke ethos is offering their consumers value for money and a stepping stone to craft beer from industrial beers. With that sort of consumer in mind, the focus with the core beers is on the malt profile, 'to provide balance and body,' says Dean McCashin.

2 Stoke (light beer)
2% ABV

One of the more readily available, better light beers on the market. Malty, with some residual sweetness.

Lager (premium lager)
4.5% ABV

A clean, dry, quenching lager. Simple, but it hits all its marks.

Pilsner
4.8% ABV

Zesty, with some aromatic floral notes, this is an entry-level Pilsner (that is, an entry-level example of an approachable style) but very focused ,with spicy hop notes and lovely golden malt.

Gold (golden ale)
4.5% ABV

A malty, clean ale with some herbal hop notes. Simple but very enjoyable.

Amber (NZ draught)
4% ABV

Sweet caramel-coloured malt with a hint of roastiness and a long, dry finish characterise this simple yet very rewarding beer.

IPA
4.8% ABV

More of a pale ale, the Stoke IPA is light-bodied, with lovely subtle aromatics and clean, long bitterness.

Dark (schwarzbier)
4.5% ABV

An excellent black lager with lovely toasty notes, creamy chocolate and a long, dry finish.

Sunshine Brewery

Brewery
Established: 1989
Location: Gisborne

Wanting to save one of New Zealand's historic craft breweries, Martin Jakicevich (brother of Jak and Jo Jakicevich, owners of the Hancock Liquor distributors, the Glengarry retail chain and Hancock Brewing, and shareholders in McCashin's Brewery), alongside a group of other Gisborne-based business owners, purchased Sunshine Brewing in 2013.

The brewery's flagship beer is Gisborne Gold (aka Gizzy Gold), which for a long time has been one of New Zealand's best pale lagers. However, the range has expanded since the takeover, with growing demand led by consistent quality and wider distribution. One of my favourite beers, Gizzy Green (a hat-tip to the illicit horticultural industry for which Gisborne is a base), has been made part of the year-round line-up but renamed, simply, Pilsner. As of mid-2015, the range will be expanding past the first two core beers.

Gisborne Gold (pale lager)
4% ABV

A lovely rich, malty lager. For many years this was one of the few craft beers on the market. Best drunk on the beach in summer.

Gisborne Pilsner
5% ABV

A citrusy, vibrant Pilsner with a hint of sweetness that distracts from the refreshing nature of the beer.

Sweatshop Brew Kitchen

Brewpub
Established: 2014
Location: Auckland CBD
Owner: Barworks Limited (owned by DB and JAG Hospitality)

Located at 1 Sale Street in central Auckland, Sweatshop Brew Kitchen is a new Lion-owned brewpub replacing what was previously called Sale Street.

Tasting tray at the Mussel Inn, Golden Bay.

There Be Dragons Brewing

Contract brewery
Established: 2012
Located: Central Otago
Brewer and owner: Mike Kush

Winemaker Mike Kush flies regularly between Queenstown, Portugal's Douro Valley and Chicago, making wine under his Chasing Harvest label in the first two locations and selling it in the third. As well as wine, he has always had a passion for beer and, since 2012, has teamed up with Wanaka Beerworks' Dave de Vylder to create a Belgian-style red ale that incorporates 10% Pinot Noir fruit and is aged in the same barrels as his wine. He has two beers: Chasing Harvest, a vintage ale, of which there have been 2012 and 2013 releases; and Royal Blood, a blend of vintage beers. He brews only once a year and makes less than 500 bottles of each beer.

Three Boys Brewery

Brewery
Established: 2005
Location: Christchurch
Owners: Ralph Bungard and
Brigid Casey

Returning to New Zealand after working in the UK, biochemist and wine scientist Ralph Bungard and his wife Brigid Casey were disappointed by the quality of beer in New Zealand, so decided to establish Three Boys, building on Bungard's academic training.

Bungard is most inspired by breweries creating 'well-crafted' beers; to him, this means beers that are 'consistently good, well made, beautiful looking and tasting'. These traits flow on to Bungard's brewing philosophy, which he describes as 'quality and consistency with our product and honesty and respect for our customers'. His ultimate goal is to create beers people want to drink again, so that Three Boys becomes its customers' 'go-to' brewery.

These two pillars have meant considerable success for Three Boys: their Oyster Stout is regarded as one of the finest stouts in the country, as well as being the country's most awarded beer. All of their core beers are among the highest regarded examples of the styles, especially their Pils, Wheat and Golden Ale.

While Three Boys do not make any collaboration beers, having several other contract-brewing companies based out of their new Three Boys brewery on Ferry Road ensures that 'there is always a good free-flow of new ideas'.

Pils (Pilsner)
5.5% ABV

Lovely rich, golden malt with spicy aromatics and clean, focused bitterness come together to create this traditional Czech-styled yet Kiwi-accented Pilsner.

Wheat (witbier)
5% ABV

Spicy and aromatic, with clove, cinnamon, a hint of fruity esters and clean citrus; this wheaten beer with a cloudy white head is the classic Kiwi example of a Belgian witbier.

Golden Ale
4.5% ABV

This is my favourite of the Three Boys beers – rich, golden malt, with beautiful lemon and citrus blossom high notes and light, refreshing bitterness. An exercise in understatement and simplicity.

IPA
5.2% ABV

A focused, firm, malty English-style IPA (and a low-ABV one at that), with woodsy, spicy English hop notes and long, refined bitterness.

Best Bitter
3.9% ABV

A very clean, nutty beer with a hint of raspy bitterness at the back of the palate. Not overly complex but very enjoyable.

Porter
5.2% ABV

A very complex beer that has an integrated nose with cocoa and spice notes. The palate is creamy and full, with a hint of iron and a flash of acidity.

Three Mountains Brewery

Brewery
Established: 2013
Location: Whangarei
Owner and brewer: Mike Jenkins

Despite having brewed beers since 2004, commercial brewing at this 140L brewery located in Whangarei began only in 2013. They brew a number of beers that are available locally, including a Pilsner, stouts and several farmhouse and Belgian ales.

Tiamana

Brewery
Established: 2014
Location: Wellington
Owner and brewer: Annika Naschitzki

The daughter of a German brewer, Annika Naschitzki moved to New Zealand in 2010. Working in the world of user-interface research and design, she decided that she no longer wanted to spend five days a week in an office 'year in and out'. Inspired by the vibrant craft beer scene in Wellington and her love of her father's craft, she decided that starting a brewery would give her 'an alternative workplace to an office... ownership and creative control in my own business... and would allow me to explore my heritage in the context of an open and supportive craft [beer] scene'.

She chose the name Tiamana, as it is Maori for both 'German' and 'Germany', and her brewing style draws strongly on her cultural heritage. While her focus is most definitely on 'German-style beers', Naschitzki does not see herself as 'bound by the Reinheitsgebot' but still has strong opinions on 'what is acceptable... and what is cheating'. She admits to not being 'impressed by heavy, hoppy, sticky beers', preferring 'beers with varied, subtle flavours that keep on changing and building sip by sip'.

Naschitzki debuted her low-alcohol 'beer' Malty at the SOBA Winter Ales Festival in 2014 – it is a traditional malztrunk (malt drink) that dates back to the fifteenth century. Fermented to about 0.8% ABV, and then chilled and pasteurised, this beverage is almost like a malt soda and is drunk in Germany after exercise, including by pregnant women and even by children. It can also be blended with beer or served with lemon. When Tiamana is at full production, it will be releasing a traditional dark version as well as a hopped pale version.

Despite being established in 2014, Tiamana had only just moved into its brewery premises at the time of writing. This is in Wellington's Mt Cook suburb and is shared with Wild and Woolly Brewing.

Totara Brewing

Brewery
Established: 2009
Location: Wai-iti Valley, Nelson
Owners: Colin Oldham, Peter Lines,
Ian Parkes and Ross Ford
Brewer: Peter Lines

Totara Brewing is the only hop farm brewery in New Zealand and is co-owned by a group of Nelson hop farmers. The brewery, located on Peter Lines's property, directly across the road from his hop farm, has been squeezed into sheds amongst his grape juice business.

Lines, a brewer, describes the owners as 'farmers, doing a bit of brewing'. Rather than using pelletised hops, the beers utilise whole hops and, where possible, fresh hops. Lines has developed a technique for preserving fresh hops without kilning them. Obviously, the beers showcase these but they do this with the same Kiwi understatement of the third-generation farmer who brews the beers. They are hoppy, yet they are also subtle, layered and extremely drinkable.

The beers, brewed in the classic Kiwi pub styles of lager, draught and dark, are wonderfully aromatic and pretty.

Gold Lager
5% ABV

Long and bright, this lager has a beautiful floral hop aroma and a malt body reminiscent of sun-kissed skin.

Drovers Draught (NZ draught)
4% ABV

This is an amazing example of a style I had virtually written off until I visited Nelson while writing this book. Hopped with Green Bullet (the hop that is used in Steinlager, as well as in many extremely commercial lagers), it is fruity and full, with refreshing bitterness and lightly aromatic hop top notes.

Ninkasi Green (NZ Pilsner)
5% ABV

A green-hopped beer, using a variety called Kahurangi that is exclusive to Totara. The beer itself is amazingly pretty and aromatic, with dank hop notes that burst out of the glass, and has a long and bitter finish.

After Dark (black lager)
5% ABV

Creamy, textured and long, this black lager has warm caramel notes, toasty coffee, long bitterness and lightly aromatic hop notes.

Townshend's

Brewery
Established: 2005
Location: Moutere, Nelson
Owner and brewer: Martin Townshend

Martin Townshend established his eponymous brewery in the Moutere hills west of Nelson in 2005. His impetus was a desire to 'produce English-style cask ales and cider', things he believed were lacking in the beer-rich Nelson region.

Townshend describes his style as 'traditional but striving to be original'. He has built a following both among lovers of British-style beers (he cask-conditions many in his range) but also among craft beer lovers looking for beers with subtlety, complexity and drinkability. Personally, I have only ever been happily surprised by these beers, and every time I drink them I think, 'I should drink these beers more!' Townshend is understated, relaxed and charming. The beers are the same.

In 2013, Townshend came runner-up to Champion Brewery in the Brewers Guild Awards, which 'gave him the confidence to persevere'. That perseverance was rewarded when in 2014 he won Champion Brewer, Champion NZ Manufacturer (an award given to recognise beers brewed under contract, as well as those under the house label), a trophy for his Oldhams Tap Pilsner and 11 other medals. Building on this success, in Feburary 2015 he spent some time in the UK brewing his beers at Everards for the Weatherspoons Real Ale Festival (one of four New Zealand brewers to so do) and is expanding the brewery to cope with demand.

Townshend is a prolific brewer (considering that for the most part he brews all the beer himself): as well as the five beers he has available all year round, he makes 11 seasonal beers and has also brewed a number of collaboration beers. Some of these have been created with members of the hop industry who live in and around the hills to the west of Nelson. His most recent collaboration, The Man at the Back, produced with a number of brewers at Invercargill

Brewery, showcases Canterbury's Gladfield malt. Townshend says that getting a better understanding of the malting process and seeing a barley kernel through malting and brewing was 'very inspiring'.

Black Arrow Pilsner
5% ABV

This beer smells like a hay field, with resinous green hop notes over the top. Long and quite fat for a Pilsner, but still extremely fresh and refreshing, with lovely citrus flower top notes and a long line of very taut bitterness.

Old House ESB
5.3% ABV

Rich and malty, with some earthy, spicy notes and long bitterness, this is a classic example of the style.

Aotearoa Pale Ale
5% ABV

A panoply of vibrant fruity New Zealand hop notes are overlaid against lovely golden malt, pineapple, gooseberry and passion fruit, along with a herbal edge and honeyed notes.

JCIPA
5.5% ABV

A very balanced IPA with generous malt and long, intense bitterness. The hop aromas are understated with sweet, zesty, ripe lemon and juicy passionfruit notes.

Sutton Hoo (American amber ale)
4.7% ABV

Spicy hop notes on the front of the palate combine with caramel notes; there is a real synchronicity between the deep, rich malt and grassy, spicy hop character. The beer is rich, but long and fresh.

TOWNSHEND'S SINCE 20 05
Founded in 2005 by Martin Townshend, this genuine real ale brewery is based in the leafy green heart of the nations hop growing region.
BANDS MAN
HOPPY ALE
WITH OLDSTYLE CHARM
3.7 PERCENT
It's worth making a song & dance about... not that we tend to blow our own trumpet.
Nelson New Zealand

TOWNSHEND'S SINCE 20 05
Founded in 2005 by Martin Townshend, this genuine true cider was produced in the leafy green heart of the nations apple growing region.
SITBEE CIDER
ANNUAL RELEASE
Renowned For DEPTH OF FLAVOUR
Made With APPLES FROM OUR OWN ORCHARDS USING TRADITIONAL CIDER VARIETIES FROM Spain.
Nelson New Zealand

TOWNSHEND'S SINCE 20 05
BLACK ARROW PILSNER
Pilsner Freshness By UK Tongs of Hops.
5.0 PERCENT
Nelson New Zealand

TOWNSHEND'S SINCE 20 05
Founded in 2005 by Martin Townshend, this genuine real ale brewery is based in the leafy green heart of the nations hop growing region.
KINGS LANDING
6.8 PERCENT
SCOTCH ALE
ANNUAL RELEASE
WITH PEATED M·A·L·T
Nelson New Zealand

TOWNSHEND'S SINCE 20 05
Founded in 2005 by Martin Townshend, this genuine real ale brewery is based in the leafy green heart of the nations hop growing region.
HM's BLACK STRAP PORTER
4.5 PERCENT
I AM RICH, DARK & COMPLEX
Nelson New Zealand

100% fresh Riwaka Hopped from Colin Oldham's Hop Garden
OLDHAM'S TAP PILSNER 5.5%
Oldham's Tap named Colin Oldham, a fine fellow and that's where his hop garden is situated. We kindly supplied the 100% fresh Riwaka hops delicately used in this 100% NZ ingredients Pilsner.
This is one third in a series of new FRESH HOPPED BEERS that belong to the Townshend's vs. Liberty collaboration. While your at it, grab the other two to compare if they are still on the shelf.
CHATHAM'S RISE Brewed with 100% NZ ingredients. Chinook & Cascade.
LAST OF THE SUMMER ALE ESB with Swags

BREWERS COLLABORATION SERIES
TOWNSHEND'S
BREWERS COLLABORATION SERIES
DONELAN'S 2XE SESSION ALE
VERY ENGLISH BUT WITH A NZ TWIST
WHO IS DOUG DONELAN? He's the guy you talk to for sage-like advise on the subject of hops. As CEO of NZ Hops he holds the keys to the brewer's hop filled toy box. Doug is one of those guys who has been passionately involved in the brewing racket for decades. As a home brewer, head brewer, then product development with Lion-Nathan , Doug talks beer language with the best of us.
The 2x6 is having a bit of a laugh at a rather ordinary beer that has it's heritage in Mangatainoka. The only thing similar is the colour. A true session ale with premium NZ Gladfield Malt and a healthy heaping of NZ Wi-iti hops. We have brewed this to be very English but with a NZ twist that you won't find in a 24 pack.

TOWNSHEND'S SINCE 20 05
Founded in 2005 by Martin Townshend, this genuine real ale brewery is based in the leafy green heart of the nations hop growing region.
SUTTON HOO
4.7 PERCENT
AMERICAN AMBER ALE
A TREASURE TROVE OF FLAVOURS Waiting To Be DISCOVERED
Nelson New Zealand

Traditional INDIA PALE ALE
AN IPA THAT WILL PUT HAIRS ON YOUR CHEST & HAVE YOU SINGING HALLELUJAH leaving you praying for more.
Nelson New Zealand

BREWERS COLLABORATION SERIES
FRESH HOPPED WITH GREEN BULLET & NELSON SAUVIN
LAST OF THE SUMMER ALE ESB 5.1%
LAST OF THE SUMMER ALE is a repeat of last years brew that is from Liberty Brewing Co. and i made up there and then with what we had kicking around on the day, then scribbled it on the back of a post card!
This beer is essentially an ESB and has a very English Malt base. It uses hops that are the last to be harvested, namely swags of fresh Nelson Sauvin and Green Bullet - bloody delicious!
This is one third in a series of new FRESH HOPPED BEERS that belong to the Townshend's vs. Liberty collaboration. While your at it, grab the other two to compare if they are still on the shelf.
CHATHAM'S RISE Brewed with 100% NZ ingredients. Chinook & Cascade fresh hops.
OLDHAM'S TAP Riwaka Pils. Delicately fresh hopped Pilsner made with 100% NZ ingredients.
Joseph came up with the bulk of the recipes for Chatham's & Oldham's and the LOTSA. He's a great guy and its great to be able to give him a nod too!
LIBERTY BREWING CO

FAT HAND
750ML
RICH AND POWERFUL
A STRONG & WARMING ALE ALLY
HUGE LIKE A GIANT IRON FIST
Standard Drinks
TOWNSHENDS

Tuatara Brewing

Brewery
Established: 2000
Location: Paraparaumu, Kapiti Coast
and Wellington
Brewer: Carl Vasta

Tired of paying for bad beer, Carl Vasta established a brewery in 2000 on family-owned land inland from Waikanae, on the Kapiti Coast. Enlisting the help (and capital) of two Wellington publicans, Sean Murrie of the Malthouse and Fraser McInnes of Bar Bodega (self-proclaimed creator of the first flat white), Tuatara 'gained an early following and began to convert the masses... one beer at a time'. Vasta describes his brewing philosophy as getting 'beautifully made beers to many by making them true to style with a distinctly Kiwi twist'.

As it has grown in popularity, Tuatara has been forced to expand several times. Vasta describes outgrowing the first brewery as 'pretty seminal', also saying that 'there's nothing like signing on for bank debt to make you sit up straight!' As well as expanding the business, Tuatara has also brought in more talent each time it has taken on capital – Vasta says that 'adding guys with business nous has been key to successfully negotiating the difficult second-album phase of our journey'.

In mid-2013, Rangitira Investments bought a 35% stake in Tuatara with Vasta and Murrie. This funded significant expansion for Tuatara, including a new brewery in Paraparaumu and the recently opened Third Eye, a brewpub in Wellington's Te Aro. This has also given Vasta the ability to experiment more; with the brewery at peak capacity producing its core range, there was little scope to produce seasonal and experimental beers. More recently, though, Tuatara has been increasing numbers of one-off and seasonal beers, such as the Tuatara Black series, a three-way collaboration with Mojo Coffee and Whittaker's Chocolate, which resulted in four beers: one each made with coffee, chocolate and 100% toasted malt, and a barrel-aged blend of these beers called Tiramisu Stout.

While Tuatara has always been known for its Belgian ale Ardennes, this has been joined by a true-to-style dubbel and tripel, as well as several highly regarded sour Belgian ales. Building on the success of their two APAs (American and Aotearoa), they have a small but growing portfolio of hoppy 'new age' styles, from the session IPA Iti through to Double Trouble, a double IPA.

Iti (session IPA)
3.3% ABV

It has only recently been introduced to the core range, now that the demand for lower-alcohol beers is growing. It is light-bodied but with more malt definition than is usually present in these beers, and has lovely grassy, citrus aromatics.

Helles Lager
5% ABV

Bone-dry with dusty malt notes and a focused, clean finish, this is a simple but incredibly enjoyable craft lager.

Bavarian Hefe
5% ABV

Aromatic with stereotypical hefe characters of clove, banana and citrus, this full-bodied and creamy beer has a fresh burst of lemony cut on the finish.

Pilsner
5% ABV

This is one of the finest examples of New Zealand-hopped Pilsner around: lovely, light, golden malt with lime blossom, lemon zest and a clean bone of bitterness running through the mid-palate.

Aotearoa Pale Ale
5.8% ABV

Originally brewed when access to US hops became more difficult, this is now a year-round beer, with Tuatara's other APA becoming a seasonal (it, too, is an excellent beer). It has great malt presence for the style, with a hint of biscuit and herbal citrus notes, goose-berry and grapefruit. A persistent bitter finish ties these aromatic notes together.

India Pale Ale
5% ABV

With a firm, malty body, spicy/woodsy hop aroma and persistent bitterness, this is an excellent entry-level IPA with a lot of character.

Porter
5% ABV

Toasty dark malts with notes of espresso, milk chocolate and a hint of grippy oats create a smooth, creamy, complete brown beer.

The Twisted Hop

Brewery
Established: 2003
Location: Christchurch
Owners: Martin and Lisa Bennett, and
Stephen and Claire Hardman

Established in 2003, The Twisted Hop – Real Ale Brewery fast became one of the centres of beer in New Zealand, especially for lovers of real ale. It was located in Poplar Lane, off High Street, which was one of the most exciting parts of Christchurch nightlife.

Sadly, the lane's area was hit hard by the 2011 February earthquakes and the brewpub was forced to close. By April, Stephen and Claire Hardman had already found the site for the new Twisted Hop in Woolston, which opened in October 2012. A brewery (on Parkhouse Road) was cobbled together from salvaged equipment and was operational by late 2011, and in mid-2012 it was upgraded to a 1800L facility.

While the Hardmans work in and on The Twisted Hop in Woolston, Martin and Lisa Bennett have established a new brewpub, The Laboratory, also in Woolston. It will serve The Twisted Hop beers as well as one-off beers brewed on site.

The Twisted Hop beers are among the finest in the country, especially those served from cask.

Sauvin Pilsner
5% ABV

A vibrant, aromatic Pilsner focused around passionfruit and gooseberry-scented Nelson Sauvin. Long, bitter and focused, with a hint of funk.

Pacifickölsh (golden ale)
4.6% ABV

A beautifully balanced golden ale with herbal notes, lemon zest and a long, aromatic finish.

Golding Bitter
3.7% ABV

A very complete beer with round golden malty notes, stonefruit and bitter herbal hop notes, and bitterness that ties the beer together.

Challenger Bitter
5% ABV

Nutty and biscuity malt notes combine with rich fruit ester notes from the English ale yeasts and grapefruit and orange marmalade hop character.

Hopback IPA
5.8% ABV

An English-style IPA with luscious caramel malts and bright, zesty citrus notes. The bitterness is focused, persistent and refreshing.

Twisted Ankle (old ale)
5.9% ABV

A complete, complex dark beer with burnt oat notes, creamy coffee and real weight. A lovely, full beer.

The Twisted Hop.

Two Thumb Brewing Co.

Brewery
Established: 2013
Location: Christchurch
Owners: Brad and Clayton Wallwork
Brewer: Clayton Wallwork

Clayton Wallwork established Two Thumb with his brother Brad and named it for the Two Thumb Range, overlooking Lake Stillwater, the site of the family's bach. The beers are approachable but generous examples of traditional styles.

NZ Pale Ale
5.4% ABV

A lovely soft, extremely aromatic New Zealand pale ale. With a biscuity malt and citrus oil, green pepper and other herbal notes, this beer is long and focused.

Oatmeal Stout
6% ABV

A full-flavoured and creamy stout with burnt coffee and a hint of bitter cocoa. Dry in style.

Valkyrie Brewing Co.

Contract brewery
Established: 2011
Location: Christchurch
Owner and brewer: Wendy Roigard

Wendy Roigard established Valkyrie after working in a number of logistics roles within the beer industry. She wanted a 'creative outlet' and to see her labour translate into a 'physical, tangible' product.

To Roigard, the Valkyrie beers are a combination of her passion for creativity and quality, but she admits to being relaxed in her brewing style, 'preferring to estimate rather than calculate… passionately tweaking and changing things, throwing in extra ingredients and being as creative as [she] can while still maintaining quality'.

Brynhild (golden ale)
5% ABV

An excellent golden ale with plush malt notes, a caramel note, and lemon, tropical fruit and subtle floral notes.

Frigg (Vienna lager)
5% ABV

Billed as a red Pilsner, this is a rich, malty lager with bitter, spicy hops and clean, focused bitterness.

Freyja (California common)
6.6% ABV

Resiny US hops are overlaid on a nutty caramel and a hint of funk. There is some sweetness and astringency, which is true to style, and aggressive effervescence.

Isis Rising (wheat)
5.5% ABV

This wheat beer has a very aromatic nose, evocative of the ingredients: oats, honey and chamomile. These flavours follow onto the palate and really pop with added baking spice. The beer's aromatics fill your mouth.

Valley Brewing and Brewery Café

Brewpub
Established: 2009
Location: Geraldine
Owners: Philip and
Raewyn Olde-Olthof

Located in Geraldine, South Canterbury, Valley Brewing is a small brewpub and café run by brewer Philip Olde-Olthof and his wife, hospitality manager Raewyn.

Vulcan Brewers

Contract brewer
Established: 2014
Location: Christchurch
Brewer and owner: Sam Miller

After seeing how difficult it can be to 'go pro' and move from homebrewing to launching a commercial beer, Sam Miller set up Vulcan Brewers to enable 'skilled homebrewers to get a commercial batch out there without having to set up all the business guff'. Currently, he is 'riding solo', getting his own beers established in the market. He describes his ideal beer as 'balance, body, romance, lust, all in a pint glass' and currently produces one year-round beer: Vulcan, a smoked bitter.

Waiheke Island Brewery

Brewery
Established: 1997
Location: Waiheke Island
Owners: Simon and Keryn Matthews
Brewer: Alan Knight

The current owners of Waiheke Island Brewery are Simon and Keryn Matthews, who also own tour and restaurant business Wild on Waiheke. They bought the brewery in 2014 and over this time have invested in it heavily. There has been a huge jump in quality in these beers recently.

Alan Knight rejoined the brewery in 2007, having worked there from its establishment in 1997 until 2000.

They have four core beers (as well as a ginger beer and cider) and a rotating seasonal beer called Tap 7. The beers are brewed using speciality German malt and New Zealand hops. Knight's aim is to create sessionable beers to complement the climate of Waiheke Island.

Wharf Road Wheat (weissbier)
4.5% ABV

Banana, wheat and lemon on the nose follow through onto the palate, while the body is creamy with a hint of zest. A very understated but complete beer.

Baroona Original Pale Ale
4.7% ABV

A clean, focused, easy-drinking pale ale with wheaten notes and citrus blossom.

Matiatia Malt Beer (American strong ale)
7.2% ABV

A big, sweet ale with layers of fruity malt notes, yeast esters and a bright bitter finish. 'Malt beer' sums this up well. Very enjoyable, especially with smoky foods.

Onetangi Dark Ale (porter)
4.3% ABV

Toasty malt gives this beer a nice grip and some tartness on the palate. Black – almost burnt – malt notes combine with creamy texture and just a hint of sweetness.

Wanaka Beerworks

Brewery
Established: 1998
Location: Wanaka
Owners: Ruenell and Mike Wing, and
Scott Beattie

Ruenell and Mike Wing, and Scott Beattie, owners of Jabberwocky Brewery, purchased Wanaka Beerworks in mid-2014 from Dave and Susan De Vylder. Originally established by expat Californian brewer Dave Gilles, Wanaka Beerworks produces classic examples of traditional Kiwi beer styles (in contrast to Jabberwocky's new-world styles).

Brewski (Pilsner)
5% ABV

A luscious beer with warming golden nectarine hop notes and focused bitterness.

Cardrona Gold (Vienna lager)
5% ABV

With biscuity malt, soft floral aromatics and clean bitterness, this is a refreshing beer.

Treble Cone (wheat IPA)
6.5% ABV

A wheat IPA with orange sherbet on the nose. It is full and creamy on the palate with firm bitterness and tangy orange hop notes.

Black Peak Coffee Stout
6% ABV

Intensely sweet but balanced by coffee bitterness, this stout pours thick and black.

Golding's Free Dive, Wellington.

Wassail Brauhaus

Brewpub
Established: 2004
Location: Egmont Village
Brewer: George Busby

Although it is not technically a brewpub, that is the best description of Wassail: a bed and breakfast that happens to produce beer. They make a variety of English-style beers that are available only to those staying at the B&B.

West Coast Brewery

Brewery
Established: 1993
Location: Westport
Owner: Coastwest Holdings
Brewer: Marc Gardiner

Now owned by Coastwest Holdings, a group of 18 investors, West Coast Brewery started its life as Miners Brewery in 1993. It became the West Coast Brewery in the mid-2000s and was directed by Queenslander Paddy Sweeney, who enlisted 371 investors to help the business grow. In 2013, the company went into liquidation and was bought by the recently formed Coastwest Holdings (originally with Sweeney as a director, and comprised largely of previous brewery shareholders), with the intention of making the brewery succeed.

Green Fern Organic Lager
5% ABV

A light-bodied, malty lager with a hint of hop funk and a long, smooth finish.

West Coast Pale Ale
5% ABV

A full, smoky malty body with bright grassy hop aroma. On the sweet side for the style, it is enjoyable and rich.

Denniston Draught
4% ABV

Rich and malty with a hint of residual sweetness, this beer has a lovely creamy texture and is very quenching.

Brewing Miners Black (porter)
4% ABV

A light, refreshing black lager with chocolate and liquorice notes and an intense charcoal-like finish.

Wigram Brewery

Brewery
Established: 2002
Location: Wigram, Christchurch
Founder: Paul McGurk
Brewer: Paul Cooper

Named after the suburb in which it is located, Wigram is a 600L brewery whose branding is inspired by the local air force museum – the suburb used to also be home to an RNZAF base.

The brewery's first beers were a lager, a New Zealand draught and a dark beer. Since 2005, the beers have won numerous awards but have continued to fly under the craft beer radar outside of their native Christchurch.

Investors came on board in 2007 and owner Paul McGurk enlisted the help of Paul 'Coops' Cooper, who he describes as 'the godfather of brewing in New Zealand'. Since then, the range has expanded (as of early 2015, some underperforming beers have got the boot so they can be replaced with new ones). The beers have won medals at New Zealand and international beer competitions every year since, including 10 trophy or best-in-class awards, two at the 2014 Brewers Guild Awards (for the Spruce Beer and Tornado Strong Ale).

Propeller Lager
5% ABV

A simple, focused, easy-drinking lager with refreshing bitterness.

Bavarian Pilsner
5% ABV

In the spicy, searingly bitter German style, with a light body and a hint of funk.

Harvard Honey Ale
6% ABV

A big, rich golden ale with warm malt notes, waxy honey, and beech and thyme high notes. Probably the most complex, enjoyable honey beer out of New Zealand.

Mustang Pale Ale
4% ABV

A lovely creamy, light pale ale with woodsy hop notes and long, refined bitterness.

Spruce Beer (herb ale)
5% ABV

Brewed with manuka and rimu tips, this is a rich, copper ale with a lovely herbal edge but also depth and complexity.

Kortegast (sparkling ale)
5% ABV

Brewed with wild hops harvested on New Zealand's West Coast, this beer is richly malted with dank green herbal notes and cutty, grassy top notes.

Vienna Lager
5% ABV

A copper lager with caramel, biscuit and a hint of toasty malt. It has lovely rich sweetness without being cloying and fine bitterness on the finish.

Dakota Dark (porter)
5% ABV

A light-bodied porter with a lovely, fruity English ale yeast note and burnt coffee.

Munchner Dunkel
5% ABV

An excellent example of the style, with roast coffee, burnt caramel and chicory. Full, but very fresh and lithe on the finish.

Bristol Best Bitter
4.5% ABV

A medium-weight, nutty brown ale with woodsy lemongrass and clean bitterness.

Tornado Strong Ale (IPA)
6.6% ABV

A big, bold, malty ale with luscious stone fruit, citrus zest and earthy, woodsy notes. A very complete beer, and big without being heavy.

Czar Imperial Stout
8.5% ABV

Undoubtedly the highlight of what is a very sound range, made in the very British (rather than hoppy American) style, with dark porty fruit and savoury elements. Rich and round.

Wild and Woolly Brewing

Brewery
Established: 2014
Location: Wellington
Owner and brewer: Llew Bardecki

Wild and Woolly is a new Wellington-based brewery, established by the 'wild and woolly' Llew Bardecki – his first beer, Basilisk, was released at X-Ale (Hashigo Zake's experimental beer festival) in early 2014. He has since gone on to create a physical brewery (shared with Tiamana's Annika Naschitzki) and released a range of beers in early 2015.

Basilisk was a Berliner weisse flavoured with Thai basil, lemon zest and kaffir lime, and it is with a similar spirit of fun and experimentation that Bardecki has created further beers. In fact, one of the beers at his release was Silver Cat Angry Gummy Bear White Stout, a beer invented a couple of months prior by Wellington beer professional Dylan Jauslin to make fun of top-20-beers-to-drink-before-you-die lists with unattainable beers – after all, what is more unattainable than a beer that does not exist? Until it did.

The beers may seem a bit crazy, but they are flavourful, enjoyable and complex.

Weezledog Brewing

Contract brewery
Established: 2014
Location: Auckland
Owner and brewer: Mark Jackman

Going against the current trend of more sessionable beers with lower ABVs is Mark Jackman of Weezledog. He believes 'sessionability is overrated', preferring to brew 'big, flavourful beers that provide an experience in every bottle'.

Hopster (NZ IPA)
6.7% ABV

A spicy, resinous nose combines with grassy, gooseberry notes. This IPA is very sweet and full for the style, with some soft bitterness but aggressive hop notes, almost to the point of astringency.

Dickle Doi (imperial red ale)
7% ABV

Big, rich caramel malt notes combine with juicy orange notes. Firm bitterness ties the beer together. It lacks depth, which is needed for a beer this big.

Brewing equipment at Zeelandt Brewery, Napier.

Yeastie Boys

Contract brewery
Established: 2008
Location: wherever Sam and Stu are
– Wellington, Auckland and London;
beers brewed in Invercargill and
Scotland
Directors and founders: Stu McKinlay
and Sam Possenneskie

The Yeastie Boys (Stu McKinlay and Sam Possenneskie) is among New Zealand's most creative breweries and, like 8 Wired, has a truly international audience – so much so that in February 2015 it launched an equity crowd-funding campaign and managed to raise a hair over half a million dollars within half an hour to fund expansion in the UK market. This will be driven by brewing in market rather than shipping their beers from New Zealand.

Their range is divisive, with beers like Gunnamatta ('hopped' with an extremely aromatic Earl Grey tea) and Rex Attitude (brewed with 100% peat malt – something even distillers of the peatiest whisky rarely do... don't even get me started on Xerrex, the imperial version of this beer) polarising the beer world. Love them or loathe them, it is hard to criticise their quality and precision.Yeastie Boys have also been active collaborators, brewing with numerous New Zealand, Australian (where they have an incredibly engaged market) and international breweries. These projects have included the Spoonbender Series, which was brewed with candi sugar made from botrytised Viognier grapes from Australian *enfant terrible* craft winery Some Young Punks. Of these beers, the porter, The Last Dictator, was the most successful. In 2014, they also travelled to Adnams in Suffolk, UK, to brew a version of Gunnamatta for the JD Wetherspoons Real Ale Festival. While I'm not a fan of the New Zealand version, this beer (tasted out of a cask imported for a function at the British High Commission) was undoubtedly my beer of 2014 – brewed with

a less aromatic English tea, it had lovely tea tannins and soft orangy aromatics.

As well as their core beers, Yeastie Boys produce regular seasonals: His Majesty and Her Majesty, and a remix of Pot Kettle Black, their hugely successful hoppy porter. These change every year, but the beers are always big, rich and often extremely cellarable.

Minimatta (session IPA)
4% ABV

A stripped-back version of Gunnamatta, with lovely rich malt notes, some very subtle bergamot, tea tannins and a hint of complementary citrusy hops. A beautiful little beer.

White Noise (wheat ale)
4.4% ABV

A creamy, wheaten ale brewed with chamomile. It has lovely, smoky honeyed notes and a herbal edge.

Gunnamatta (tea-leaf IPA)
6.5% ABV

Bursting with intense bergamot Earl Grey tea notes, this IPA is extremely floral and aromatic. It has firm malt and is complemented by grapefruit and zesty orange hop notes. This beer is totally over the top but remains balanced, focused and complete. I personally don't like this beer but I cannot criticise its exceptional quality.

Stairdancer (Pacific ale)
4.4% ABV

A vibrantly fruity wheaten pale ale packed full of tropical fruit. Very integrated and drinkable.

Digital IPA
5.7% ABV

Recently retooled from a 7% IPA, this beer is a light-bodied IPA bursting with New Zealand hop character. Gooseberry, lemon blossom, aromatic Asian herbs and grapefruit all jump out of the glass.

Divine Hammer (amber ale)
6.2% ABV

A peachy, nutty, amber ale with oxidised caramel notes, a hint of spicy rye malt and vibrant mandarin, and long, firm bitterness.

Pot Kettle Black (hoppy porter)
6% ABV

A generous, malty dark porter with mocha notes, orange marmalade and resinous, herbal pine notes. Fuller and richer than a black IPA, it is described by Yeastie Boys as a South Pacific Porter.

Rex Attitude (peat-smoked golden ale)
7% ABV

A golden ale bursting with peat smoke, saline saltiness and a sweaty note. I find this beer to be a monolith of peat, although more developed palates tell me there is depth and complexity to be found. It's too much for me, but if you are a fan of Islay malts you will love it.

Stu McKinlay and Sam Possenneskie at the Yeastie Boys crowd-funding equity event.

Zeelandt Brewery

Brewery
Established: 2012
Location: Eskdale, Napier
Owner and brewer: Chris Barber

One of the first true craft breweries to establish in Hawke's Bay, Zeelandt was established by Scotland-trained Chris Barber on his family vineyard in Eskdale (his brother tends the vines and makes some outstanding wine under the Petane Station label). The beers are malt-driven, balanced and sessionable, and have quickly converted local drinkers. Their seasonal and pilot batch beers are exceptional examples of old-world and new-world styles. Expect understatement, refinement and drinkability rather than huge hop-forward beers.

Helles (lager)
5% ABV

A simple but beautifully balanced and drinkable German-style lager with generous, golden malt and clean bitterness.

Pale Ale
5% ABV

With biscuity malt and zesty citrus, this is an integrated, easy-drinking pale ale. Subtle, linear bitterness provides focus and urges another sip (or glass).

New Zealand beer destinations

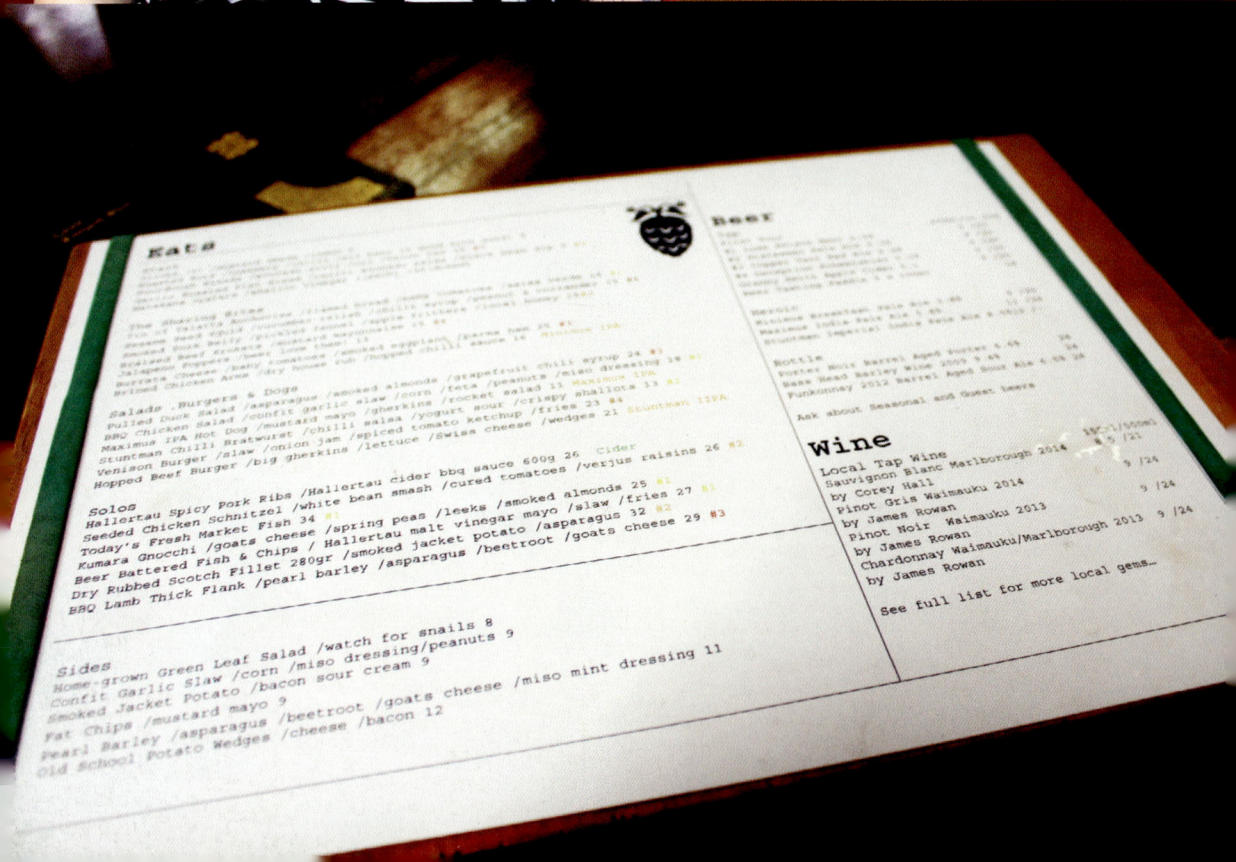

Where to find craft beer

The following guide features 160-plus specialist beer bars, retailers, brewpubs, tasting rooms and restaurants that all have serious beer lists.

There are dedicated listings for the main centres of beer tourism – Auckland, Wellington, Nelson–Tasman and Christchurch. Likewise, there are guides for the North and South islands, broken down by region. Don't overlook some of the smaller centres – there are little towns like Oamaru and regional centres like Hawke's Bay and the Waikato that have flourishing local beer scenes.

Regardless of whether you are travelling specifically to visit and explore beer and breweries, or are using this guide to find spots to visit on holiday or otherwise, please enjoy and support these excellent businesses. The more that we as beer lovers support these businesses, the more likely breweries of all sizes will flourish.

OPPOSITE, CLOCKWISE FROM TOP LEFT Ava Wilson from Beer Baroness, Christchurch; bartender at Twisted Hop Brewery, Christchurch; menu at Hallertau, West Auckland. *BELOW:* Hop Federation Brewery, Riwaka.

New Zealand beer destinations

Auckland

If you have picked up this guide after landing in New Zealand, chances are you are in Auckland. This is the biggest city in New Zealand and has a beer scene that has recently begun to thrive. With breweries, brewpubs (both old and new), and some amazing retailers and excellent restaurants with amazing beer lists, there is something for everyone in almost every corner of the city. In addition to the establishments listed below, excellent craft beer is also available at the many Glengarry, Liquorland and Super Liquor stores, as well as New World supermarkets.

Andrew Andrew
andrewandrew.co.nz
201 Quay Street, Viaduct Harbour
From 4 p.m., 7 days
A very 'cool' craft beer bar – six taps, dark wood and velvet.

Blanc
blanc.kiwi.nz
130 Lincoln Road, Henderson
From 9 a.m. weekdays
From 10 a.m. weekends
An excellent off-licence in West Auckland, with an interesting range of bottled beer and half a dozen taps; also hosts annual beer festivals.

Brew on Quay
brewonquay.co.nz
102 Quay Street, Auckland CBD
From 11 a.m., 7 days
Nestled in a beautiful red-brick building on Auckland's waterfront, Brew on Quay is one of Auckland's oldest craft beer pubs. There is an excellent selection of beer on tap, and it's the kind of pub where you can sidle up to the bar and chat to regulars.

Brothers Beer
brothersbeer.co.nz
City Works Depot, Shed 3D, corner of Wellesley and Nelson streets
From midday, 7 days
Brothers Beer is the epicentre of beer in Auckland. Multiple breweries brew out of the site and it has an amazing selection of tap and bottled beer that you can drink in or take out. They also make delicious pizzas. A great place to while the day away in the sun! Brothers Beer is opening another branch, Brothers Brewing, in Mt Eden in mid-2015.

Coco's Cantina
cocoscantina.co.nz
376 Karangahape Road, Auckland CBD
Dinner from 5 p.m., Tuesday to Saturday
Rustic Italian food with Mediterranean influences and a well-formed beer list. It's loud, busy and fun.

Deep Creek Brewing Co pubs
dcbrewing.co.nz

Cove Bites and Brews
149 Oceanview Road, Oneroa, Waiheke Island
From 11 a.m., 7 days

Deep Creek Brews and Eats Browns Bay
111 Clyde Road, Browns Bay
From 11 a.m., 7 days
This is the original Deep Creek brewpub, which still sports the original brewkit that is now used for seasonals and special beers.

Coast Bites and Brews
342 Hibiscus Coast Highway, Orewa
From 11 a.m., 7 days

One of the bastions of craft beer on the North Shore, with pubs serving great food in Browns Bay, Orewa and on Waiheke Island. Like the beers, the food has a Western/Texicana feel. The ribs are a standout.

Depot
eatatdepot.co.nz
86 Federal Street, Auckland CBD
From 7 a.m., 7 days
Depot is Al Brown's flagship restaurant. Inspired by the informal New Zealand bach, this is the epitome of casual Kiwi cuisine. And they have a great beer list.

Galbraith's Alehouse
alehouse.co.nz
2 Mt Eden Road, Grafton
From midday, 7 days

Galbraith's is a must-not-miss for beer lovers visiting Auckland, with a range of cask-conditioned beers available only at the pub, all of which are exceptional (some of the most exciting are the Great Brewers Series), and an outstanding kitchen putting out classy takes on traditional pub food.

Golden Dawn
goldendawn.co.nz
Corner of Ponsonby and Richmond roads, Ponsonby
From 4 p.m., Tuesday to Thursday
From 3 p.m., Friday to Sunday

I've heard Golden Dawn described many times as 'very Ponsonby'... that is, too school for cool. The fact is they have a full selection of Hallertau beer on tap and a great range of bottles in the fridge. If your companion is a wine lover, come here – you can drink tasty beer while they geek out, and you both eat simple, yet inventive, food.

Hallertau Brewbar and Restaurant
hallertau.co.nz
1171 Coatesville Riverhead Highway,
West Auckland
From 11 a.m., 7 days

One of my personal favourites in Auckland. Only 20 minutes from the heart of the city, Hallertau is an oasis with a stunning menu, great beer and terrific service.

Hopscotch
hopscotch.co.nz
2/2 Shaddock Street, Eden Terrace
From midday, Tuesday to Saturday

With 30 taps and a small but perfectly formed range of bottled beer, Hopscotch is one of Auckland's best specialist beer retailers.

The Lumsden Free House
thelumsden.co.nz
444–448 Kyber Pass Road, Newmarket
From 11.30 a.m., 7 days

With 15 taps and excellent food, The Lumsden Free House is an excellent pub that also holds regular craft beer tastings and events.

Masu
masu.co.nz
90 Federal Street, Auckland CBD
Lunch from midday, 7 days
Dinner from 5.30 p.m., 7 days

Masu is high-end Japanese dining at its finest. The Haru Orchard Ale is a collaboration brew between Hallertau in West Auckland and Baird Beer in Japan, and the restaurant has an excellent selection of Japanese craft beer. It's also a great place to take wine lovers to geek out.

16 Tun
16tun.co.nz
10–26 Jellicoe Street, Wynyard Quarter
From 11.30 a.m., 7 days

One of Auckland's newest and coolest beer bars. It has 19 taps, an excellent bottle selection and a food menu designed to complement whichever beer you choose to imbibe.

Skysport Grill
skysportgrill.tv
95–99 Customs Street West, Viaduct Harbour
From 11.30 a.m., 7 days

A sports bar with great beer – what more can you ask for? The 25 TVs are eclipsed only by the 40 beers (mostly craft) on tap. The food, provided by next door's Foodstore, is classy pub fare.

Sweat Shop Brew Bar
sweatshopbrew.co.nz
7 Sale Street, Freemans Bay
From 11.30 a.m., 7 days

Sweat Shop is located just down the hill from the Sky Tower. In addition to beers brewed on site, they specialise in traditional barbecued food.

The Thirsty Dog
thirstydog.co.nz
469 Karangahape Road, Auckland CBD
From 10 a.m., Monday to Saturday
From 2 p.m., Sunday

An old-fashioned pub serving a small selection of craft beers.

Vultures' Lane
vultureslane.co.nz
10 Vulcan Lane, Auckland CBD
From 11 a.m., 7 days

With 19 taps and a huge selection of bottled beer, Vultures' Lane is a lively craft beer bar with clever bar food and a great vibe.

Map legend

$ beer retailer

craft beer bar

brewery

restaurant

brewpub

tasting room

Beer destinations in Auckland central

See map opposite for places you can visit for beer in Auckland central.

1. 16 Tun
2. Andrew Andrew
3. Skysport Grill
4. Brew on Quay
5. The Thirsty Dog
6. Vultures' Lane
7. The Lumsden Free House
8. Depot
9. Masu
10. Coco's Cantina
11. Galbraith's Alehouse
12. Sweat Shop Brew Bar
13. Hopscotch

Keith Galbraith at Galbraith's Alehouse, Auckland.

AUCKLAND CENTRAL

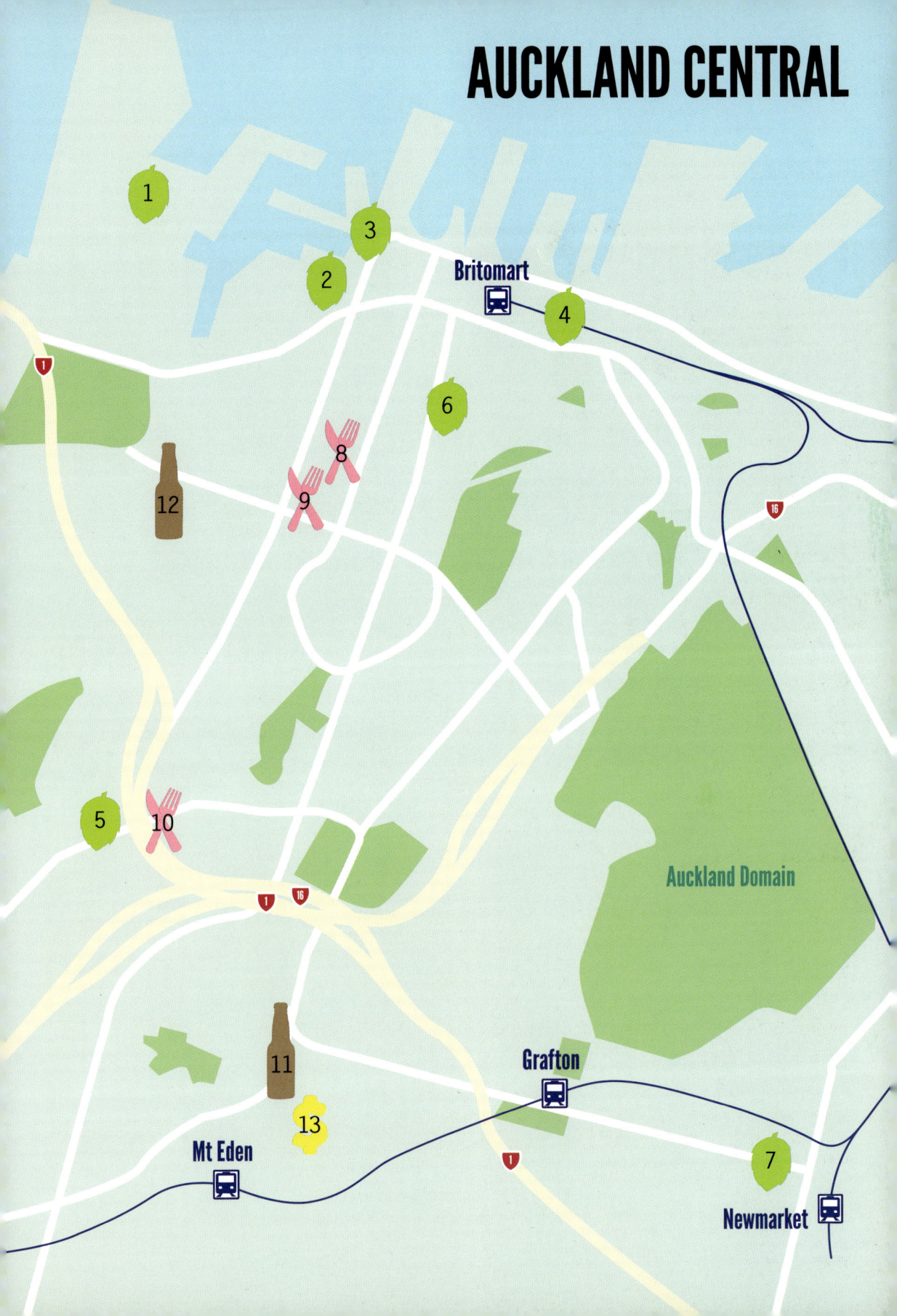

1

3

2

Britomart

4

6

8

9

12

5

10

Auckland Domain

11

13

Grafton

Mt Eden

7

Newmarket

Wellington

Wellington has one of New Zealand's most developed beer cultures and it is hard to go into even the most commercial pub or restaurant without finding at least a couple of craft beer options. It boasts a number of breweries within walking distance of each other and some excellent craft beer bars, each with their own specialities. Lovers of beer and food will always find something to suit as there are numerous restaurants – from informal to white tablecloth – that offer exceptional ranges of craft beer.

The region also includes Lower and Upper Hutt, Kapiti and the Wairarapa, all of which host a number of excellent breweries. As well as those listed here, there are several Brew'd pubs in the suburbs, which have excellent food and a good selection of craft beer. And in addition to the speciality retailers, excellent craft beers are available from most Liquorland and Super Liquor stores, as well as all New World supermarkets.

Craft Beer Capital (craft beer capital.com) is a wonderful resource for locating bars and finding out what's on tap and where.

Basque
basque.co.nz
8 Courtney Place, Te Aro
From 3 p.m., Sunday to Thursday
From midday, Friday and Saturday

A Spanish-themed bar with an excellent offering of New Zealand and international craft beers.

Baylands Brewery and Brewing Supplies
baylandsbrewery.com
22 Victoria Street, Petone
Midday – 6 p.m., Tuesday to Thursday
Midday – 7 p.m., Friday
10 a.m. – 6 p.m., Saturday
11 a.m. – 4 p.m., Sunday

Black Dog Brewery
blackdogbrewery.co.nz
17–19 Blair Street, Te Aro
From 2 p.m., Tuesday to Saturday

An excellent brewpub off Courtney Place, with especially enjoyable seasonals.

The Butcher and Brewer
thebutcherandbrewer.co.nz
175 Jackson Street, Petone
From 11 a.m. weekdays
From 10 a.m. weekends

Newly refurbished, The Butcher and Brewer is an excellent brewpub with meat-focused fare: think steaks, ribs, burgers and barbecues.

Centre City Wines & Spirits
centrecity.co.nz
2–4 Waring Taylor Street, Wellington CBD
9 a.m. – 7 p.m., Monday; 9 a.m. – 7.30 p.m., Tuesday to Thursday; 9 a.m. – 8 p.m., Friday
11.30 a.m. – 6.30 p.m., Saturday

One of the few excellent craft beer retailers in the middle of the CBD, Centre City offers a range of bottled beers and pre-filled riggers.

Fork & Brewer
forkandbrewer.co.nz
14 Bond Street, Te Aro
From 11.30 a.m., Monday to Saturday

The Fork & Brewer offers 26 taps pouring beer brewed both in the on-site brewery and by other New Zealand and international craft breweries, off-licence sales and a comprehensive menu featuring dishes matched to the house-brewed beers.

Garage Project Cellar Door
garageproject.co.nz
66 Aro Street, Aro Valley
Midday – 6 p.m., Monday
Midday – 8 p.m., Tuesday to Thursday
10 a.m. – 9 p.m., Friday and Saturday
10 a.m. – 7 p.m., Sunday

Golding's Free Dive
goldingsfreedive.co.nz
15 Leeds Street, Te Aro
From midday, 7 days

Taking inspiration from North America and Europe, Golding's Free Dive strives to be a neighbourhood bar.

Think Cheers, only with better beer. Food wise, they offer sandwiches and pizzas from Pizza Pomodoro, located just across the lane from the bar. They also offer one of Wellington's only outside non-smoking areas.

Grill Meats Beer
grillmeatsbeer.co.nz
227 Cuba Street, Te Aro
From midday, Tuesday to Sunday

Grill Meats Beer is the brainchild of Steve Logan and Shaun Clouston, the two principal partners of Logan Brown. They offer a range of beer-friendly cuisine such as burgers, steaks and ribs (the banh mi is amazing) cooked to order in an open kitchen and matched to a well-selected, rotating range of craft beer.

Hashigo Zake
hashigozake.co.nz
25 Taranaki Street, Te Aro
From midday, 7 days

Hashigo Zake offers nine regularly changing taps and two on hand-pull, as well as a plethora of bottled beers. With a motto of 'No crap on tap' and specialising in imports (the company owns its own beer importer and distributor, Beer Without Borders), but also featuring the best beers of New Zealand, especially hard-to-find and seasonal beers, Hashigo Zake is a must-visit for beer lovers spending time in Wellington.

Hillside Kitchen & Cellar
www.hillsidekitchen.co.nz
241 Tinakori Road, Thorndon
7 a.m. – 4 p.m. & from 4.30 p.m. Tuesday to Friday
8 a.m. – 4 p.m. Saturday

A little bit of shameless self-promotion here – this is my baby. We serve three- and four-course menus matched to an eclectic selection of craft beer (or wine).

The Hop Garden
thehopgarden.co.nz
13 Pirie Street, Mt Victoria
From 3 p.m., Monday and Tuesday
From 11.30 a.m., Wednesday to Friday
From 10.30 a.m., Saturday and Sunday

Kereru Brewing Brewery
kererubrewing.co.nz
415A Maidstone Terrace, Upper Hutt
10 a.m. – 5 p.m., 7 days

Little Beer Quarter
littlebeerquarter.co.nz
6 Edward Street, Te Aro
From 3.30 p.m., Monday
From midday, Tuesday to Saturday
From 3 p.m., Sunday

With 14 beers on tap, two on hand-pull and over 100 bottle options, Little Beer Quarter also offers a comprehensive menu of beer-friendly dishes, including pizza, tasting plates and a full dinner menu.

Logan Brown
loganbrown.co.nz
912 Cuba Street, Corner of Cuba and Vivian streets, Te Aro
Dinner from 5.30 p.m., Tuesday to Saturday
Lunch midday – 2 p.m.,
Friday and Saturday

Logan Brown is one of Wellington's finest formal restaurants, and alongside a formidable wine list they offer a discerning selection of craft beer. They also offer an exceptionally priced bistro menu at lunchtime and in the early evenings.

Long Beach

longbeach.net.nz
40 Tutere Street, Waikanae Beach
From 9 a.m. weekdays
From 8.30 a.m. weekends

Long Beach is a café and pub offering an excellent selection of craft beer. Its menu includes everything from simple breakfasts through to sophisticated evening dining.

The Malthouse

themalthouse.co.nz
48 Courtenay Place, Te Aro
From 3 p.m., Monday and Tuesday
From midday, Wednesday to Sunday

The Malthouse is the original Wellington craft beer bar, now over 21 years old, offering 26 beers on tap and two on hand-pull, alongside a huge list of bottled beers.

Martinborough Brewery Tasting Room

martinboroughbeer.com
8 Ohio Street, Martinborough
11 a.m. – 4 p.m., Sunday and Monday
11 a.m. – 7 p.m., Thursday to Saturday

Moore Wilson's Wine, Beer and Spirits

moorewilsons.co.nz
93 Tory Street, Te Aro
8 a.m. – 7 p.m. weekdays
8 a.m. – 6 p.m., Saturday
9 a.m. – 5 p.m., Sunday

Servicing much of the Wellington trade, and now with an online outlet, Moore Wilson's is a cash and carry that has a significant offering of local and imported craft beer. The branches in Porirua and Masterton also offer a wide range of bottled craft beer.

New World Thorndon

41 Murphy Street, Thorndon
7 a.m. – 11 p.m., 7 days

With over 600 bottled beer options, New World Thorndon offers the largest selection of retail craft beer in New Zealand.

Ortega Fish Shack

ortega.co.nz
16 Majoribank Street, Mt Victoria
From 5.30 p.m., Tuesday to Saturday

Within this 'Shack' lies one of Wellington's best restaurants focused, but not limited to, the best seasonal seafood available. Run by chef patron Mark Limacher, Ortega offers 60 different bottled beer options from New Zealand's and the world's best breweries.

ParrotDog Brewery

parrotdog.co.nz
29 Vivian Street, Te Aro
From 10 a.m. weekdays
From midday, Saturday

Queen of Jackson

queenofjackson.co.nz
181 Jackson Street, Petone
From midday, Wednesday to Friday
From 11 a.m., Saturday and Sunday

A gastro-pub with a good range of beers on tap and clever, focused, beer-friendly food.

Regent 58 Ale House

1A Stubbs Lane, Carterton
2 p.m. – 9 p.m., Thursday to Saturday
Open Sundays in summer

Regional Wines & Spirits

regionalwines.co.nz
15 Ellice Street, Mt Victoria
9 a.m. – 7.30 p.m., Monday and Tuesday
9 a.m. – 9 p.m., Wednesday to Saturday

Regional Wines & Spirits offers 10 fill-your-own taps and countless bottle options, including an excellent selection of Belgian, American, British and other imported craft beers.

Rogue & Vagabond

rogueandvagabond.co.nz
18 Garett Street, Te Aro
From 11 a.m., 7 days

Located in Glover Park, Rogue & Vagabond has 16 craft beers on tap and specialises in pizza and burgers. It also hosts regular live music gigs.

Sprig & Fern Taverns

sprigandfern.co.nz

342 Tinakori Road, Thorndon
From 4 p.m., Monday
From 2 p.m., Tuesday to Thursday
From midday, Friday to Sunday

146 Jackson Street, Petone
From 2 p.m., Monday and Tuesday
From midday, Wednesday to Sunday

With locations in Thorndon and Petone, the Sprig & Fern offers a wide selection of Nelson-brewed Sprig & Fern beers. The pubs are warm, inviting and family-friendly.

Taylors on Jackson

taylorsonjackson.co.nz
282 Jackson Street, Petone
Dinner from 5 p.m., Tuesday to Saturday

The eponymous bistro of Wellington culinary identity Glen Taylor offers an excellent selection of craft beer that is taken just as seriously as the wine list.

Tuatara Brewery

tuatarabrewing.co.nz

Brewery Tasting Room
7 Sheffield Street, Paraparaumu
From 3 p.m., Thursday
From midday, Friday to Sunday
Off-licence sales from midday,
Wednesday to Sunday

A cellar-door experience at the Tuatara brewery in Paraparaumu on the Kapiti Coast, offers drinks, bar snacks and pizza.

The Third Eye
30 Arthur Street, Te Aro
From midday, 7 days

Just of Cuba Street, Tuatara's 'temple of taste' has a small but beautiful copper brewkit, a good selection of Tuatara beers and a couple of guest taps, and simple but well-executed pub food.

Beer destinations in Wellington central

See map opposite for places you can visit for beer in Wellington central.

1. Garage Project
2. ParrotDog Brewery
3. Black Dog Brewery
4. Fork & Brewer
5. Sprig & Fern Thorndon
6. Basque
7. Golding's Free Dive
8. Hashigo Zake
9. Little Beer Quarter
10. The Malthouse
11. Rogue & Vagabond
12. The Third Eye
13. Hillside Kitchen & Cellar
14. The Hop Garden
15. Logan Brown
16. Ortega Fish Shack
17. Centre City Wines & Spirits
18. Moore Wilson's Wine, Beer and Spirits
19. New World Thorndon
20. Regional Wines & Spirits

WELLINGTON CITY

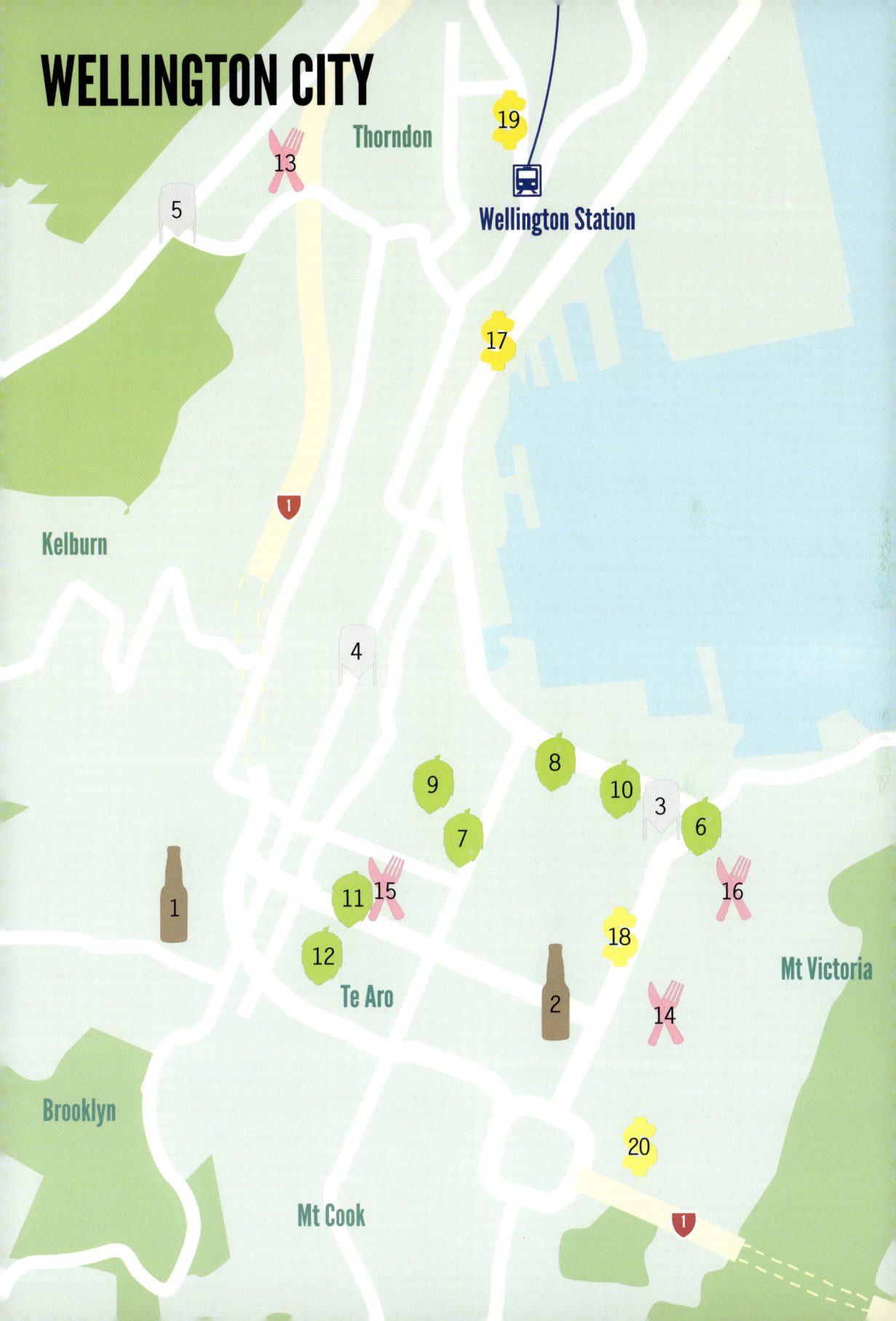

Thorndon

Kelburn

Te Aro

Brooklyn

Mt Cook

Mt Victoria

Wellington Station

13

5

19

17

4

9

8

10

3

6

7

16

11

15

18

12

1

2

14

20

Rest of the North Island

North of Auckland

Brauhaus Frings
frings.co.nz
104 Dent Street, Whangarei
From 10 a.m., 7 days
Brewpub with regular live music.

Leigh Sawmill Café and Brewery
sawmillcafe.co.nz
142 Pakiri Road, Leigh
From 10 a.m., 7 days (27 December–17 February)
From midday, Thursday, and from 10 a.m., Friday to Sunday, rest of year

Tahi Bar
tahibar.com
1 Neville Street, Warkworth
From 3.30 p.m., Tuesday–Thursday
From midday, Friday–Sunday

Coromandel

Hot Water Brewery and Brasserie
www.hotwaterbrewingco.com
1043 Tairua Whitianga Road, Whitianga
From 11 a.m., 7 days

The Pour House/Coromandel Brewing Company
coromandelbrewingcompany.co.nz
7 Grange Road, Hahei
From 11 a.m., 7 days, summer
From 3 p.m. weekdays and from midday weekends, rest of year
A relaxed, family-friendly brewpub.

Waikato

BREW Rotorua
brewpub.co.nz
1103 Tutanekai Street, Rotorua
From 11 a.m., 7 days
Owned by Croucher Brewing, this brewpub features the Croucher beers as well as a selection from other Kiwi breweries. It is sister to BREW Tauranga.

Good George Brew Pubs
goodgeorge.co.nz

Good George Dining Hall and Brewery
32a Somerset Street, Hamilton
From 11 a.m., Monday to Thursday
From 10.30 a.m., Friday to Sunday

Good Neighbour
44 Horsham Downs Road, Rototuna
From 11 a.m. weekdays
From 10 a.m. weekends

Little George
15 Hood Street, Hamilton
From 4 p.m. weekdays
From 2 p.m. weekends

With three brewpubs, Good George has quickly cemented itself into the fabric of the Hamilton beer scene. The Dining Hall and Good Neighbour are both traditional pubs where you can get a full meal. Little George is more of a bar with pizzas and snacks.

The Hamilton Beer and Wine Company
beerandwine.co.nz
856 Victoria Street, Hamilton
10 a.m. – 6 p.m., Sunday to Wednesday
10 a.m. – 7 p.m., Thursday and Saturday
10 a.m. – 8 p.m., Friday

A truly wonderful off-licence with some of the most interesting bottled beers and an ever-changing tap bank that is usually focused on one-off and seasonal beers.

Raukura Campus Club
raukara-club.co.nz
Raukura Road, Hamilton
4.45 p.m. – 6.30 p.m., Monday
4.45 p.m. – 7 p.m., Tuesday and Wednesday
4.45 p.m. – 8 p.m., Thursday
4 p.m. – 9 p.m., Friday

Raukura Campus Club, on the Waikato University campus, is a private club, which means that to enter you will need to be a member, a guest of one or an affiliate.

Shunters Yard Brewery
woodsideestate.co.nz
130 Woodside Road, Matangi
Brewery tours by appointment

Taupo and Bay of Plenty

Aotearoa Breweries
mata.net.nz
57 Onslow Street, Kawerau
From 10 a.m. weekdays
Most weekends – call to check (07) 323 8370
Home of MATA beer.

BREW Tauranga
brewpub.co.nz
107 The Strand, Tauranga
From 4 p.m., Monday and Tuesday
From 11 a.m., Wednesday to Sunday

Owned by Croucher Brewing, this brewpub features the Croucher beers as well as a selection from other Kiwi breweries. It is sister to BREW Rotorua.

Crafty Trout Brewing Co.
craftytrout.co.nz
131–135 Tongariro Street, Taupo
Trout Shoppe and Brewery: 10 a.m. – 4 p.m.,
   Wednesday to Monday
Bier Kafe: from midday, Wednesday to Monday

With a tasting room downstairs and the Austrian-styled Bier Kafe upstairs, you can sip away with an excellent view over the lake.

Lakehouse
lakehousetaupo.co.nz
10 Roberts Street, Taupo
From 7.30 a.m., 7 days

A café, restaurant and craft beer bar, Lakehouse is a splendid 'all things to all people' place that just works.

Mount Brewing Co.
mountbrewingco.co.nz

Mount Brewing Co. Bar
109 Maunganui Road, Mt Maunganui
From 11 a.m., 7 days

Brewers Bar
107 Newton Road, Mt Maunganui
From 11 a.m., 7 days

Hawke's Bay and Gisborne

Common Room
commonroombar.com
227 Heretaunga Street East, Hastings
From 3 p.m., Friday
From 4 p.m., Wednesday, Thursday and Saturday

A cosy locals' bar with live music and local craft beer on tap.

Fat Monk Brewing Co. (at Abbey Cellars)
fatmonk.co.nz
1769 Maraekakaho Road, Hastings
From 11 a.m., Wednesday to Sunday

Roosters Brew House
roosters.co.nz
1470 Omahu Road, Hastings
From 10 a.m., Monday to Friday
From 2 p.m., Saturday

Rose and Shamrock Village Inn
roseandshamrock.co.nz
Corner of Napier Road and Porter Driver,
Havelock North
From 10.30 a.m., 7 days

A traditional Irish pub, but one with dedicated and ever-revolving domestic and international craft beer taps.

Sunshine Brewery Tasting Room
sunshinebrewery.co.nz
49 Awapuni Road, Gisborne
Tap Room: from 3 p.m., Monday to Wednesday;
from midday, Thursday to Sunday
Off-licence: from 10 a.m., Monday to Saturday;
from midday, Sunday

Ten Twenty Four
tentwentyfour.org
1024 Pakowhai Road, Hastings
Lunch: Tuesday to Sunday
Dinner: 5 p.m. – 8 p.m. Tuesday (tacos); Friday and
Saturday (chef's choice)

Featuring the cuisine of Kent Baddeley, who prides himself on pushing the boundaries, Ten Twenty Four isn't a beer restaurant per se but does offer beers from local craft breweries.

Westshore Beach Inn and Beer Garden

westshorebeachinn.co.nz
84 Meeanee Quay, Westshore, Napier
From 11.30 a.m., 7 days

A favourite with locals and tourists alike, Westshore serves a range of craft beer on tap that is also available to take away.

Zeelandt Brewery

zeelandt.co.nz
14 Shaw Road, Eskdale, Hawke's Bay
From 1 p.m., Thursday and Friday
From 10.30 a.m., Saturday

Taranaki

The Hour Glass

49 Liardet Street, New Plymouth
From 4 p.m., Tuesday to Saturday

A great craft beer bar with a real cellar that you can venture into (with the bartender's permission) to select your own beer. It also has a selection of local, domestic and international beers on tap.

Liquorland Fitzroy

liquorland.co.nz
594 Devon Street East, Fitzroy, New Plymouth
9 a.m. – 9 p.m., Monday to Thursday; until 10 p.m.,
9 a.m. – 10 p.m., Friday and Saturday
10 a.m. – 6 p.m., Sunday

Mike's Tasting Room and Brewery Shop

organicbeer.co.nz
487 Mokau Road, New Plymouth
From 10 a.m., 7 days

Palmerston North, the Tararuas and Whanganui

Liquorland Albert Street

liquorland.co.nz
105 Albert Street, Palmerston North
10 a.m. – 8 p.m., Monday and Tuesday
10 a.m. – 9 p.m., Wednesday and Thursday
10 a.m. – 10.30 p.m., Friday and Saturday
10.30 a.m. – 7.30 p.m., Sunday

Rutland Arms Inn

rutlandarms.co.nz
Corner of Victoria Avenue and Ridgway Street, Whanganui
From 7 a.m., 7 days

A warm pub with good food and 25 domestic and international craft beers to choose from.

Tui Brewery and HQ Café

tui.co.nz
State Highway 2, Mangatainoka
10 a.m. – 4 p.m., 7 days

Tours by appointment.

Village Inn Kitchen

villageinnkitchen.co.nz
360 Albert Street, Hokowhitu Village, Palmerston North
From 3.30 p.m., Tuesday and Wednesday
From midday, Thursday and Friday

A gastro pub with great food and a rotating selection of fine domestic and international craft beers.

Owner Ron Trigg at Mike's, North Taranaki.

Nelson–Tasman

With hop fields galore in the surrounding hills, Nelson has always been a brewing centre and today it is a beer-lover's dreamland. If you live outside the region, it's ideal for a weekend trip, although you will need the better part of a day to drive out to the Mussel Inn (stop at Hop Federation on the way), which is an absolute must-do. There are heaps of pubs serving great beer in this small city and it also happens to be pretty damn beautiful. With updated craft beer trails and details on breweries, bars and events, the Nelson Craft Brewing website (craftbrewingcapital.co.nz) is a terrific resource.

Bays Brewery

baysbrewery.co.nz
89 Pascoe Street, Nelson
11 a.m. – 5.30 p.m., Monday to Thursday
11 a.m. – 6 p.m., Friday and Saturday
Midday – 5.30 p.m., Sunday

Bel-Aire Tavern

belairetavern.co.nz
37 Tahunanui Drive, Nelson
From 3 p.m. weekdays
From 1 p.m. weekends

Choose from 27 taps featuring the best beers of Nelson (and a few others from the rest of the country). Beers are available to take away in flagons as well.

Founders Brewery Café and Bar

foundersbrewery.co.nz
Founders Heritage Park, 87 Atawhai Drive, Nelson
10 a.m. – 4.30 p.m., 7 days

Aside from tasting the full range of Founders beer while relaxing in the Hop Garden, you can learn about what you're drinking at the Hop and Beer Museum, or the family it's brewed by at Duncan House – both located in Founders Heritage Park.

The Free House

thefreehouse.co.nz
95 Collingwood Street, Nelson
From 4 p.m. weekdays (3 p.m. in summer)
From midday weekends

A free house (that is not tied to a brewery), which boasts that it has poured over 650 beers since 2009. Great food, great beer (including the only real ale in town) and even better company.

Fresh Choice Richmond

richmondfreshchoice.co.nz
21b Queen Street, Richmond
7 a.m. – 9 p.m., 7 days

Supermarket with a world-class beer selection.

Golden Bear Brewery

goldenbearbrewing.com
12 Aranui Road, Mapua
Weekday hours vary depending on season
From midday Saturday and Sunday

Enjoy big US-styled beers accompanied by Mexican food overlooking the stunning Mapua Wharf.

Hop Federation Brewerey

hopfederation.co.nz
483 Main Road, Riwaka
From 11 a.m., 7 days

Hopgoods Restaurant and Bar

hopgoods.co.nz
284 Trafalgar Street, Nelson
Lunch: Friday only
Dinner: Monday to Saturday

One of Nelson's best restaurants, housing an excellent beer cellar alongside its wine one.

Lighthouse

nzcraftbeer.tv/lighthouse-brewery
21 Echodale Place, Stoke
Tuesday to Saturday

One of the smallest breweries in New Zealand.

CLOCKWISE FROM TOP LEFT Founders Heritage Park, Nelson; Dick Tout at Lighthouse Brewery, Nelson; James Connell leading a tour at McCashin's Brewery, Nelson.

McCashin's Brewery, Café and Bar

mccashins.co.nz; stokebeer.co.nz
660 Main Road, Stoke
7 a.m. – 8 p.m., Sunday to Wednesday
7 a.m. – 9 p.m., Thursday to Saturday

McCashin's hold regular tours at 11 a.m. and 2 p.m. (bookings essential), if you want to learn how beer is brewed and see a lot of Kiwi brewing history. I cannot recommend this highly enough.

Moutere Inn

moutereinn.co.nz
1046 Moutere Highway, Moutere
From midday, 7 days

The oldest pub in the country, serving a rotating selection of craft beers – 10 on tap and three on hand-pull, including their own Moutere Brewing Company range. They also have a couple of well-appointed, affordable rooms for the weary traveller.

The Mussel Inn

musselinn.co.nz
1259 State Highway 60, Onekaka, Golden Bay
From 11 a.m., 7 days (closed mid-July to mid-September)

An eclectic pub and brewery at the heart of Golden Bay – an absolute must-visit.

Roots Bar

rootsbar.co.nz
1 Commercial Street, Takaka
From 2 p.m., Tuesday to Sunday

Sprig & Fern Taverns

sprigandferntaverns.co.nz

Brightwater
54 Ellis Street, Nelson
From 2 p.m., Tuesday to Friday
From 11.30 a.m. weekends

Hardy Street
280 Hardy Street, Nelson
From 11 a.m., 7 days

Mapua
67 Aranui Road, Mapua
From 2 p.m., 7 days

Milton Street
134 Milton Street, Nelson
From 10 a.m., 7 days

Motueka
Wallace Street, Motueka
From 2 p.m. weekends
From 11 a.m. weekends

Richmond
126 Upper Queen Street, Nelson
From 3 p.m., Sunday to Tuesday
From 2 p.m., Wednesday to Saturday

Tahuna
13 Beach Road, Tahunanui, Nelson
From midday weekdays
From 10 a.m. weekends

With locations all over Nelson, the Sprig & Fern taverns offer the full selection of Nelson-brewed Sprig & Fern beers. The pubs are warm, inviting and family-friendly. Rigger sales are available from all outlets.

Urban Oyster Bar and Eatery

urbaneatery.co.nz
From 4 p.m., Monday
From 11 a.m., Tuesday to Saturday

Beer destinations in Nelson

See map opposite for places you can visit for beer in Nelson and its immediate suburbs.

1. *Lighthouse*
2. *McCashin's Brewery, Café and Bar*
3. *Bays Brewery*
4. *Sprig & Fern Hardy Street*
5. *Sprig & Fern Milton Street*
6 *Sprig & Fern Richmond*
7. *Sprig & Fern Tahuna*
8. *Founders Brewery, Café and Bar*
9. *The Free House*
10. *Bel-Aire Tavern*
11. *Hopgoods Restaurant and Bar*
12. *Urban Oyster Bar and Eatery*
13. *Fresh Choice Richmond*

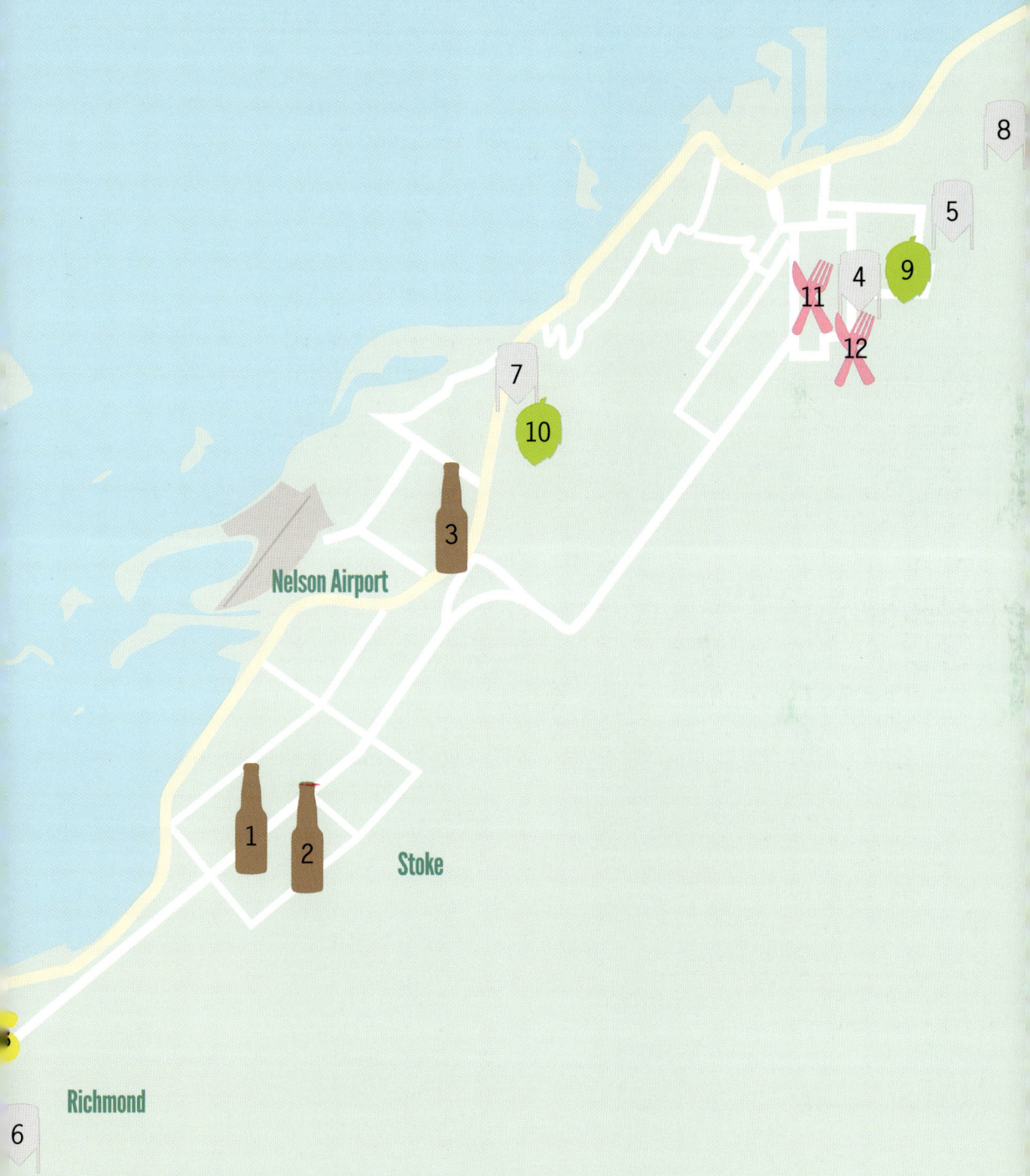

NELSON

Nelson Airport

Stoke

Richmond

Christchurch

Parts of Christchurch were all but destroyed by a series of earthquakes and aftershocks in 2010 and 2011. Prior to this, Christchurch already had an active craft beer scene and since the earthquakes numerous breweries, contract brewing operations, bars, pubs and restaurants have popped up with abandon. It is an amazing city to visit, with a beer culture very much influenced by its English heritage (cask ale lovers take note). In addition to the establishments listed, most Liquorland, Super Liquor stores and New World supermarkets have excellent selections of craft beer.

The Beer Library
thebeerlibrary.co.nz
363 Colombo Street, Sydenham
From 10 a.m., 7 days

The largest selection of craft beer in Christchurch, with a strong focus on imported beer.

Brew Moon Brewing Company
brewmoon.co.nz; brewmooncafe.co.nz
12 Markham Street, Amberley
Opening spring 2015

Burgers and Beers Inc.
burgersandbeersinc.co.nz

355–357 Colombo Street, Sydenham
From 11 a.m., 7 days

478 Cranford Street, Redwood
From 11 a.m., 7 days

Two locations with a name that says it all.

Cassels & Sons: The Brewery
casselsbrewery.co.nz
The Brewery
3 Garlands Road, Woolston
From 7 a.m., 7 days

Located in the beautiful Tannery complex, allowing you to leave your non-drinking friends or family to shop (and there is something for everyone) while you nurse a pint of Milk Stout. The kitchen is also excellent.

CBD Bar
208 Madras Street, Christchurch
From 9 a.m., 7 days

An excellent watering hole located inside the four avenues that demarcate the inner city.

TOP *Andrew Dixon at the Mussel Inn, Golden Bay.*
BOTTOM *Grain mill at McCashin's Brewery, Nelson.*

Fresh Choice Merivale
Merivale Mall, 189 Papanui Road
7 a.m. – 9 p.m., 7 days

Fresh Choice Parklands
myfreshchoice.co.nz
60 Queenspark Drive, Parklands
7 a.m. – 11 p.m., 7 days

Golden Eagle Brewery and Raindogs Brewery
goldeneaglebrewery.co.nz
55 Riccarton Road, Christchurch
10 a.m. – 5 p.m., Monday to Wednesday
10 a.m. – 7 p.m., Thursday to Saturday

Harlequin Public House
hphchch.com
32 Salisbury Street, Christchurch
From 11 a.m., 7 days

Chef Jonny Schwass's flagship restaurant. The beer on tap is mediocre but there is an excellent list of local beers by the bottle that can be matched to beer-friendly food.

Harrington's Breweries
harringtonsbreweries.co.nz
199 Ferry Road, Christchurch
9 a.m. – 5 p.m. weekdays

As well as the brewery at Ferry Road, Harrington's have a chain of retail outlets around the city:

Harrington's Belfast
808 Main North Road, Belfast

Harrington's City
199 Ferry Road, Phillipstown

Harrington's Elmwood
1 Normans Road, Merivale

Harrington's Hills Road
205 Hills Road, Shirley

Harrington's New Brighton
52 Hawke Street, New Brighton

Harrington's Wainoni
165 Pages Road, Wainoni

The Institution

theinstitution.co.nz
28 New Regent Street, Christchurch
From 5.30 p.m., Monday
From 4 p.m., Tuesday to Friday
From 2 p.m., Saturday and Sunday

Craft beer speakeasy is the best way to describe The Institution – one of the many new hospitality ventures on New Regent Street (don't miss The Last Word whiskey bar across the road).

The Laboratory

thelaboratory.net.nz
17 Westbelt, Lincoln
Opening mid-2015

Set up by Twisted Hop co-owners Martin and Lisa Bennett, The Laboratory is scheduled to open mid-2015. It will feature the Twisted Hop range as well as serving more experimental beers from its own onsite brewery.

Pomeroy's Old Brewery Inn

pomeroysonkilmore.co.nz
292 Kilmore Street, Christchurch
From 3 p.m., Tuesday to Thursday
From midday, Friday to Sunday

Housed in a beautiful red-brick building with lovely (and good-value) accommodation, this is a cozy pub with beers from on-site brewery Four Avenues as well as the best breweries around the country. The food is terrific – have the crackling and ask for extra apple sauce.

Three Boys Brewery

threeboysbrewery.co.nz
592 Ferry Road, Woolston
7 a.m. – 3 p.m., Monday to Friday

The Twisted Hop Pub

thewoolstonhop.co.nz
616 Ferry Road, Woolston
From 3 p.m. weekdays
From midday weekends

Pre-quake, The Twisted Hop was one of the most highly regarded brewpubs in the country, especially for lovers of real ale. This is its post-quake incarnation, as the original building was destroyed. Now, the beers are brewed offsite but it is still a must-visit, particularly for cask ale lovers. Great food, better beer and regular events.

Two Thumb Brewing Co. Beerhouse

twothumb.com
352 Manchester Street, Christchurch
3 p.m. – 6 p.m., Wednesday to Friday
Rigger sales are available.

Volstead Trading Company

volstead.co.nz
55 Riccarton Road, Christchurch
From midday, 7 days

With 13 taps, no fewer than nine beers on hand-pull and a Mexican-influenced menu, this is an excellent craft beer bar.

Wigram Brewing Company

wigrambrewing.co.nz
34 Sonter Road, Wigram
From 8 a.m., weekdays

Beer destinations in Christchurch

See map for beer destinations in Christchurch.

1. Cassels and Sons: The Brewery
2. Golden Eagle and Raindogs Brewery
3. Three Boys Brewery
4. Wigram Brewing Company
5. Two Thumb Brewing Co. Beerhouse
6. The Twisted Hop Pub
7. Pomeroy's Old Brewery Inn
8. Volstead Trading Company
9. The Institution
10. Harlequin Public House
11. The Beer Library
12. CBD Bar
13. Burgers and Beers Inc., Sydenham
14. Harrington's Belfast
15. Harrington's Elmwood
16. Harrington's Hills Road
17. Harrington's New Brighton
18. Harrington's Wainoni
19. Harrington's City
20. Fresh Choice Merivale
21. Fresh Choice Parklands
22. Burgers and Beers Inc. Redwood

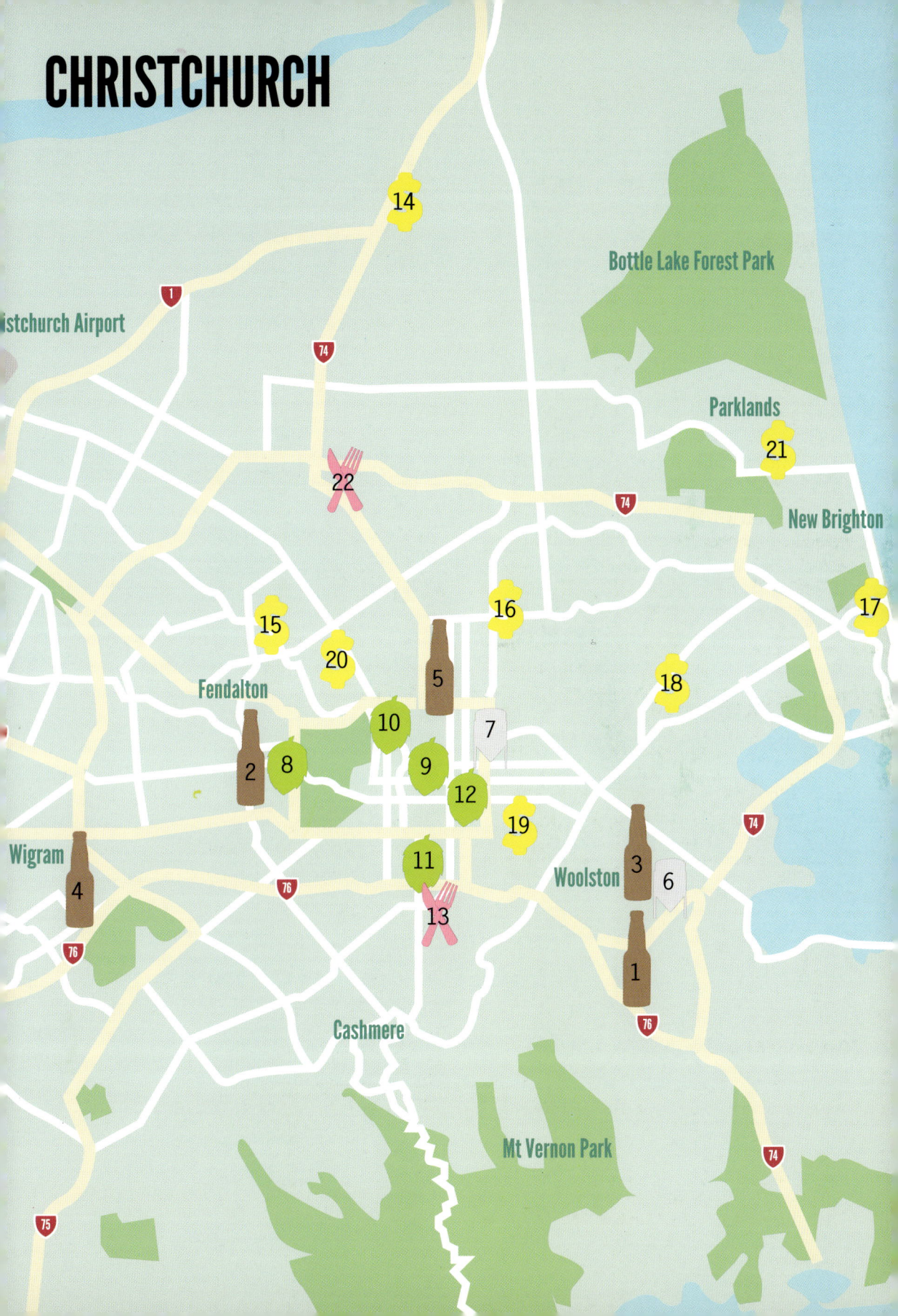
CHRISTCHURCH

Christchurch Airport

Bottle Lake Forest Park

Parklands

New Brighton

22

14

1

74

74

21

17

16

15

20

18

Fendalton

5

10

7

2   8

9

12

19

Woolston

3

11

Wigram

4

76

13

1

76

Cashmere

Mt Vernon Park

74

74

76

75

Rest of the South Island

Marlborough

Dodson Street
dodsonstreet.co.nz
1 Dodson Street, Blenheim
From 11 a.m., 7 days

Located on the same site as Renaissance Brewing, Dodson Street serves the Renaissance beers alongside a wide variety of other Kiwi craft beers. They serve pizza and traditional German food.

Grovetown Hotel
2470 State Highway 1, Grovetown, Blenheim
From 3 p.m. weekdays
From midday weekends

This is a classic, Kiwi country pub that serves great beer.

Moa Brewery and Cellar Door
moabeer.com
258 Jacksons Road, Blenheim
From 11 a.m., 7 days

The Old Bank Tavern
theoldbank.co.nz
81 Cleghorn Street, Redwood Village, Blenheim
From 11 a.m., 7 days

Owned by craft beer enthusiast Mike Pink, The Old Bank has 12 beers on tap and one cask ale (usually from Townshend's in Nelson). Off-licence sales are available.

Renaissance Brewing
renaissancebrewing.co.nz
1 Dodson Street, Blenheim
From 9 a.m. weekdays

Off-licence sales.

Scotch Bar
scotchbar.co.nz
26 Maxwell Road, Blenheim
From 4 p.m., Monday to Saturday

A wine and beer bar in the heart of wine country.

West Coast

Monteith's Brewing Co.
monteiths.co.nz
Corner of Turumaha and Herbert streets, Greymouth
From 10 a.m., 7 days

Brewery tours at 10.30 a.m., 3 p.m., 4.30 p.m. and 6 p.m. (bookings essential)

The West Coast Brewery
westcoastbrewery.co.nz
10 Lyndhurst Street, Westport
From 9.30 a.m. weekdays

South Canterbury and North Otago

Craftwork Brewery
craftworkbrewery.co.nz
59 Tyne Street, Oamaru
By appointment

Riverstone Kitchen
riverstonekitchen.co.nz
1431 State Highway 1, Oamaru
From 9 a.m., Thursday to Monday
Dinner: Thursday to Sunday

Chef Bevan Smith's award-winning farm-to-table restaurant, with a craft beer list designed around the food.

Scotts Brewing Co. Brewery and Brewbar
scottsbrewing.co.nz
1 Wansbeck Street, Oamaru
From 11 a.m., 7 days

Valley Brewing Company Brewery Café and Tasting Room
valleybrewing.co.nz
Corner of Gaulter Road and State Highway 79, Geraldine
From 9 a.m., 7 days
Dinner: Friday and Saturday

Off-licence sales available.

Dunedin

Albar
135 Stuart Street, Dunedin
From 11 a.m., 7 days
One of the best pubs in the country, with a great offering of craft beer and an even better whisky selection.

Emerson's Brewery Shop
emersons.co.nz
14 Wickliffe Street, Dunedin
From 9 a.m., Monday to Friday
From early 2016, Emerson's will have larger guest facilities at their Anzac Avenue site.

Eureka Café and Bar
eurekadunedin.co.nz
116 Albany Street, Dunedin
From 11.30 a.m. weekdays
From 10.30 a.m. weekends

McDuff's Brewery Shop
mcduffsbrewery.co.nz
695 Great King Street, Dunedin
From 10.30 a.m., Monday to Saturday

Ombrellos
ombrellos.co.nz
10 Clarendon Street, North Dunedin
From 11 a.m. weekdays
From 10 a.m. weekends
Closed Monday evenings
An excellent café with a good selection of local beer.

Plato Café and Birch Street Brewery
platocafe.co.nz
Corner of Birch, Roberts and Wharf streets, Dunedin
Brunch: 11 a.m. – 2 p.m., Sunday
Lunch: midday – 2 p.m., Wednesday–Sunday
Dinner: from 6 p.m., 7 days
One of Dunedin's top restaurants, which even has a brewery on site. A must-visit for beer or food lovers.

The Portsider
31 George Street, Port Chalmers
From 3 p.m. weekdays
From 11 a.m. weekends
A beautifully appointed pub in a Victorian-era wooden building. It has good food and an even better selection of local and international beers, plus an off-licence.

Speight's Ale House
thealehouse.co.nz
200 Rattray Street, Dunedin
From 11.45 a.m., 7 days
With regular brewery tours (book online), lunch until 2 p.m. and dinner from 5 p.m., this is the original Speight's Ale House, attached to the brewery.

Tonic
tonicbar.co.nz
138 Princes Street, Dunedin
From 4 p.m., Tuesday to Friday
From 6 p.m., Saturday
An excellent craft beer bar with an array of local, national and international beers.

Central Otago

Atlas Beer Café
atlasbeercafe.com
Steamer Wharf, Queenstown
From 9 a.m. weekdays
From 10 a.m. weekends

Wanaka Beerworks Tasting Room and Flat Head Café
wanakabeerworks.co.nz
891 Wanaka–Luggate Highway, Wanaka
From 8 a.m., 7 days

The Deep South

Invercargill Brewery Cellar Door
72 Leeds Street, Invercargill
From 10 a.m., Monday to Saturday

Endnotes

1. Dominic Kelly, 'Random End of Year Rant' on *The Liquor Ladder*, December 2014, http://theliquorladder.blogspot.co.nz/2014/12/random-end-of-year-rant.html

2. ANZ Bank Report into the New Zealand Craft Beer Industry, August 2014, https://bizhub.anz.co.nz/media/2431529/craft-beer-industry.pdf

3. Ibid.

4. Luke Nicholas, 'How Many Craft Beer Drinkers in New Zealand', June 2014, www.luke.co.nz/2014/06/many-craft-beer-drinkers-new-zealand

5. Rob Stock, '42 Below's Ross takes stake in Moa Beer', December 2010, www.stuff.co.nz/business/4449659/42-Belows-Ross-takes-stake-in-Moa-beer

6. Jonathan Underhill, 'Rangatira pumps $5 million into Tuatara – biggest stakeholder', June 2013, www.nbr.co.nz/article/rangatira-emerges-biggest-investor-tuatara-after-investment-about-5-mln-bd-142191

7. Mike O'Donnell, 'Brass Monkey offers chilling insight into Moa's decline', June 2014, www.stuff.co.nz/business/opinion-analysis/10128673/brass-monkey-offers-chilling-insight-into-Moas-decline

8. 'American Hops', Garrett Oliver (ed.), *The Oxford Companion to Beer*, 2012 (Oxford University Press, New York), p. 41.

9. 'Water', *The Oxford Companion to Beer*, p. 826.

10. Rogue/Voodoo Doughnut Bacon Maple Ale.

11. Three Boys' Oyster Stout.

12. Cock ale, a historical style.

13. Mamma Mia Pizza Beer.

14. Lost Abbey's Gift of the Magi, which also contains frankincense and myrrh.

15. Wynkoop Brewing Company's Rocky Mountain Oyster Stout.

16. Mikkeller Beer Geek Brunch Weasel.

17. Paulaner, Spatenbräu, Löwenbräu, Augustiner-Bräu, Staatliches Hofbräu-München and Hacker-Pschorr-Bräu.

18. Decoction brewing is where a proportion of the grains is boiled and returned to the mash.

19. German/Bavarian Purity Laws that state only water, malt and hops may be used in beer production.

20. 'Weissbier', *The Oxford Companion to Beer*, p. 829.

21. A Belgian sugar commonly used in brewing, converted from sucrose to a mixture of fructose and glucose by heating with water and some acid.

22. The trend toward hoppy US beer styles like IPA began on the west coast.

23. Sound is a surprisingly powerful medium when it comes to enjoying beer (and food and wine), and there is a lot of research being done in this field. For an example of how sound affects your drinking experience, just think of the reassuring subtle hiss of a new bottle being opened or the warming glug of beer being poured into a glass. If you want to experience the effect of sound on sensory perception, make sure you visit The Auricle – a sonic arts gallery and wine bar in Christchurch (auricle.org.nz).

24. Once you have gained some confidence, try pairing up with a friend to describe beers blind (that is, without sighting the label). This can be a very useful skill – so often we are influenced by what we think a beer should taste like.

25. Now everyone knows my trick.

The following supported the Kickstarter project that allowed for the production of this book

Ava Wilson (*Beer Baroness*), *New Zealand Hops Limited*, Joseph Wood (*Liberty Brewing*), *The Free House*, *Emerson's Brewery*, Jacques van Cruysen, *Martinborough Brewery*, Clayton Wallwork (*Two Thumb Brewing*), *Society of Beer Advocates*, *Yeastie Boys*, Tammy Viitakangas (*Mata Brewing*), *ParrotDog Brewing*, Chris Mills (*Kereru Brewing*), Wendy Roigard (*Valkyrie Brewing*), Nigel Gregory (*Croucher Brewing*), Lea Boodee (*MarchFest*), Jarred MacLachlan (*Deep Creek Brewing*), *Crafty Trout Brewing Co.*, *Moa Brewing Company*, Steven Schekter, Gabriella and Doug Michael (*Gladfied Malt*), Paul Donaldson, Helen Hancox, Ian D. Kitto, *Baylands Brewery*, Bill Xu, Ben Middlemiss (*Ben Middlemiss Brewing*), Colin Mallon (*The Malt House*), Lile Ramsay, *Fork and Brewer*, Dominic Kelly (*Hashigo Zake* and *Beer Without Borders*), *Regent 58 Brewery*, Claire and Dean van der Plas, Lauren and Chris Heslop, Mark Jackman (*Weezledog Brewing*), Scott Bell, Kent Baddelely (*1024*), Ted and Francis Verrity, Pip Honeychurch, Geoff and Hillary Munn, *Tuatara Brewing*, *BeerCellar.com*, Andrew Childs (*Behemoth Brewing*), Simon Edwards, Tom Ormond (*Giant Brewing*), David Johnson, Deirdri and Peter Costello, Bill O'Bryne, Andrew Cole, Tui Wilson and Jeremy Morris-Jarrett, Michael O'Brien (*Craftwork Brewing*), Gordon Russell, Miyuki McGuffie, Gerard Baron (*Common Room*), Dale Cooper, Rachel Pugh, Pauline Sutton, Sharon Payne, Simon Rodger, Elissa Jordan, Nicola and Mike Woodman, Daniel McCarthy, Damon Taylor, Chris Ormond (*Giants Brewing*), Dean Stewart, Clayton Chisholm, Shane Bell, Lisa and Graeme Fletcher, Jed Soane, Kylie Harris, Stacey Jane Walsh (*LBQ*), Brendon Le Comte, *Beertique NZ*, Greg Huddelstone, Alex Bazeley, Maree Shaw, Ben Lawrie, Rich Swain, Hayden Esau, Jennifer Wilbanks, Colin Palmer, David Strange, Barbara Joppa, *Vulcan Brewers*, Tracey Gibbs, Greig McGill (*Brewaucracy*), Christina Oatham, Ian McLoughlin, Peter Moran, Therese Costello, Kelly Ryan (*Brew Mountain*), Annika Naschitzki (*Tiamana*), Mike Stearne, Phil Olyott, *Big Growler Brewery*, Scott Feehan, Ryan Jennings, Dave Waugh, Jeremy Greenbrook-Held, Shane Cowlishaw, David Wu, Robin Sheat, Lance Morell, Keane Chan, Jesse Says, Krystal Smith, Stephen Jones, Derek Shanks, Liz Thomas, Andy McKenzie, Nick Goodall, Keith Charlton, Kylie Hunter, Daniel Richards, *Hopswillers*, Kent Lambert, David Powell, Beth Pottinger-Hockings, Christopher Barber (*Zeelandt*), Curtis Baird, Jackson Beavis, Julie Fitzjohn, Russell James Smith, Catriona Petrie and Alex Carr, Nicole Anfang, Cameron Meade, Martin Barry, Wilma van Cruysen and Richard Mansell, Andrew Lees, James Stuntman, Julian Hart, Eloise Page, Martha Machin, Matthew Seale, Ffion Jones, Nigel Marx, Shiggy Takagi (*Funk Estate*), Simon Allen, Brian Lacey, Jonathan Galuszka, Sian Beattie, Murray McLeod, Tony Chandler, Gillian Topping, James Radcliffe, Caleb DeFrees, Ben Taylor, Jula Goebel, Clare Heslop, Ben Hoskin, Caroline Hellaby, Michelle Kelly, Wendy Potts, John Kotrosos, Amanda Ra, Brendon Doran, Steven Wells, Kit Benham, Dylan Vernall, Lee Jackson, Steve Cossaboom, Guillaume Corgnet, Dave, Grant Shannon, Geoff Griggs, Sam Huges, Rory Horne, Craig Boon, Daniel Bellhouse, Simon Woods, Mick Bromwich, Hamish Hann, Tom Cornford, Paul Hicks, Aaron McKoy, Graham Witts, Mike Kush (*Chasing Harvest*), Kelly and Graham Eyres, Michael Julian, *Jaberwocky Brewery*, Ben Chapman, Justin Flitter, Josh Bycroft, Bevan Lord, Jayden Elley, Okewa Rainwear, *Beer Cartel*, Zane Smith, Paul Chilton, Glynn Rudolph, Richard Sherriff, Patricia Hetherington, Justin Robinson, Chris Cormac, Leo Innovations, Camile Wright, Ed Blaze, Sean Golding (*Golding's Free Dive*), *Golden Eagle*, *Renaissance*, *Bach Brewing*, Trish Paino, *Sprig & Fern*, *Wild and Woolly Brewing*, and Lisa and Martin Benett (*The Laboratory*).

Please know, this book would not have been possible without your support!

First published in 2015 by Potton & Burton

Potton & Burton
98 Vickerman Street, PO Box 5128, Nelson, New Zealand
pottonandburton.co.nz

© Jules van Cruysen

Interior design: Lauren Costello
Cover design: Lisa Noble

ISBN 978 1 927213 52 0

Printed in China by Midas Printing International Ltd

This book is copyright. Apart from any fair dealing for the purposes of private study, research, criticism or review, as permitted under the Copyright Act, no part may be reproduced by any process without the permission of the publishers.